PLENTY MORE

PLENTY MORE

YOTAM OTTOLENGHI

EBURY
PRESS

CONTENTS

INTRODUCTION

VEGI-RENAISSANCE

Chunky green olives in olive oil; a heady marinade of soy sauce and chilli; crushed chickpeas with green peas; smoky paprika in a potent dip; quinoa, bulgar and buckwheat wedded in a citrus dressing; tahini and halva ice cream; savoury puddings; fennel braised in verjuice; Vietnamese salads and Lebanese dips; thick yoghurt over smoky aubergine pulp… I could go on and on with a list that is intricate, endless and exciting. But I wasn't always aware of this infinite bounty; it took me quite a while to discover it. Let me explain.

As you grow older, I now realise, you stop being scared of some things that used to absolutely terrify you. When I was little, for example, I couldn't stand being left on my own. I found the idea – not the experience, as I was never really left alone – petrifying. I fiercely resented the notion of spending an evening unaccompanied well into my twenties; I always had a 'plan'. When I finally forced myself to face this demon, I discovered, of course, that not only was my worry unfounded, I could actually feast on my time alone.

Eight years ago, facing the prospect of writing a weekly vegetarian recipe in the *Guardian*, I found myself gripped by two such paralysing fears.

First, I didn't want to be pigeonholed as someone who only cooks vegetables. At the time, and in some senses still today, vegetables and legumes were not precisely the top choice for most cooks. Meat and fish were the undisputed heroes in lots of homes and restaurant kitchens. They got the 'star treatment' in terms of attention and affection; vegetables had the supporting roles, if any.

Still, I jumped into the water and, fortunately, just as I was growing up and overcoming my fear, the world of food was also growing up. We have moved forward a fair bit since 2006. Overall, more and more confirmed carnivores, chefs included, are happy to celebrate vegetables, grains and legumes. They do so for a variety of reasons related to reducing their meat consumption – animal welfare is often quoted, as well as the environment, general sustainability and health. However, I am convinced there is an even bigger incentive, which relates to my second big fear when I took on the *Guardian* column: running out of ideas.

It was in only the second week of being the newspaper's vegetarian columnist that I felt the chill up my spine. I suddenly realised that I had only about four ideas up my sleeve – enough for a month – and after that, nothing! My inexperience as a recipe writer led me to think that there was a finite number of vegetarian ideas and that it wouldn't be long before I'd exhausted them all.

Not at all! As soon as I opened my eyes I began discovering a world of ingredients and techniques, of dishes and skills that ceaselessly informed me and fed me. And I was not the only one. Many people, initially weary of the limiting nature of the subject matter (we are, after all, never asked in a restaurant how we'd like our cauliflower cooked: medium or medium-well), had started to discover a whole range of cuisines, dishes and ingredients that make vegetables shine as brightly as any star.

Just like me, other cooks are finding reassurance in the abundance around them that turns the cooking of vegetables into the real deal. They are becoming more familiar with different varieties of chillies, with ways of straining yoghurt, with new kinds of citrus (like pomelo or yuzu), with whole grains and pearled grains, with Japanese condiments and North African spice mixes, with a vast number of dried pasta shapes and with making their own fresh pasta. They are happy to explore markets and specialist shops or go online to find an unusual dried herb or a particular brand of curry powder. They read cookery books and watch television programmes exploring recent cooking trends or complex baking techniques. The world is their oyster, only a vegetarian one, and it is varied and exciting.

TURNING IDEAS INTO RECIPES

I get my recipe inspiration in a variety of ways. When travelling, I am constantly on the lookout for new ideas. A trip to Tunisia is a waste of time unless I come back with the ultimate method for making harissa; Christmas on the beach in Thailand will be cut short (much to my partner Karl's dismay) in favour of a search through swarming Bangkok alleys for the elusive best-ever oyster omelette.

My collection of cookery books and magazines takes me on journeys into the creative minds of other cooks, or their heritage, or both. It might start off from an image or an idea that I find in a book – combining sorrel with mustard seeds, for example, or roasting carrots with orange halves – which sparks a chain reaction leading to a brand new dish. Over the past few years I have been on a long journey to Iran – alas, a virtual one – through the pages of some of my favourite books (may I mention Najmieh Batmanglij's marvellous *Food of Life*?); I have been on similar tours to Lebanon and Japan (Michael Booth's *Sushi and Beyond* is exemplary); and I was made privy to the ins-and-outs of various unusual grains (through Liana Krissoff's *Whole Grains for a New Generation*) and vegetables (by Deborah Madison's *Vegetable Literacy*).

My colleague chefs at Ottolenghi and NOPI – Sami, Scully, Helen and many others – also constantly stimulate me with their ideas, which turn into dishes and products that we serve in our shops and restaurants.

Pivotal to this book's content is the way in which initial, nascent ideas are turned into actual recipes. Since *Plenty* and my early *Guardian* columns I have expanded my range of ingredients and techniques, but I have also vastly changed the way I work and *Plenty More* is the result and expression of this change.

In the early days it was all pretty simple (as things often are). On a recipe-testing day I would get up early in the morning and go out shopping for ingredients in a local market or supermarket. I'd then return home, unpack, draw out my notes and my key dry staples and start cooking and scribbling. In the early afternoon I'd clear up and go to the computer to note down the recipes. By the evening there were two recipes ready to go, three if I'd been efficient and lucky.

As my shopping, prepping and writing workload increased I needed some help, and this was when Tara came on board. Eventually, however, all this activity outgrew my domestic kitchen: poor Karl had his home turned into a big food lab, with bowls of half-made concoctions here or a plate of some semi-eaten thing there. There weren't many 'proper' meals.

Two years ago we took over a railway arch in Camden, central London, next door to the Ottolenghi bakery, and turned it into the official test kitchen. The story of the last two years, as well as of *Plenty More*, is in many ways the story of Arch 21, where the recipes presented to you in this book were conceived, tested, tasted, evaluated and now finally released to the world. It is also the story of growth: from *Plenty* as a sole venture to *Plenty More* as a project shared by a group.

THE SET AND THE MAIN CHARACTERS

The Ottolenghi 'hub' now occupies three railway arches. The first, taken on in 2007, we call the 'bakery', yet it is so much more. It is the powerhouse behind Ottolenghi and NOPI.

If you happened to walk into Arch 20, you would most likely come across Artur, headphones on as a permanent fixture, grating lemons and squeezing juice: litre upon litre of the cloudy yellow liquid on which our little empire runs. Next you'd find Aga, hair net on (new health and safety imperative every day) rolling grissini sticks. Upstairs Mariusz and Irek dispense terrifying quantities of Lescure butter into brioche dough, puff pastry or croissant mix. At night Carlos lines large square tins with almond cream and rhubarb while Robert fills breadbaskets with a bubbly sourdough. Twenty-four hours a day something – flour-related, jam-related, curd-related, chocolate-related – is happening in Arch 20.

To our left is the youngest member of the family, Arch 22, where Maria works on world domination through the Internet: a recently opened Ottolenghi online shop dispensing all those exotic ingredients you either love or loathe us for having brought into your life. Upstairs there's a little office and Ottolenghi accounts, with Angelita at the helm, as close as we get to a corporate headquarters.

Arch 21 is the creative hub from which dishes, recipes and many of our products sprout. Every day kohlrabis are diced, chickpeas soaked, yoghurt blitzed with a bunch of herbs, or a leg of lamb goes in the oven with seasonal root veg and a bottle of wine. By midday there are usually a couple of dishes ready to put together.

All the office dwellers then huddle together for a taster and give their two pennies' worth. Lucy, who's in charge of Ottolenghi's purchasing and of my life in general, isn't hard to please but *can* be highly observant; Sarah is often harsher – a love-it or leave-it kind of girl – but always happy to be surprised by a 'goner'; Tara tends to deliver short verdicts with effective proposals for improvement; Esme, a perfectionist in the kitchen, is mostly positive and willing to go to take-5, -6 or -7 to make the recipe work.

Once the robust discussion is over we go back to the ingredients list with a bunch of adjustments. Through the testing process a dish could completely transform itself from one thing to another: rice stuffing may end up as risotto, an aubergine sauce as beef-rib marinade. As painstaking as this sounds, it is highly enjoyable. Hitting on the missing piece that 'solves' a dish like a puzzle is a moment of revelation. Everything falls into place when deep-fried onions add the richness so lacking in an otherwise delicious barley dish with lentils and mushrooms; or when a finishing touch of burnt butter with Urfa chilli is spooned over courgette with yoghurt. Often this last effort properly punctuates the dish and brings all the other elements into the correct light.

In *Plenty More* I have aimed to capture some of the techniques involved in constructing a dish, in putting together components and arranging them in layers of flavour, texture and colour. If *Plenty*, through its structure and recipe selection, tried to shed light on groups of ingredients – my favourite ingredients – this book takes these favourites, adds a few new members to the happy family (kashk, dakos and black garlic, to name just a few) and then focuses on cooking techniques and methods that best utilise their potential. Roasting lemon, for example, or braising lettuce was novel to me a few years ago. Now I am eager to share these ideas.

Exposing parts of the process that lead to the creation of a dish, telling about the culinary journeys I have recently been on, and focusing on some simple cooking techniques that elevate an ingredient and properly reveal it, will, I hope, offer an additional perspective on an ever-expanding world of vegetables, grains and legumes, a world with plenty of fantastic ingredients and dishes and plenty more to discover.

YOTAM OTTOLENGHI

....

A SHORT NOTE ABOUT INGREDIENTS

Vegetable weights in brackets are always net: that is, after peeling, chopping, etc. Unless otherwise specified, all salt is table salt, pepper is freshly cracked, eggs are large, parsley is flat-leaf, olive oil is extra-virgin, peppers are deseeded, lemon and lime pith is to be avoided when the zest is shaved, and onions, garlic and shallots are peeled.

TOSSED

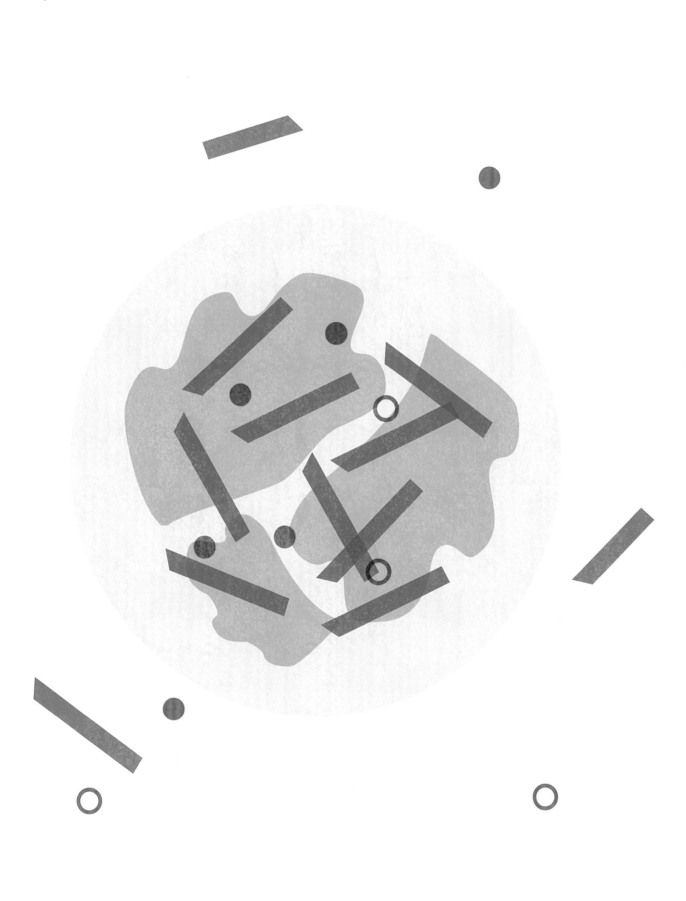

TOMATO AND POMEGRANATE SALAD

I rarely rave about my own recipes but this is one I can just go on and on about. The definition of freshness with its sweet and sour late-summer flavours, it is also an utter delight to look at. But the most incredible thing about it is that it uses a few ingredients that I have been lovingly cooking with for many years, and believed I knew everything there was to know about, yet had never thought of mixing them in such a way. That is, until I travelled to Istanbul and came across a similar combination of fresh tomatoes and pomegranate seeds in a famous local kebab restaurant called Hamdi, right by the Spice Bazaar. It was a proper light-bulb moment when I realised how the two types of sweetness – the sharp, almost bitter sweetness of pomegranate and the savoury, sunny sweetness of tomato – can complement each other so gloriously.

I use four types of tomato here to make the salad more interesting visually and in flavour. You can easily use fewer, just as long as they are ripe and sweet.

200g red cherry tomatoes, cut into 0.5cm dice

200g yellow cherry tomatoes, cut into 0.5cm dice

200g tiger (or plum) tomatoes, cut into 0.5cm dice

500g medium vine tomatoes, cut into 0.5cm dice

1 red pepper, cut into 0.5cm dice (120g)

1 small red onion, finely diced (120g)

2 garlic cloves, crushed

½ tsp ground allspice

2 tsp white wine vinegar

1½ tbsp pomegranate molasses

60ml olive oil, plus a little extra to finish

seeds of 1 large pomegranate (170g)

1 tbsp small oregano leaves

salt

Mix together the tomatoes, red pepper and onion in a large bowl and set aside.

In a small bowl whisk the garlic, allspice, vinegar, pomegranate molasses, olive oil and ⅓ teaspoon of salt, until well combined. Pour this over the tomatoes and gently mix.

Arrange the tomatoes and their juices on a large flat plate. Sprinkle over the pomegranate seeds and oregano. Finish with a drizzle of olive oil and serve.

SORT-OF-WALDORF

My first foray into the weird and wonderful world of presenting on national television was when I took part in the BBC's Great British Food Revival *and was given the somewhat trying task of selling British nuts to the great British public. The combination of my inexperience in front of the camera and my lacklustre attitude to the subject matter resulted in a performance you could fairly describe as not my finest hour ('Have you not watched the programme?' was my reaction when asked about it the following year).*

Still, I did manage to develop a taste for an English eccentricity called pickled walnuts and for cobnuts, which have a fresher flavour than any other nut I know. They go brilliantly well with autumnal fruit and young varieties of cheese. Here I roast them very slowly to make them totally crunchy and enhance their flavour. Normal hazelnuts, lightly toasted and gently crushed with the flat side of a large knife, are a good substitute. (Also pictured overleaf.)

....

Preheat the oven to 160°C/140°C Fan/Gas Mark 2.

Scatter the cobnuts (or hazelnuts) in an ovenproof dish and roast in the oven for 30 minutes or until they take on some colour and turn perfectly dry and crisp. Let them cool down and then crush roughly.

For the mayonnaise, place the shallot, egg yolk, mustard, maple syrup, vinegar and ½ teaspoon of salt in the small bowl of a food processor. Whisk together and, with the machine still running, slowly add the oils in a steady stream until you get a smooth and thick mayonnaise. Set aside.

Place the cabbage, celery, apples and onion in a large mixing bowl. Add the soured cream, dill, mayonnaise, sour cherries, ½ teaspoon of salt and some black pepper. Use your hands to thoroughly mix everything together – don't worry if you break the apple slices; it's all part of the look. Transfer to individual plates, scatter the nuts on top and serve.

50g shelled cobnuts (or hazelnuts)

¼ red cabbage, finely shredded (300g)

6 celery stalks, thinly sliced (350g)

2 Granny Smith apples, cored and thinly sliced (300g)

½ medium red onion, thinly sliced (60g)

140g soured cream

50g dill, finely chopped

100g dried sour cherries or cranberries (optional)

salt and black pepper

Mayonnaise

1 small shallot, finely chopped (20g)

1 egg yolk

1 tsp Dijon mustard

1 tsp maple syrup

1 tbsp cider vinegar

80ml sunflower oil

80ml rapeseed oil

FANCY COLESLAW

2 medium carrots,
  peeled and cut into thin
  matchsticks (140g)
1 small fennel bulb,
  shredded 3mm thick
  (120g)
60ml lemon juice
¼ small Savoy cabbage,
  shredded 3mm thick
  (120g)
1 large radicchio, shredded
  3mm thick (200g)
1 medium red pepper, thinly
  sliced (100g)
1 red chilli, thinly sliced
100g Greek yoghurt
40g mayonnaise
1½ tsp Dijon mustard
1½ tsp honey
1 tbsp olive oil
30g parsley, chopped
20g dill, chopped
10g tarragon, chopped
salt and white pepper

Spiced cashews
120g cashew nuts, roughly
  chopped
¾ tsp ground turmeric
¾ tsp ground cumin
1½ tsp paprika
¾ tsp caster sugar

After a bit of shredding and chopping, you'll have a refreshing bowlful of fresh vegetables. To save time, use a food processor to slice the vegetables: the end result won't be quite as beautiful but it will be just as delicious. Likewise, to save time, any toasted nuts can be used to replace the spiced cashews, but if you do make them, double or triple the amount stipulated: they make a great nibble to serve with drinks. (Pictured on previous page.)

Preheat the oven to 180°C/160°C Fan/Gas Mark 4.

Place the carrots, fennel and 2 tablespoons of the lemon juice in a large bowl and mix well. Set aside for 20 minutes and then strain.

Put the cashew nuts in a small bowl along with the turmeric, cumin, paprika, sugar and a pinch of salt. Stir through 1 tablespoon of water so that the spices cling to the nuts. Spread out on a parchment-lined baking tray and roast for about 12 minutes, until golden and crunchy. Remove and leave aside to cool.

Return the carrots and fennel to the large bowl, add the cabbage, radicchio, red pepper and chilli and stir well.

Make the dressing by whisking together the yoghurt, mayonnaise, mustard, honey, olive oil, remaining lemon juice, ¼ teaspoon of salt and a pinch of white pepper. Pour this over the vegetables and mix well. Add the herbs and spiced nuts, stir to combine and serve.

RAW BEETROOT AND HERB SALAD

This crunchy and fresh salad, with tons of sharp, peppery, 'healthy' flavours, is a good way to start a meal or end it, or simply to have with lots of other summery, vegetable-based dishes. It is also very effective served with grilled lamb or oily fish from the barbecue. Prepare all your ingredients in advance, keeping the delicate herb leaves refrigerated in a sealed container with a moist cloth at the bottom, and toss together when you are ready.

30g flaked almonds

15g sesame seeds

45g pumpkin seeds

3 medium beetroots, peeled and cut into thin strips (300g)

40g basil leaves, torn

20g parsley leaves

30g dill leaves

20g coriander leaves

10g tarragon leaves

1 tsp chilli flakes

2 tsp grated lemon zest

3 tbsp lemon juice

75ml olive oil

salt and black pepper

Preheat the oven to 200°C/180°C Fan/Gas Mark 6.

Mix together the almonds, sesame and pumpkin seeds and spread out on a baking tray. Place in the oven and roast for 6 minutes. Remove from the oven and set aside to cool.

Place the beetroot, herbs, chilli and lemon zest in a large bowl. Add the seeds and nuts, lemon juice and olive oil, along with ¼ teaspoon of salt and a grind of black pepper. Toss together and serve at once.

CELERY SALAD WITH FETA AND SOFT-BOILED EGG

Adding feta, a bit like lemon juice or coriander, is one of the oldest tricks in my book when trying to 'fix' a recipe. 'We can do the obvious and add some feta', we always say in the test kitchen when faced with a dish that seemed wow-ish on paper but didn't quite live up to the promise; 'but that would just be too easy'. It is, indeed, easy and it does work but I do try to limit the number of times I resort to feta, just so that it remains special (I am less successful with lemon and coriander, I am happy to concede).

In this recipe, though, the feta is instrumental in bridging the gap between the sharp, crunchy and healthy-tasting salad and the warm, creamy, rich egg. The result is the most comforting of dishes.

....

Place the celery, green pepper and onion in a bowl, sprinkle over the sugar, along with ½ teaspoon of salt and mix well. Set aside for 30 minutes, for the vegetables to soften and draw out some of the juices, which will make up part of the dressing.

Take the lemons and use a small sharp knife to slice off the top and tail. Cut down the side of each lemon, following its natural curve, to remove the skin and white pith. Over a small bowl, cut in between the membranes to remove the individual segments.

Add the lemon segments to the softened vegetables, along with the celery leaves, parsley, coriander, capers, chilli, olive oil and some black pepper. Mix gently to combine.

Just before you are about to serve, carefully spoon the eggs into a pan of boiling water and simmer gently for 6 minutes. Run under cold water until the eggs are just cool enough to handle but still warm inside, then peel them gently; the yolk should still be runny.

Arrange the salad on plates, dot with the feta and place a soft-boiled egg on top of each plate, broken in the middle. Finish with a few drops of olive oil and some black pepper and serve at once.

8 celery stalks, finely sliced on the diagonal (400g)

2 green peppers, sliced into 0.5cm strips (200g)

1 medium onion, finely sliced (150g)

1 tsp caster sugar

4 lemons

20g celery leaves

15g parsley leaves

15g coriander leaves

4 tbsp capers

2 green chillies, deseeded and finely sliced

2 tbsp olive oil, plus extra to finish

4 eggs

200g feta, broken into 2cm chunks

salt and black pepper

WATERCRESS SALAD WITH QUAIL'S EGGS, RICOTTA AND SEEDS

12 quail's eggs
2 small garlic cloves,
  crushed
1½ tbsp lemon juice
50ml olive oil, plus extra to
  finish
15g dill leaves
15g basil leaves, torn
15g coriander leaves
30g watercress
50g ricotta
salt and black pepper

Seeds
1½ tbsp flaked almonds
1½ tbsp pumpkin seeds
2 tsp sesame seeds
⅓ tsp nigella seeds
¼ tsp chilli flakes
¼ tsp olive oil

The seeds sprinkled over this salad at the end give it a real boost in look, texture and flavour. Make more of the mix than you need and keep it in a jar ready for your next creation that's lacking crunch.

Many an Ottolenghi salad has benefitted from the addition of these seeds over the years, so one day we decided to start selling them in jars labelled 'Sami's Seeds', alongside a new range of spicy nuts that were also going to bear Sami's name in a similar fashion. Lisa Reynolds, a sassy ex-Ottolenghi shift manager, rightly pointed out that these names might not necessarily enhance the eating experience we were hoping to give our customers and, luckily, got us to change the labels before too many were printed.

Start with the seeds. Place all the ingredients in a small pan with a pinch of salt and cook on a medium heat for 3–5 minutes, stirring frequently, until the sesame seeds take on colour. Remove from the heat and set aside to cool.

Place the quail's eggs in a saucepan, cover with cold water and bring to the boil. Simmer for 30 seconds for semi-soft, or 2 minutes for hard-boiled. Refresh in cold water, then peel.

For the dressing, place the garlic, lemon juice and olive oil in a small bowl with ¼ teaspoon of salt and some black pepper. Whisk to combine and set aside.

To assemble the salad, mix the herbs and watercress together and then divide half of the salad between four starter plates. Halve the quail's eggs and put a few halves on every plate. Use a teaspoon to deposit tiny dollops of ricotta over the salad and drizzle the dressing on top. Pile the remaining salad leaves over each portion, giving it as much height as possible. Carefully dot the salad with any remaining egg halves and cheese and drizzle with a tiny amount of oil. Finish with a sprinkle of the seeds on top before serving, at once.

RAW VEGETABLE SALAD

200g cauliflower (about a
third of a head), broken
into small florets

200g radishes (long variety
if possible), thinly sliced
lengthways

200g asparagus, thinly
sliced lengthways

30g watercress

100g fresh or frozen peas,
blanched for 1 minute and
refreshed under cold water

20g basil leaves

75g pitted Kalamata olives

Dressing

1 small shallot, finely
chopped (20g)

1 tsp mayonnaise

2 tbsp champagne vinegar
or good-quality white wine
vinegar

1½ tsp Dijon mustard

90ml good-quality
sunflower oil

salt and black pepper

Certain vegetables – cauliflower, turnip, asparagus, courgette are all good examples – are hardly ever eaten raw in the UK. When I travel back home to visit my parents, I always enjoy a crunchy salad like this one, where the vegetables of the season are just chopped and thrown into a bowl with a fine vinaigrette. The result is stunning; it properly captures the essence of the season and is why I would only make this salad with fresh, seasonal, top-notch vegetables. This really is crucial. Ditto for the dressing: if you can use a good-quality sunflower oil – one that actually tastes of sunflower seeds – it will make a real difference.

The best way to cut the asparagus into strips is by using a vegetable peeler.

First make the dressing. Mix together the shallot, mayonnaise, vinegar and mustard in a large mixing bowl. Whisk well as you slowly pour in the oil, along with ¾ teaspoon of salt and a good grind of black pepper.

Add the salad ingredients to the dressing, use your hands to toss everything together gently and serve.

CRUNCHY ROOT VEGETABLES

Narrowing down the raw vegetable salads for this book was a very meaty task. Beetroot, carrot and red cabbage slaw, beetroot and celeriac slaw, fancy coleslaw, raw vegetable salad, crunchy root vegetable salad, tart apple and celeriac salad: a great many vegetables were sacrificed (to our tummies) for you, in pursuit of the perfected and very prized shortlist. A mandoline or food processor with the appropriate attachment will aid you still further in the preservation of hassle and time.

....

Place the sliced vegetables in a large bowl and add the chilli, lemon juice, vinegar, sugar, oil and a ⅓ teaspoon of salt. Mix well and set aside.

Place the almonds in a small pan and toast for 1 minute, stirring all the time. Add the poppy seeds and fry for another minute, taking care not to over-colour the almonds. Remove from the pan and set aside.

Just before serving, add the almonds, poppy seeds, coriander and dill to the vegetables and mix together. Transfer to serving bowls or a large platter, spoon over the pomegranate seeds and serve.

1 small kohlrabi, peeled and cut into very fine strips, roughly 5cm long and 1–2mm thick (100g)

¼ small swede, peeled and cut into very fine strips, roughly 5cm long and 1–2mm thick (100g)

1 small turnip, peeled and cut into very fine strips, roughly 5cm long and 1–2mm thick (80g)

1 small carrot, peeled and cut into very fine strips, roughly 5cm long and 1–2mm thick (60g)

1 red chilli, finely chopped

1 tbsp lemon juice

1 tbsp cider vinegar

1½ tsp caster sugar

1½ tbsp rapeseed oil

25g flaked almonds

2 tsp poppy seeds

20g coriander leaves

15g dill leaves

seeds of ½ small pomegranate (50g)

salt

FIG SALAD

2 small red onions (200g in
  total)
3 tbsp olive oil
50g hazelnuts, skins on
60g radicchio leaves,
  roughly torn
40g basil leaves
40g watercress leaves
6 large ripe figs (300g in
  total)
1 tbsp balsamic vinegar
¼ tsp ground cinnamon
salt and black pepper

*Late summer and early autumn are peak time for figs. At any other time of the
year you will probably be getting fruit from great distances and, as figs don't
ripen after picking, this normally means bland and dry. A great fig should look
like it's just about to burst its skin. When squeezed lightly it should give a little
and not spring back. It must be almost unctuously sweet, soft and wet. Once
you've managed to find a fig that meets all these criteria, I guarantee a heavenly
experience. Assemble this salad at the last minute and serve as a starter.*

Preheat the oven to 220°C/200°C Fan/Gas Mark 7.

Peel and halve the onions, lengthways, and cut each half into 3cm-wide
wedges. Mix together with ½ tablespoon of olive oil, a pinch of salt and
some black pepper and spread out on a baking tray. Roast in the oven for
20–25 minutes, stirring once or twice during cooking, until the onion is
soft and golden and turning crispy in parts. Remove and set aside to cool
before pulling the onions apart with your hands into bite-sized chunks.

Reduce the oven temperature to 160°C/140°C Fan/Gas Mark 3. Scatter
the hazelnuts in a small roasting tray and toast for 20 minutes. Remove
from the oven and, when cool enough to handle, roughly crush with the flat
side of a large knife.

Assemble the salad on four individual plates. Mix the three leaves together
and place a few on the bottom of each plate. Cut the figs lengthways into
four or six pieces. Place a few fig pieces and some roasted onion on the
leaves. Top with more leaves and continue with the remaining fig and
onion. You want to build up the salad into a small pyramid.

In a small cup, whisk together the remaining olive oil, vinegar and
cinnamon with a pinch of salt and some black pepper. Drizzle this over the
salad, finish with the hazelnuts and serve.

POMELO SALAD

Once in a while, not very often, my mother brought home a pomelo. This used to just sit there, on the kitchen counter, a massive old thing, and we, the children, couldn't do much with it. It took an adult to peel off the thick skin with a serious knife and then get the juicy flesh out of the tight, bitter membrane. It was a proper ceremony that my mum used to conduct after dinner. We would all sit and wait, like chicks in a nest, for the precious pieces to come our way, never quite fast enough.

These days I think of the pomelo as one of the most underappreciated of fruit. Oranges and grapefruit are almost mundane staples, yet many people don't have a clue about the third party in this citrussy trio. Well, I am happy to champion its bitter-sweet, sharpish flavour and firm yet juicy texture to anyone who is willing to listen. It is refreshing, delicious and worth a bit of peeling effort.

Pomelos vary in size. Here you'll need at least three, if they are grapefruit size, or only one of the large standard pomelos.

This salad is perfect alongside some grilled prawns or calamari, and if you're already willing to go non-veggie, add a few drops of fish sauce to give the fruit extra depth. Cold cooked rice noodles will bulk up the salad and turn it into a fresh vegetarian main course.

....

First make the marinade. Place the vinegar and sugar in a small saucepan and warm gently, stirring, until the sugar dissolves. Remove from the heat, add the orange blossom, star anise, cinnamon, ginger and chilli and set aside.

Use a sharp knife to peel the pomelo skin. Divide into segments and use the knife to remove and discard the pith and membrane. Break the fruit segments into 1 or 2 bite-size chunks, put in a shallow dish and pour over the marinade. Leave for at least 30 minutes – the longer the better.

Remove and discard the star anise and cinnamon. Drain and save the marinade juice. Place the pomelo, ginger and chilli in a large bowl and add 3 tablespoons of the reserved juice and all the remaining salad ingredients, except for the sesame seeds and peanuts, along with ¼ teaspoon of salt. Gently toss, add more marinade juice, if needed, and serve, sprinkled with the sesame seeds and peanuts.

Marinade
75ml rice wine vinegar
40g palm (or caster) sugar
1 tbsp orange blossom
  water
2 star anise
1 cinnamon stick, broken
  in two
10g fresh root ginger,
  peeled and cut into thin
  strips
2 red chillies, deseeded and
  cut into thin strips

Salad
1 large (or 2 small) pomelo
  (1kg in total; 350g once
  peeled and segmented)
1 small green (or regular)
  mango, peeled and cut
  into thin strips (140g)
10g coriander leaves
10g mint leaves
4 baby red (or regular)
  shallots, thinly sliced (40g)
60g watercress
2 tsp groundnut oil
¾ tbsp lime juice
2 tsp black sesame seeds (or
  white, if unavailable)
40g roasted unsalted
  peanuts, roughly chopped
salt

PINK GRAPEFRUIT AND SUMAC SALAD

6 pink or red grapefruit
(2.2kg in total)

2 tbsp caster sugar

1 small dried red chilli (use
less if it is very hot)

60ml olive oil

1½ tbsp lemon juice

1 tbsp sumac

½ medium red onion, very
thinly sliced (70g)

2–3 small red chicories,
leaves separated and any
large leaves cut in half at
an angle (280g)

80g watercress

20g basil leaves

salt

Something about the word or connotations of grapefruit often stops people from ordering it from a menu, but I urge you to give this a go: its astringency is more than balanced here by the sweetness of the basil and the dressing. It works as a palate-awakening starter or in between courses, but also as a side dish served alongside fried firm tofu pieces or a spicy roasted chicken. Preparing the grapefruit takes a little time but can be done well in advance.

Take 5 of the grapefruit and use a small sharp knife to slice off each top and tail. Now cut down the side of each grapefruit, following its natural curve, to remove the skin and white pith. Over a small bowl, cut in between the membranes to remove the individual segments. Place in a colander to drain and gently squeeze any remaining juices into a small saucepan.

Squeeze enough juice from the last grapefruit to make the juice in the pan up to 300ml. Add the sugar and chilli and bring to the boil. Reduce the heat to medium and simmer until the sauce thickens and you have about 5 tablespoons left, about 30 minutes. Set aside to cool down, then whisk in the olive oil, lemon juice, sumac and ¼ teaspoon of salt.

To assemble the salad, put the grapefruit segments, onion, chicory, watercress and basil in a large bowl. Pour over three quarters of the dressing and toss very gently. Add the remainder of the dressing if the salad seems dry; otherwise, keep in the fridge for another leafy salad. Serve immediately.

TART APPLE AND CELERIAC SALAD

120g quinoa

3 tbsp white wine vinegar

2 tbsp caster sugar

1 medium red onion, thinly
  sliced (130g)

60ml rapeseed oil

½ large head of celeriac
  (300g in total)

60ml lemon juice

2–3 Granny Smith apples
  (400g in total)

2 tsp poppy seeds

1 red chilli, thinly sliced at
  an angle

15g coriander leaves,
  roughly chopped

salt

*This salad hits you on the head with its sharp sweetness and oniony heat and
it's exactly what I'd prescribe to shake you up a little on a drowsy wintry night.
Serve it alongside a seasonal stew and you'll get a perfect balance. If serving on
its own, try adding a handful of chopped walnuts and a few baby leaves. Use
a mandoline, if you have one, for the celeriac and apple.*

Bring a small saucepan of water to the boil, add the quinoa and simmer for
9 minutes. Drain in a fine sieve, run under cold water and then shake well
to remove all the water. Set aside to dry.

Place the vinegar, sugar and 1 teaspoon of salt in a mixing bowl and whisk
to combine. Add the onion and rub the liquids into it using your hands.
Add the oil, stir, and set aside for 30 minutes to marinate.

Peel and cut the celeriac into very thin strips and place it in a bowl with
the lemon juice to prevent discoloration. Quarter the apples, remove the
cores and cut each quarter into similarly thin strips. Add to the celeriac
and mix well. Add the onion along with the quinoa, poppy seeds, chilli and
coriander. Mix well and taste to see if you need any more salt, sugar or
vinegar: you are aiming for a pungent, sweet and sour flavour.

PARSLEY, LEMON AND CANNELLINI BEAN SALAD

100g red quinoa

20g parsley, finely shredded

20g mint leaves, finely
  shredded

50g spring onion, finely
  sliced

250g cooked cannellini
  beans, drained (tinned are
  fine)

½ large lemon, skin and
  pips removed, flesh finely
  chopped (70g)

½ tsp ground allspice

60ml olive oil

salt and black pepper

*I ate a lot of this sort of salad when travelling around the southern and eastern
Mediterranean filming for my first series of* Mediterranean Feasts. *It's super-
simple, ready in minutes and absolutely delicious. The red quinoa looks great
against the cannellini but use white, which needs a minute or two less cooking,
if that's what you have to hand.*

Bring a medium saucepan of water to the boil. Add the quinoa and cook
for 11 minutes. Drain in a fine sieve, refresh under cold water and set aside
to dry completely. Transfer the cooked quinoa to a large bowl, along with
the remaining ingredients, ¾ teaspoon of salt and some black pepper. Stir
together and serve.

ORANGE AND DATE SALAD

For one logistical reason or another, this heavenly salad didn't make it to the final cut of my Moroccan episode of Mediterranean Feasts. *Budget and pressures on timing aside, the crew were delighted to keep re-shooting it in different locations – on riad rooftops and in the kitchens of kind strangers – if only to devour the offerings once the 'wrap' was called.*

Make the dressing by whisking together the lemon juice, garlic, orange blossom water, cinnamon and fennel seeds. Add the olive oil, ½ teaspoon of salt and a generous grind of pepper and whisk until well combined. Set aside.

Take the oranges and use a small sharp knife to trim off their tops and tails. Now cut down the sides of the oranges, following their natural curve, to remove the skin and white pith. Cut widthways into 0.5cm-thick slices and remove the pips.

Put the oranges, along with the remaining salad ingredients, in a large but shallow salad bowl. Stir the dressing and pour it over the salad. Gently stir everything together and serve.

5 medium oranges (1kg in total; 500g after peeling and slicing)

3 large Medjool dates, pitted and quartered lengthways (60g)

120g radishes, sliced 1–2mm thick

⅓ small red onion, very thinly sliced into rings (30g)

60g rocket

30g lollo rosso lettuce, torn into 3cm pieces

15g coriander, roughly chopped

15g parsley, roughly chopped

15g mint, roughly torn

Dressing
2 tbsp lemon juice
1 garlic clove, crushed
1 tsp orange blossom water
½ tsp ground cinnamon
2 tsp fennel seeds, toasted and lightly crushed
3 tbsp olive oil
salt and black pepper

SPROUT SALAD

1½ tbsp cumin seeds

450g mixed sprouts (mung beans, chickpeas, aduki beans, lentils, etc.)

1 daikon, peeled and thinly sliced (250g), or plain radishes or kohlrabi if unavailable

2 large carrots, peeled and thinly sliced (250g)

20g parsley, roughly chopped

10g coriander, roughly chopped

2 garlic cloves, crushed

3 tbsp sunflower oil

2 tbsp rapeseed oil

2 tbsp white wine vinegar

2 tbsp cider vinegar

300g baby plum tomatoes, halved lengthways

80g baby spinach leaves

salt and black pepper

My Camden test kitchen is an autonomous unit, separate from our shops and restaurants by distance and pervading atmosphere. Calm and collected is how I'd describe it, nothing like the frenzied air of the 'professional' kitchens we run; those can become pretty mad at times, churning out tons of food at a heart-stopping pace. Still, when Cornelia, Noam or Sami pop over from one of the shops to have a chat and, invariably, sample the day's recipes, things can turn a bit thorny even in my little paradise. Few words are minced by my discerning and hard-to-please business partners. Praise is rarely without qualification, improvements are often suggested.

Sami is quick to disqualify; Noam to reject anything white; but Cornelia who, generally, would always prefer a piece of raw, minced steak over anything, is the hardest to please. So, as you can probably imagine, bets were not placed on her rooting for this virtuous-sounding salad. We were all wrong. She absolutely loved it. And when Cornelia loves something she makes it over and over again. This salad has made it into her all-time Top 10, the biggest accolade imaginable!

Different oils and vinegars are used here, to add a certain richness, but you can use just one of each and the daikon can be substituted with normal radishes or kohlrabi. Walnuts and chunks of creamy blue cheese would move this away from the land of the virtuous and turn it into a sumptuous main course. (Pictured on page 39.)

Place the cumin seeds in a small frying pan. Toast on a high heat for a minute or two, shaking the pan to move the seeds around, until they give off their aroma and begin to pop. Transfer to a mortar and crush with a pestle until powdery.

Put the sprouts, daikon and carrot in a large mixing bowl. Add the herbs, garlic, oils, vinegars, ground cumin seeds, 1 teaspoon of salt and some black pepper. Stir well, taste and adjust the seasoning if you need to. Add the tomatoes and spinach leaves, stir gently and serve.

I'm not entirely sure of the etiquette surrounding sequels to recipes but, three years on from the January when the first sprout salad was devised, I found myself in a similar state of post-festive-season excess, in need of a detox. This was the result and, again, it will make not eating cheese and drinking red wine for a while seem like a very good idea indeed. The salty-sour umeboshi purée, made from pickled plums, can either be found in large supermarkets with other Japanese ingredients or in specialist shops. (Pictured overleaf.)

....

Preheat the oven to 170°C/150°C Fan/Gas Mark 3½.

Place the sunflower seeds and almonds on a small baking tray and roast for 15–20 minutes or until golden. Remove from the oven and set aside to cool.

Put all the ingredients for the dressing in a small bowl, along with ⅓ teaspoon of salt. Whisk well until combined and set aside.

Bring a medium pan of water to the boil, add the edamame beans, bring back to the boil and then immediately drain and refresh under cold water. Shake well to dry before transferring them to a large bowl along with the remaining ingredients. Pour over the dressing, mix to combine and serve.

20g sunflower seeds
20g flaked almonds
150g frozen edamame beans
15 medium radishes, sliced into 2mm rounds (140g)
1 small kohlrabi, peeled and cut into thin strips (100g)
1 medium carrot, peeled and cut into thin strips (100g)
120g mung bean sprouts
2 large ripe avocados, peeled and cut into 1.5cm dice (280g)
20g coriander, chopped

Dressing
1½ tsp umeboshi purée
1 tbsp rice wine vinegar
1½ tbsp lime juice
1 tbsp soy sauce
½ tsp sesame oil
2 tsp caster sugar
1 small shallot, finely chopped (25g)
3 tbsp sunflower oil
salt

SPRING SALAD

350g asparagus, trimmed
  and sliced widthways, at a
  sharp angle, into 3–4 thin
  pieces
200g French beans,
  trimmed
300g broad beans, fresh or
  frozen
50g baby spinach leaves
1 banana shallot, very
  thinly sliced (50g)
1 red chilli, finely diced
½ tsp sesame oil
2 tbsp olive oil
1 tbsp lemon juice
1 tbsp black and white
  sesame seeds, toasted
1 tsp nigella seeds
salt

I love dishes that feature the various shades of a single colour, making you stop to check what's in there. Spring and early summer are the time to do this with green – with artichoke, rocket, asparagus, broad beans, watercress, peas, cabbage, all kinds of lettuce and many, many more to choose from. When you put a few of these in one bowl, you get the most glorious celebration of colour and spring.

Bring a large pan of water to the boil, add the asparagus and blanch for 3 minutes. Use a slotted spoon to transfer the asparagus to a bowl of ice-cold water. Add the French beans to the boiling water and blanch for 5 minutes. Use the slotted spoon to transfer them to the bowl with the asparagus, drain both and then set aside to dry. Add the broad beans to the boiling water and blanch for 2 minutes. Drain, refresh under cold water and then remove and discard the skins by pressing each bean gently between your finger and thumb.

Place all the greens in a large mixing bowl. Add the remaining ingredients, along with ½ teaspoon of salt, stir gently and serve at once.

DAKOS

I sometimes worry that my mild obsession with these Cretan barley rusks is in excess of their status as, essentially, a type of crispbread. I fell in love with them one summer in Crete and, with apologies to Turkey's apple tea, these flings don't always stand the test of time once the holiday bags have been unpacked. The second I snack on dakos, though, piled high with sweet chopped tomatoes and dotted with feta cheese or wrinkly black olives, I'm more convinced than any smitten seventeen-year-old that this is a relationship that will last. The barley in the rusks makes them sweeter, nuttier, crunchier (and more utterly addictive) than their wheat-only counterparts. If you can't find the Greek dakos then other rusks are fine here: I particularly like the wholemeal Swedish Krisprolls, which are widely available.

As with all simple tomato-based salads, the quality of the tomatoes is key. If yours are anything other than bursting with flavour, a pinch of sugar or a few drops of balsamic vinegar will help to draw out their natural sweetness.

6 large tomatoes, cut into 1cm dice (500g)

½ red onion, cut into 0.5cm dice (50g)

1½ tbsp red wine vinegar

3 tbsp olive oil

½ tsp ground allspice

150g Cretan dakos or other rusks, roughly broken

70g feta, roughly crumbled

40g black olives, pitted and halved

30g capers, whole or very roughly chopped

5g chopped parsley, to serve

salt and black pepper

Place the tomato, onion, vinegar, 2 tablespoons of oil and the allspice in a large mixing bowl, along with ⅓ teaspoon of salt and a good grind of black pepper. Stir gently and set aside.

Spread the dakos out on a serving platter and spoon the tomato mixture on top. Sprinkle over the feta, olives and capers, followed by the parsley and remaining tablespoon of olive oil. Leave to sit for 5 minutes before serving.

CARAMELISED FIG, ORANGE AND FETA SALAD

100g caster sugar

16 fresh figs, cut in half lengthways (530g)

4 medium oranges, topped and tailed, peeled and sliced into 1cm-thick rounds (750g)

2 tbsp lemon juice

1½ tbsp raki, Pernod or another aniseed-flavoured liqueur

1 tsp aniseed or fennel seeds, lightly toasted

1 garlic clove, crushed

80ml olive oil

200g feta, roughly crumbled into 1cm chunks

1 tbsp oregano, small leaves whole and larger ones chopped

60g rocket

coarse sea salt and black pepper

Bringing caramel to just the right point of caramelisation whilst trying to look good for a camera is no mean feat – one I didn't manage to pull off, I hasten to add, when filming in Mallorca for Mediterranean Feasts. *I was granted the benefit of three takes to get the dish (and myself) looking right for the shoot but I suggest you keep focused on the dish alone. This was the first ever dish that Esme tested for me in Camden. In classic day-one madness, her attempts to caramelise were impeded by the fact that she had reached for the salt, rather than the sugar, to add to the pan!*

Working with caramel may seem intimidating but you needn't worry: the juicy fruit will be fine even if the caramel is slightly crystallised or lumpy. It won't be thanking you, though, if the caramel burns, so you need to work fast when the caramel reaches the desired colour and not to worry if you add the fruit before all of the sugar has melted. If you can look cute and talk to the camera at the same time then all credit to you. There is nothing strictly 'tossed' about this recipe, I know, but the other salads insisted on taking it under their wing. (Also pictured overleaf.)

Place a large frying pan on a medium heat and add half the sugar. Leave for 2–3 minutes, or until it turns a golden caramel colour; don't stir the sugar at this stage. Once nice and golden, add half the figs, cut-side down. Cook for 2 minutes until starting to soften, before turning to cook for a further minute. Remove from the pan and add the second batch of figs and repeat the cooking process. You might need to add a tablespoon or two of water to the pan if the figs aren't very juicy.

Add the remaining sugar to the pan, return to the heat and let it start to caramelise before adding the oranges and leaving for 1 minute on each side. They should take on a rich caramel colour. Remove and add to the plate of figs.

Take the caramel off the heat and whisk in the lemon juice, alcohol, aniseed or fennel seeds, garlic, ¾ teaspoon of salt and a generous grind of black pepper. Once combined, whisk in the olive oil and set aside.

Arrange the oranges and figs on a large platter and dot with the feta pieces. Drizzle over any juices left on the fruit plate, followed by the dressing. Sprinkle with the oregano and rocket and serve.

STEAMED

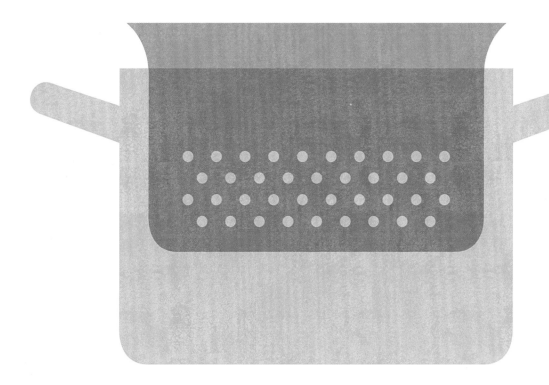

STEAMED AUBERGINE WITH SESAME AND SPRING ONION

2 medium aubergines,
  topped and peeled (650g)
2½ tsp mirin
½ tsp sesame oil
1½ tbsp light soy sauce
2½ tsp rice vinegar
1½ tsp maple syrup
2 tsp peeled and finely
  chopped fresh root ginger
1 garlic clove, crushed
5 spring onions, thinly
  sliced at an angle (70g)
10g toasted mixed black
  and white sesame seeds
salt

That rare Ottolenghi combination: an aubergine without olive oil, due only to the Japanese heritage of the dish. Steaming maintains some of the vegetable flesh's texture, which doesn't happen if you cook it any other way, giving the dish a particularly substantial quality. It's suitable to serve as a main course with just plain rice or fried tofu. The black sesame seeds look fantastic but use white if that's all you have to hand.

Fill a large pot (for which you have a lid) with water to a quarter of the way up the sides and bring to the boil. Place the aubergines in a steamer or a colander, set over the water, making sure the water doesn't touch the base of the steamer. Cover tightly, using foil to seal the edges if you need to, and steam for 30 minutes, turning once. Once cooked, remove the steamer from the pot and leave the aubergine to cool and drain inside the colander. Shred the flesh by hand into long, thin strips 0.5cm wide, and continue to drain for another 20 minutes.

Meanwhile, make the dressing. Mix together the mirin, sesame oil, soy sauce, vinegar, maple syrup and ¼ teaspoon of salt. Stir through the ginger and garlic and set aside.

Once the aubergine is cool, gently toss it with the dressing before adding the spring onion and sesame seeds. Leave to marinate for at least 10 minutes and then serve.

RICE SALAD WITH NUTS AND SOUR CHERRIES

150g wild rice

220g basmati rice

80ml olive oil

100g quinoa

60g almonds, skins on,
  roughly chopped

60g pine nuts

60ml sunflower oil

2 medium onions, finely
  sliced (320g)

30g parsley, roughly
  chopped

20g basil, roughly chopped

10g tarragon, roughly
  chopped

40g rocket

80g dried sour cherries

60ml lemon juice, plus the
  grated zest of 1 lemon

2 garlic cloves, crushed

salt and black pepper

Forgive me for all the pots and pans here. They are all left fairly clean so a good wipe with a tea towel between uses will save some washing up. The sour cherries have a welcome bite, which sweet raisins lack, so they are worth seeking out in larger shops. You could substitute chopped cranberries soaked in a little lemon juice, if need be. This salad makes a satisfying meal-in-a-bowl and will keep in the fridge for at least a day. Just remember not to serve it cold and to adjust the seasoning before serving.

Place the wild rice in a medium saucepan, cover with plenty of water, bring to the boil and then reduce to a gentle simmer for 35 minutes until the rice is cooked but still firm. Drain, rinse under cold water and set aside to dry.

Mix the basmati rice with 1 tablespoon of olive oil and ½ teaspoon of salt. Place in a medium saucepan with 330ml of boiling water, cover and cook on the lowest possible heat for 15 minutes. Remove from the heat, place a tea towel over the pan, replace the lid and set aside for 10 minutes. Then uncover and allow to cool down completely.

Bring a small saucepan of water to the boil and add the quinoa. Cook for 9 minutes, then drain in a fine sieve, refresh under cold water and set aside.

Place the almonds and pine nuts in a small pan with 1 tablespoon of olive oil and a pinch of salt. Cook on a medium–low heat for about 5 minutes, stirring frequently. Transfer to a small plate as soon as the pine nuts begin to colour, and set aside.

Heat the sunflower oil in a large frying pan and add the onions, along with ¼ teaspoon of salt and some black pepper. Cook on a high heat for 5–8 minutes, stirring often, so that parts of the onion get crisp and others just soft. Transfer to kitchen paper to drain.

Place all the grains in a large mixing bowl along with the chopped herbs and rocket, fried onion, nuts and sour cherries. Add the lemon juice, zest, remaining olive oil, garlic, ½ teaspoon of salt and some pepper. Mix well and set aside for at least 10 minutes before serving.

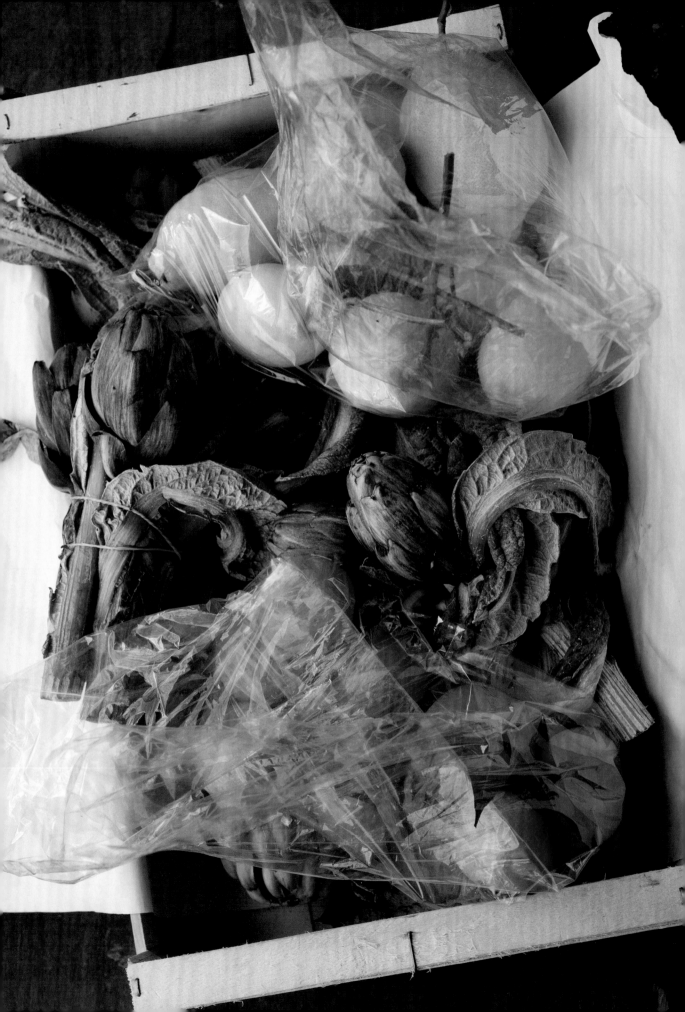

LEMON AND CURRY LEAF RICE

This will be a revelation to those who tend towards plain steamed basmati. The method is fail-safe and the result is stunning. Serve this rice with an Asian savoury pickle to make a vegetarian meal, or next to a freshly roasted chicken. Try to look for fresh curry leaves for this dish, using them on the stem. They freeze well so don't worry if you end up getting a large bunch. (Pictured overleaf.)

....

Preheat the oven to 200°C/180°C Fan/Gas Mark 6.

Put the cinnamon sticks, cloves, lemon rind, curry leaves, 1½ teaspoons of salt and ½ teaspoon of pepper in a medium saucepan. Cover with 680ml of water and place on a high heat. As soon as the water boils, remove the pan from the heat.

Spread the rice out in an ovenproof dish or roasting tray, approximately 24cm x 30cm, cover with the boiled water and aromatics and stir well. Lay a piece of greaseproof paper over the surface of the water and cover the dish with foil. Cook in the oven for 25 minutes, then remove and leave to sit, covered, for 8–10 minutes.

Just before serving, melt the butter in a small saucepan. Once it's melted and very hot, carefully add the lemon juice and swirl together to mix. Pour this over the hot rice and fluff it up with a fork. Transfer to a serving bowl and serve at once (you can remove the curry branches and cinnamon sticks or keep for the look).

5 short cinnamon sticks (10g)
10 cloves
shaved rind of 1 lemon, plus 1 tbsp lemon juice
3 stems of fresh curry leaves (about 25 leaves) or 35 dried curry leaves
400g basmati rice, rinsed, soaked in water for 15 minutes and drained well
60g unsalted butter
salt and white pepper

SAFFRON, DATE AND ALMOND RICE

I have been having a long literary love affair with Claudia Roden, instigated initially by my crippling dependence on her Book of Jewish Food, *which I consulted whenever I needed to cook anything typically Jewish. Later I met my idol in the flesh and immediately fell for her charm, captivating modesty and endless stream of stories. It is a real honour to count her as a friend.*

Apart from her Jewish cookery bible, Claudia has written several masterpieces covering the cuisines of Italy and Spain and many other illuminating recipe collections. Her Book of Middle Eastern Food, *in particular, has paved the way for many writers on the subject and still feels as current as it did when it was first published in 1968. This recipe is inspired by a marvellous Iranian dish from that book.*

I have said it before and I am happy to repeat myself: Iranians make the best rice. Their technique of washing and parboiling the rice, and then allowing it to steam in the residual moisture, makes it worthy of being included in this chapter much more than other rice-cooking methods that, technically, are more about absorption than steaming. The result is light rice, every grain perfectly defined from the rest of the clan. Don't be alarmed by the amount of salt called for in the water before the rice is drained and rinsed, and also don't worry about some rice sticking to the bottom and burning a little: it makes it nice and crunchy, just as the Iranians like it. The rice will go fantastically well with the Indian Ratatouille (see page 140) or the Iranian Vegetable Stew (see page 146).

400g basmati rice
110g unsalted butter
100g whole blanched almonds, roughly chopped
80g Medjool dates, pitted and roughly chopped
¼ tsp saffron threads, soaked in 2 tbsp hot water
salt and white pepper

....

Rinse the rice well under cold running water. Put it in a large bowl, cover with plenty of lukewarm water and stir through 2 tablespoons of salt. Allow the rice to sit for 1–2 hours, then drain and wash in lukewarm water.

Bring a medium pot of water to the boil and add 2 tablespoons of salt, then the rice. Gently boil the rice for 3–4 minutes, until the rice is almost cooked. Check this by removing a grain and biting into it: it should still have a tiny bit of bite. Drain the rice and rinse under lukewarm water. Set aside to drain.

In the same saucepan, melt 80g of the butter and sauté the almonds for 4 minutes, until they turn slightly golden. Add the dates and cook for a couple more minutes. Stir through ½ teaspoon of white pepper, ¼ teaspoon of salt and half the rice. Gently flatten this layer of rice and then place the remaining rice on top. Melt the remaining butter and drizzle this over the top, along with 3 tablespoons of water. Cover the pan tightly with a lid and cook on the lowest heat possible for 35 minutes. Remove from the heat and spoon over the saffron and its soaking water. Cover the pan immediately with a tea towel, seal with the lid and set aside for 10 minutes.

To serve, don't stir the rice, just use a large serving spoon to remove portions with the distinct two layers kept separate. Serve at once.

MISO VEGETABLES AND RICE WITH BLACK SESAME DRESSING

300g sushi rice

1½ tsp dashi stock powder
or a light vegetarian stock
powder

1½ tbsp tamari soy sauce

1½ tbsp mirin

30g dark red (or brown)
miso paste

1½ tsp caster sugar

220g broccolini, trimmed
and cut in half widthways
(180g); if thick, halve
lengthways as well

165g buna-shimeji
mushrooms, divided into
small clumps

1 large carrot, peeled and
cut into 0.5cm x 6cm
batons (140g)

50g mangetout, cut into fine
matchsticks

1 baby cucumber, cut into
0.5cm x 6cm batons (100g)

10g coriander leaves

Black sesame dressing

40g peanuts, toasted and
roughly chopped

15g black sesame seeds (or
white, as an alternative)

1 tbsp rice vinegar

1 tsp maple syrup

1 tsp groundnut oil

½ tsp chilli flakes

This is my go-to dish for winter evening comfort food. You can buy dashi stock powder in oriental or health food shops but most varieties are not suitable for vegetarians. A decent vegetarian dashi can be made by boiling kombu (which your oriental or health food shop should sell), an edible kelp, for just 5 minutes. Use the cooking liquid, instead of the water specified in the recipe, omitting the stock powder but still adding the soy, mirin, miso and sugar.

Soak the rice for 15 minutes in cold water, drain, place in a medium saucepan for which you have a lid and cover with 375ml water. Cover the pan, bring to the boil, then reduce the heat to the lowest setting. Cook for 10 minutes, remove from the heat and leave, covered, for a further 15 minutes.

Meanwhile, place all of the ingredients for the black sesame dressing in a small bowl and mix together well.

Pour another 375ml water into a separate medium pan and add the dashi powder, soy sauce, mirin, miso paste and sugar. Bring to the boil, stirring occasionally, and then reduce the heat to medium. Add the broccolini and simmer for 4 minutes. Use a slotted spoon to remove from the pan and set these aside in a large bowl whilst you cook the other vegetables. Add the mushrooms, cook for 3 minutes, remove and add these to the bowl with the broccolini. Repeat with the carrots – they need 2 minutes; mangetout, 1 minute; cucumber, just 15 seconds. When all the vegetables have been cooked and set aside, increase the temperature under the stock and reduce the liquid until there is about 60ml left: this should take about 10 minutes. Divide the rice between four bowls and place the vegetables on top. Spoon over the reduced cooking liquid, followed by the black sesame dressing. Finish with the coriander leaves and serve at once.

BLANCHED

TOMATO AND ROASTED LEMON SALAD

2 medium lemons, halved
lengthways, pips removed
and cut widthways into
2mm slices (260g)

3 tbsp olive oil

½ tsp caster sugar

8 sage leaves, finely
shredded

400g baby tomatoes, yellow
or red or a mixture of
both, halved

⅓ tsp ground allspice

10g parsley leaves

15g mint leaves

seeds of 1 small
pomegranate (120g)

1½ tbsp pomegranate
molasses

½ small red onion, finely
sliced (50g)

salt and black pepper

I cooked a recipe similar to this in Sardinia when I shot my Mediterranean Island Feast *series. I was performing in front of two cameras and our small crew when suddenly a bunch of chirpy Aussie ladies arrived to check in. By coincidence they had come straight from London, which they had visited especially in order to eat in the restaurants of their favourite chef; that chef turned out to be your humble servant. The raucous exhilaration was hard to contain but it did, I must admit, seriously boost my performance. There's nothing like a noisy home crowd!*

Seek out the sweetest tomatoes you can for this salad in order to balance the bitterness of the lemon. You can bulk it up, as I did in Sardinia, by adding lots more leaves and fresh herbs and some cooked fregola. This will turn the salad into a whole meal. Otherwise, serve it with oven-roasted potatoes or pan-fried fish.

Preheat the oven to 170°C/150°C Fan/Gas Mark 3½.

Bring a small saucepan of water to the boil, add the lemon slices and blanch for 2 minutes. Drain well and then place the lemon in a bowl and pour over 1 tablespoon of the oil, ½ teaspoon of salt, the sugar and sage. Gently mix and then spread out everything on a parchment-lined baking tray. Place in the oven and cook for 20 minutes, until the lemons have dried out a little. Remove and set aside to cool.

Place the rest of the ingredients in a bowl along with the remaining oil, ¼ teaspoon of salt and some black pepper. Add the lemon slices, stir gently and serve.

RICE NOODLES WITH SPRING ONIONS AND SOY BEANS

These noodles are unchallenging in the best sense of the term: they are easy to make and very comforting. As they are they'd be lovely with the Steamed Aubergine with Sesame (see page 52), omitting the spring onion from that recipe. Or, as a stand-alone dish, adding 120g of picked crabmeat with some lime juice at the final stage is a delicious upgrade.

....

Bring a large pot of salted water to the boil and cook the noodles for about 5 minutes, or as instructed on the packet, until al dente. Drain well, rinse under hot water, and set aside in a large mixing bowl with ½ tablespoon of sunflower oil stirred through. Keep the bowl somewhere warm, covered, until ready to use.

Heat the remaining sunflower oil in a large wok or sauté pan on a high heat. Add the spring onions and chilli. Cook for 2–3 minutes, stirring frequently, until the onions soften a little but don't turn mushy. Add the soy beans and heat them for about 30 seconds.

Give the noodles a quick rinse under warm water if they have become stuck together and then, when drained, pour the contents of the wok over them, followed by the sesame oil, sesame seeds, vinegar, coriander and ¾ teaspoon of salt. Stir well, sprinkle over the lime zest and serve at once, with the wedges alongside.

250g dried wide rice noodles
2½ tbsp sunflower oil
450g spring onions (about 35 small ones), trimmed and cut at an angle into 3cm slices, white and green parts
2–3 green chillies, depending on heat, deseeded and thinly sliced
250g frozen soy beans, blanched for 3 minutes, refreshed under cold water and left to dry
1 tbsp sesame oil
3 tbsp sesame seeds (a mix of black and toasted white or just toasted white)
2 tbsp rice wine vinegar
15g coriander, roughly chopped
1 lime, zest finely grated and fruit cut into 6 wedges
salt

SEAWEED, GINGER AND CARROT SALAD

40g dried sea spaghetti

40g fresh root ginger,
   peeled and cut into very
   thin strips

3 medium carrots, peeled
   and cut into very thin
   matchsticks (200g)

80ml rice wine vinegar

1 tbsp caster sugar

1 large cucumber, peeled,
   quartered lengthways,
   deseeded and cut into
   very thin strips (275g)

1 large mango, peeled and
   cut into very thin strips
   (260g)

100g peanuts, toasted and
   salted, roughly chopped

2 tbsp sesame seeds,
   toasted

2 tsp lime juice

1 tbsp groundnut oil

20g coriander, chopped

20g mint, shredded

salt

I originally made this using hijiki seaweed, which looked and tasted great, but as I was about to press the 'send' button and email it to the Guardian, *I received an urgent note from Tara pointing out that the* Food Standards Agency *actually advised against eating hijiki because of its high levels of inorganic arsenic. This was after I had already eaten buckets of the stuff (!) and enjoyed it thoroughly. Luckily, for my readers at least, the salad tastes just as good and looks equally striking made with sea spaghetti or other varieties of seaweed. A range of stunning dried Irish seaweed is available in various shops and online.*

Start by rinsing the sea spaghetti in cold water, drain and then cover generously with cold water. Set aside for 30 minutes.

Bring a large pot of water to the boil. Drain the spaghetti and place it in the boiling water along with the ginger. Boil for 2 minutes and then add the carrots. Boil for another 2 minutes, strain and immediately pat dry. Transfer everything to a large mixing bowl and, whilst still hot, add the vinegar, sugar and 1¼ teaspoons of salt. Mix well and leave aside to cool.

Add the remaining ingredients, stir well and serve.

SPICY TURNIP

20g dried ancho chilli,
  deseeded and stalk
  removed
½ tsp Aleppo chilli flakes,
  or just a pinch if using
  other very hot chilli flakes
2 small garlic cloves,
  roughly chopped
½ tsp ground cumin
⅛ tsp ground cardamom
1 tsp caraway seeds,
  toasted
1½ tbsp olive oil
1½ tbsp sunflower oil
1½ tsp caster sugar
3 tbsp cider vinegar
2 tbsp lemon juice
5 or 6 small turnips,
  unpeeled and stalks
  removed (700g)
90g preserved lemon,
  halved, flesh and skin
  thinly sliced, seeds
  removed
15g coriander, chopped
salt

For all turnips in need of a makeover: this is the dish. Sassy and show-stealing, this heady condiment is everything that people won't expect of the Plain Jane of the root vegetable world. A bit like pickle, this can be stored in the fridge for a few days, ready to eat with grilled meat or fish, to add to sandwiches and salads or even just to serve alongside steamed rice. Ancho chilli is mild on heat, big on aroma and well worth seeking out. Supermarkets are beginning to stock a range of dried chillies but you can also buy them very easily online.

Place the ancho chilli in a small bowl and pour over enough boiling water so that it is just covered. Leave to soak for 30 minutes, until soft. Remove the chilli from the water and squeeze out some of the moisture. Set aside 2 tablespoons of the chilli water and discard the rest.

Place the ancho in the small bowl of a food processor along with 1 teaspoon of salt and all the remaining ingredients except the turnips, preserved lemon and coriander. Add the reserved chilli water and blitz to form a rough paste. Transfer to a medium bowl and set aside.

Bring a medium pan of water to the boil, add the turnips and blanch for 3 minutes. Drain and refresh under cold water, pat dry and cut into 1cm-wide wedges. Add these to the chilli paste, along with the preserved lemon, and mix well. Cover and leave to marinate for at least an hour. Sprinkle with the coriander and serve.

SOBA NOODLES WITH QUICK-PICKLED MUSHROOMS

SERVES FOUR

as a starter or light lunch

Cold noodles are a Japanese art form. On a trip to Tokyo a few years ago I queued with a bunch of suited businessmen to have lunch in one of the city's most renowned soba noodle restaurants. It was incredibly humbling to watch a bunch of very busy people putting aside time to sit quietly for half an hour and completely immerse themselves in appreciation of the profound subtlety of the noodles. Enlightenment still escapes me but I've had my own little 'life moments' in various London noodle bars in recent months.

....

In a small saucepan mix together the vinegar, sugar, ginger and ¾ teaspoon of salt. Gently warm to dissolve the sugar, remove from the heat and add the mushrooms. Set aside to cool, stirring occasionally.

Blanch the carrots in a small saucepan of boiling water for 30 seconds. Drain, refresh under cold water, drain again and dry well.

Throw the noodles into a medium pan with plenty of boiling salted water and cook as instructed on the packet, about 7 minutes or until al dente. Refresh under cold water and set aside in a colander to drain.

Just before serving, place all of the ingredients together in a large mixing bowl, including the mushroom marinating liquid. Toss together gently and serve.

60ml rice vinegar
2½ tsp caster sugar
10g fresh root ginger, peeled and cut into very thin strips
150g buna-shimeji mushrooms, separated into individual mushrooms
2 small carrots, peeled and cut into very thin matchsticks (100g)
80g dried soba noodles
100g radishes, thinly sliced
20g salad cress (or another cress or tender leaf)
1 spring onion, trimmed and very finely sliced (15g)
1 red chilli, finely diced
2 tbsp chopped coriander
5 nori (dried seaweed) sheets (20cm x 20cm), cut into 1cm x 4cm strips
1 tsp groundnut oil
1 tbsp sesame seeds, toasted
50g mange tout, finely shredded
salt

SPROUTING BROCCOLI AND EDAMAME SALAD WITH CURRY LEAVES AND COCONUT

420g purple sprouting
broccoli, trimmed, or 350g
broccolini

220g French beans,
trimmed

200g podded frozen
edamame beans

3 tbsp olive oil, plus 1 tbsp
to finish

1 medium onion, finely
diced (150g)

2½ tsp black mustard seeds

30 fresh (or 40 dried) curry
leaves

3 whole dried chillies (or
fewer, depending on how
hot they are)

shaved rind of 1 lime, plus
1½ tbsp lime juice

10g coriander leaves

50g fresh coconut, coarsely
grated

salt

This salad works just as well without the coconut; it's your call, although the chewy texture of the freshly grated flakes contrasts brilliantly with the more yielding beans. Cracking open a coconut is a fun family challenge that children love to get involved in (from a distance, please!). For the non-thrill-seekers, punnets of fresh coconut pieces are available in many shops and supermarkets. As ever, I urge you to look out for fresh curry leaves – they make a world of difference. If you find yourself with an abundance, it wouldn't be overkill to serve this with the Lemon and Curry Leaf Rice (see page 57). They also freeze very well.

Bring a large pot of salted water to the boil. Add the broccoli and French beans and blanch for 3–4 minutes, or until they are cooked but still have bite. Use a slotted spoon to transfer the vegetables to a colander and run under cold water. Drain, pat dry well, transfer to a large mixing bowl and set aside.

Return the pan of water to the boil, add the edamame and blanch for 2 minutes. Transfer to the colander, run under cold water, pat dry and add to the broccoli and beans. Sprinkle ½ teaspoon of salt over the vegetables, stir and set aside.

Heat the olive oil in a sauté pan on a medium–high heat. Add the onion, along with ¼ teaspoon of salt, and cook for about 4 minutes, until soft. Add the black mustard seeds and, when they begin to pop, add the curry leaves, chillies and lime rind. Fry for a final 2 minutes before pouring everything over the vegetables. Stir and set aside for 10 minutes.

Just before serving, add the lime juice, coriander and coconut. Give everything a very gentle stir and serve.

BEETROOT, AVOCADO AND PEA SALAD

The possibility of blanching beetroot could do with some championing to those who always incline towards the hour-long boil or roast: keeping a bite on the purple root adds another layer of texture in a salad. Prepare everything in advance (keep the herbs in the fridge), combine when you're ready and serve with something substantial like the Bread and Pumpkin 'Fondue' (see page 276). (Also pictured overleaf.)

....

Bring a large pot of water to the boil and add the beetroot. Blanch for 3–5 minutes, until semi-cooked but still retaining a bite. Refresh under cold water and pat dry before transferring to a large bowl. Add the onion, vinegar, oil, sugar, chilli sauce, 1 teaspoon of salt and some black pepper. Toss gently and then leave aside for 15 minutes.

When ready to serve, spread half of the beetroot mixture on a large platter or in a shallow bowl. Top with half the avocado, coriander, mint, pea shoots and peas. Add the rest of the beetroot and arrange the remaining ingredients on top. Finish with a drizzle of oil and serve.

4 medium beetroots, peeled and sliced 2–3mm thick (if the beets are large, halve them after peeling) (400g)

1 small red onion, thinly sliced (100g)

3 tbsp sherry vinegar

60ml olive oil, plus extra to finish

½ tsp caster sugar

1–3 tsp savoury chilli sauce or paste such as Tabasco or Mexican Cholula Hot Sauce

2 medium avocados, peeled and thinly sliced (200g)

10g coriander leaves

10g mint leaves

20g pea shoots, or lamb's lettuce if you can't get them

150g peas, fresh or frozen, quickly blanched and refreshed under cold water

salt and black pepper

SPROUTING BROCCOLI WITH SWEET TAHINI

This is my take on a Japanese favourite, Goma-dare (sweet sesame sauce), using another much-loved seasonal ingredient, purple sprouting broccoli. I mix it here with other greens for a refreshing blend of textures but you can also use it solo. Please forgive me for the unorthodox mix of tahini and soy; my only defence is that it works perfectly.

300g purple sprouting
  broccoli or 250g broccolini
120g French beans,
  trimmed
180g mange tout, trimmed
1 tbsp groundnut oil
20g coriander leaves
2½ tbsp black and white
  sesame seeds, toasted
1 tsp nigella seeds

Sauce
about 50g tahini paste
1 small garlic clove,
  crushed
½ tsp tamari soy sauce
½ tbsp honey
1 tbsp cider vinegar
salt

Whisk together all the ingredients for the sauce in a bowl along with ½ teaspoon of salt and about 2 tablespoons of water: you want the consistency to be smooth and thick but pourable, a bit like honey; add a tiny bit of extra water or tahini paste if needed and whisk well.

Trim off the broccoli leaves. If the stems are thick, cut them into two or four lengthways, so you are left with long and thinner stems, similar in proportion to the French beans.

Bring a medium pot, with plenty of unsalted water, to the boil. Blanch the beans for about 4 minutes, until just cooked but still retaining a bite. Use a slotted spoon to lift the vegetables out of the water: transfer them to a colander, run under plenty of cold water and then dry well with a tea towel. In the same water boil the mange tout for 2 minutes. Use the slotted spoon to remove them from the water, refresh and dry as before. Repeat the same process with the broccoli, cooking it for 2–3 minutes.

Once all the vegetables are cooked and dry, mix them together in a bowl with the oil. You can now serve the salad in one of two ways. Mix most of the coriander and seeds with the vegetables and pile up on a serving dish. Pour the sauce on top and finish with the remaining coriander and seeds. Alternatively, pile the vegetables on a serving plate, dotting them with coriander leaves and sprinkling with seeds as you go, and serve the sauce in a bowl on the side.

PEAS WITH SORREL AND MUSTARD

300g peas, fresh or frozen
and defrosted
2 tsp Dijon mustard
1½ tsp English mustard
powder
¾ tsp caster sugar
2 tbsp olive oil
220g spring onions,
trimmed and sliced at
an angle into 1cm-thick
pieces
2 garlic cloves, finely sliced
1 tbsp black mustard seeds,
toasted
75g Greek yoghurt
100g sorrel leaves and
stalks, roughly shredded
salt

I once said that I look for 'drama in the mouth' when eating. I don't need every spoonful to make a statement but I am always on the lookout for bursts of pronounced flavour and mouthfuls that surprise and delight. These can come in many forms: preserved lemon skin, barberries, thin stem ginger in syrup. Give any of these a mellow background and they'll shine. Sorrel is another ingredient with this in-built 'wow' factor. When paired with more evenly balanced flavours, this sour leaf can turn even the most frugal of meals into something very special.

I hope that supermarkets will begin to stock more sorrel when it's in season in the summer months. A few do but it's still hard to find, so you'll need to hunt it down at good grocers' stores and farmers' markets.

This dish snuck into the book at the eleventh hour, when things were being wrapped up and new recipes were being developed for future Guardian *columns. One bite secured its late entry to the book and will always be the recipe that heralded the end of the shoot, the beginning of spring and a celebration of all good things. It's delicious by itself but goes very well with some simply cooked fish or chicken and plain rice or bread.*

Bring a medium pan of water to the boil, add the peas and blanch for just 30 seconds. Refresh under cold water and set aside.

Place both mustards in a small bowl with the sugar, 3 tablespoons of water and ½ teaspoon of salt. Mix together to form a smooth paste and set aside.

Place a large sauté pan on a medium–high heat and add the oil. Once hot, add the spring onion and garlic and fry for 8 minutes, stirring frequently, until golden brown. Reduce the heat to low and add the mustard sauce, peas, 2 teaspoons of the mustard seeds and the yoghurt. Stir through for 1 minute until everything is combined and the yoghurt is warmed through. Remove from the heat, stir through the sorrel and serve at once, with the remaining mustard seeds sprinkled on top.

SIMMERED

TAGLIATELLE WITH WALNUTS AND LEMON

SERVES TWO

When this recipe was first published in the Guardian *it sparked a short discussion between two readers about the ideal quantity of pasta in a single portion. This debate demonstrates a point we always discuss at length in my test kitchen: how many people does the recipe serve? This question is almost as redundant as 'How long is a piece of string?', yet all cookery writers engage in it seriously every time we write a recipe, because that's the convention: a good recipe must indicate the number of servings.*

When I mentioned in my article that a main course should have 100– 150g of dried pasta per person, one reader accused me of greediness – though not in so many words – and claimed 75g is absolutely enough, while another agreed with my estimate. If I am totally honest, I can eat anywhere between 100g and 300g of pasta depending on how hungry I am and, more importantly, how delicious it is. I am sure this applies to most people.

This is why I would like to suggest a new system of portion indication, which will take these two factors into consideration. So a recipe may 'serve two people with a medium level of hunger but absolutely in love with white truffles', or 'serve a single diner with a massive appetite but only when expertly prepared', or 'will satisfy ten little stomachs when the cook is pressed for time'. I think my system should illuminate the subject and both prevent food going to waste and people going hungry.

On a more serious note, this recipe is pretty simple and quick to prepare yet delivers an unexpected richness of flavour. Make sure you use fresh walnuts, without any bitterness in them.

60g walnuts, roughly broken up
30g unsalted butter
10g sage leaves, finely shredded
grated zest of 1 medium lemon
3 tbsp double cream
300g dried tagliatelle (or tagliolini, if you prefer)
50g Parmesan, shaved
15g parsley, chopped
2 tbsp lemon juice
salt and black pepper

....

Preheat the oven to 160°C/140°C Fan/Gas Mark 2.

Spread out the walnuts on a baking tray and roast in the oven for 15 minutes. Remove and set aside to cool.

Place a medium frying pan on a high heat and add the butter. Cook for a minute, add the sage and fry for about 2 minutes, until the butter starts to brown. Add the lemon zest, cream, ½ teaspoon of salt and plenty of black pepper, stir and cook for just a few seconds so the sauce thickens a little. Remove from the heat at once so the cream doesn't split. Set aside until ready to use.

Bring a large pan of salted water to the boil and add the pasta. Cook for 8 minutes, or according to the packet instructions, until al dente. Drain, reserving a few tablespoons of the cooking liquid, and place in a large bowl.

Warm the sauce, adding some of the pasta cooking liquid if it has become very thick, before adding it to the pasta, along with the walnuts, Parmesan and parsley. Stir in the lemon juice and serve at once.

BRUSSELS SPROUT RISOTTO

30g unsalted butter
2 tbsp olive oil
2 small onions, finely chopped (200g)
2 large garlic cloves, crushed
2 tbsp thyme leaves
2 lemons, rind shaved in long strips from one; finely grated zest of the other
300g risotto rice
500g trimmed Brussels sprouts, 200g shredded and 300g quartered
200ml dry white wine
900ml hot vegetable stock
about 400ml sunflower oil
40g Parmesan, roughly grated
60g Dolcelatte, broken into 2cm chunks
10g tarragon, chopped
2 tsp lemon juice
salt and black pepper

If you wonder about a risotto full of Brussels sprouts, please trust me and set your doubts aside. My recipe tester, Claudine, said she had similar misgivings but totally loved it. The fried sprout quarters add a layer of texture and crunch that risottos often lack: they are so good that you'll quickly be figuring out other dishes they can be sprinkled over. (Also pictured overleaf.)

Place the butter and olive oil in a large sauté pan on a medium–high heat. Add the onion and fry for 10 minutes, stirring occasionally, until soft and lightly caramelised. Add the garlic, thyme and lemon strips and cook for a further 2 minutes. Add the rice, along with the shredded sprouts, and cook for another minute, stirring frequently. Pour over the wine and let it simmer for a minute before you start adding the stock, along with 1 teaspoon of salt and a good grind of pepper. Reduce the heat to medium and carry on adding the stock in ladlefuls, stirring often, until the rice is cooked but still retains a bite, and all the stock is used up.

While the rice is cooking, pour the sunflower oil into a separate large saucepan; it should come 2cm up the sides. Place on a high heat and, once very hot, use a slotted spoon to add a handful of the quartered sprouts: take care that they are completely dry before being fried; they will still splutter so be careful. Fry the sprouts for less than a minute, until golden and crispy, then transfer them to a plate lined with kitchen paper. Keep somewhere warm whilst you continue with the remaining sprouts.

Add the Parmesan, Dolcelatte, tarragon and half the fried sprouts to the cooked risotto and stir gently. Serve at once with the remaining sprouts spooned on top, followed by the grated lemon zest and juice.

LEGUME (NOODLE) SOUP

125g dried chickpeas,
   soaked overnight in water
   with 2 tsp bicarbonate of
   soda
125g dried butterbeans,
   soaked overnight in water
   with 2 tsp bicarbonate of
   soda
80g clarified butter
2 large onions, thinly sliced
   (400g)
10 garlic cloves, thinly
   sliced
1½ tsp ground turmeric
225g yellow split peas
2 litres vegetable stock
35g parsley, chopped
35g coriander, chopped
15g dill, chopped
100g trimmed spring
   onions, thinly sliced
150g baby spinach
100g dried reshteh noodles
   or linguine
150g soured cream, plus 1
   tsp per portion to finish
1½ tbsp white wine vinegar
4 limes, halved
salt and black pepper

My previous life must have been somewhere in old Persia. I am absolutely convinced of this. I am completely infatuated by the richness of Persian cuisine, by its clever use of spices and herbs, by the ingenuity of its rice making, by pomegranate, saffron and pistachios, by yoghurt, mint and dried limes. It seems that my palate is just naturally honed for this set of flavours.

Unfortunately, I have never been able to travel to Iran, but my love affair with its food has been abundantly fed in recent years by the inspirational books of Najmieh Batmanglij. These are where I go to for a peep into a sweet, yet forbidden, culinary world.

This heart-warming thick soup, called ash-e reshteh, is the Iranian answer to minestrone. It is wonderfully wholesome and nourishing and leaves a real smile on your face. I found reshteh noodles at an Iranian grocer's near me but linguine would do the job just as well. As suggested by the parentheses in the recipe name, you can dispense with the noodles altogether if you like. There is plenty going on, body-wise, without.

Drain and rinse the chickpeas and butterbeans. Bring two pans of water to the boil and cook the chickpeas and butterbeans separately: this should take anywhere between 20 and 40 minutes. Drain and set aside.

Put the butter, onion and garlic in a large pan and place on a medium heat. Cook for 20 minutes, stirring occasionally, until soft and golden-brown. Stir in the turmeric, ½ teaspoon of salt and some black pepper and remove a third of this mix from the pan to use later.

Add the chickpeas and butterbeans to the pan, then add the split peas and stock. Simmer for about 35 minutes, skimming the froth occasionally, or until the peas are tender.

Add the herbs, spring onion and spinach, stir well and cook for another 15 minutes; add more stock or water if the soup is very thick. Add the noodles and cook for about 10 minutes so that they are just done. Stir in the soured cream and vinegar and serve at once, garnished with a teaspoon of soured cream per portion and the reserved cooked onion. Serve lime halves to squeeze over every portion.

FREGOLA AND ARTICHOKE PILAF

3 globe artichokes (900g in total), or 300g artichoke hearts

2 tbsp lemon juice

2 tbsp olive oil

2 medium onions, thinly sliced (300g)

20g unsalted butter

250g fregola, rinsed well under cold water and left in a colander to drain

600ml boiling vegetable stock

1½ tbsp red wine vinegar

60g pitted black Kalamata olives, torn in half

60g flaked almonds, toasted

10g parsley, chopped

salt and black pepper

Green chilli sauce

3 green chillies, deseeded and roughly chopped

1 garlic clove, roughly chopped

1 small preserved lemon, deseeded and roughly chopped (40g)

1 tbsp lemon juice

3 tbsp olive oil

30g parsley, chopped

Unlike many of my dishes, this one doesn't excel on the visual front. What it has going for it is its surprisingly fresh set of flavours and wonderfully warm and comforting texture; I am quite happy to scoff this down every day of the week. Fregola is a type of pasta from Sardinia, similar to giant couscous. Couscous, giant couscous, fregola, mograbiah, maftoul: confused? Don't be! Though springing from different countries and going by various names, they are all variations on the theme of very little (or quite little), round (or pretty-much-round) balls of pasta. They are happiest when supporting flavourful ingredients in soups, stews, salads or sauces, but they are also great simply served alongside meat and fish.

Use commercial frozen and defrosted or jarred, drained artichoke hearts here if you like, to save yourself time and labour.

Place all the ingredients for the chilli sauce in the small bowl of a food processor. Blitz to form a rough paste and set aside until ready to use.

Cut most of the stalk off each of the artichokes and remove the tough outer leaves by hand. Once you reach the softer leaves, cut 2cm off the top and trim the base around the stalk. Cut in half, lengthways, so that you can reach the heart, scrape it clean of hairs and cut each half into three triangular segments. Put the artichokes in a medium saucepan, pour over enough water to cover, around 500ml, along with the lemon juice. Bring to the boil, reduce the heat to medium and simmer gently for about 8 minutes, until the artichokes are semi-cooked but still firm. Drain, season with ¼ teaspoon of salt and set aside.

Place the oil in a large sauté pan for which you have a lid and place on a medium–high heat. Add the onions, along with ¾ teaspoon of salt, and cook for 10 minutes, stirring often, until the onion is brown and caramelised. Add the butter and stir until it melts before adding the semi-cooked artichoke or artichoke hearts, if using, fregola, stock and a good grind of black pepper. Stir once, cover the pan and place on a low heat for about 18 minutes, until the fregola is cooked and all of the liquid has been absorbed. Avoid the temptation to stir as this will lead to a starchy dish.

Remove the pan from the heat and leave to sit, covered, for 10 minutes. Remove the lid, add the vinegar, olives and almonds and stir gently. Sprinkle with the parsley and serve warm or at room temperature, with a generous spoonful of the chilli sauce on top.

HOT AND SOUR MUSHROOM SOUP

This takes its inspiration from Asian soups, such as Thai tom yum or Vietnamese pho. The key to these is a rich and hearty stock, with many layers of flavour hitting the palate at different stages, a bit like a great aged wine. This is why my list of ingredients – please forgive me for it – is so long here. I have a hunch you will find it worthwhile. This soup is intentionally light but it can be bulked up with cooked rice noodles. Add more tamarind paste if you like this super-sharp. Coriander roots, available in many Indian and oriental grocers', have a deeper and more intense flavour than the leaves. If you can't get hold of any, tie together a small bunch of coriander stems with a piece of string, gently bruise them with a rolling pin to help release their flavour, and use those instead. (Pictured overleaf.)

....

Begin by heating the oil in a large saucepan and add the onion, carrot, celery, garlic and ginger. Cook on a high heat for about 5 minutes until the edges begin to colour. Pour in 2.25 litres of water and add the lemongrass, prunes, chilli, star anise, soy, lime leaves and coriander root. Bring to the boil, then reduce to a low simmer and cook for 45 minutes.

Strain the stock and return to the pan. You can discard the vegetables, though I love eating the carrot and celery. Bring the stock back to a very low simmer, add the tamarind paste, followed by the enoki and white mushrooms and cook for 1 minute. Then add the remaining ingredients, apart from the sesame oil, along with 1½ teaspoons salt, and allow to heat through for a further minute. Ladle into warm bowls and finish with a little drizzle of sesame oil, no more than a few drops in each bowl.

1 tbsp sunflower oil

3 small onions, roughly chopped (350g)

3 medium carrots, peeled and roughly chopped (250g)

6 celery stalks, roughly chopped (350g)

6 garlic cloves, peeled and left whole

75g fresh root ginger, peeled and roughly chopped

3 lemongrass stalks, roughly chopped (50g)

12 prunes (120g)

3 red chillies, roughly chopped

6 star anise

2 tbsp tamari soy sauce

6 lime leaves

30g coriander root, chopped

2 tbsp tamarind paste

toasted sesame oil, to finish

salt

150g enoki mushrooms, separated into individual mushrooms

150g white mushrooms, sliced

150g buna-shimeji mushrooms, separated into individual mushrooms

65ml lime juice (about 2 limes)

20g coriander leaves, plus extra to garnish

20g Thai basil leaves

160g bean sprouts

160g green beans, cut into thirds, boiled for 4 minutes and refreshed under cold water

SPICY CHICKPEA AND BULGAR SOUP

2 tbsp olive oil

2 small onions, cut into 1cm dice (180g)

4 garlic cloves, crushed

2 large carrots, peeled and cut into 1cm dice (250g)

4 celery stalks, cut into 1cm dice (250g)

2 tbsp harissa paste (less if you don't like things very hot)

1 tsp ground cumin

1 tsp ground coriander

1½ tsp whole caraway seeds

500g cooked chickpeas (tinned are fine)

1.2 litres vegetable stock

100g coarse bulgar wheat

salt and black pepper

Creamed feta paste (optional)

100g feta, broken into large chunks

60g crème fraîche

15g coriander, roughly chopped

15g mint leaves

This simple and soothing soup, minus the optional feta paste, can most likely be made with ingredients you already have in your cupboards and fridge (and if you don't have some celery stalks and a couple of carrots regularly lying around in your fridge, plus a jar of good harissa, I highly recommend that you do; they form the base of some of my favourite sauces). The dairy-free soup works well without the paste, but a spoonful on top elevates a midweek supper into something pretty special.

Place the oil in a medium saucepan on a medium heat. Add the onions and sauté for 5 minutes, stirring from time to time, until translucent. Add the garlic, carrots and celery and continue cooking for another 8 minutes. Add the harissa, cumin, coriander and caraway seeds and cook for a further 2 minutes, stirring well. Gently mix the chickpeas into the pot – you don't want them to break up – along with 1 teaspoon of salt and plenty of black pepper. Add the stock and bring to the boil. Reduce the heat and simmer gently for 10 minutes.

Meanwhile, rinse the bulgar, put in a small saucepan and cover generously with cold water. Bring to the boil and immediately remove from the heat. Drain, refresh under cold water, drain again and set aside.

If you are making it, put all the ingredients for the feta paste in the small bowl of a food processor, along with ⅛ teaspoon of salt. Blitz for a couple of minutes to form a smooth and creamy paste and then keep in the fridge until needed.

Before serving, add the cooked bulgar to the soup and bring to a light simmer. Divide between bowls, add a spoonful of feta paste to each bowl, if using, and serve at once.

SPRING ONION SOUP

Kashk is a relatively recent addition to my pantry and it has become an absolute favourite. Kashk, kash and kishk signify different things throughout the Middle East, Turkey and Greece, but each refers to a type of foodstuff produced by the process of fermentation and then drying of yoghurt or curdled milk; they are then turned into a powder that can later be reconstituted. Iranian kashk is used to bulk up soups and stews and gives them a wonderfully deep and sharp aroma: a bit like feta but in runny form. You can get it from specialist Iranian shops but don't worry if you cannot get hold of it: I'm aware it's not easy to come by – a mixture of crème fraîche and grated Parmesan or another mature cheese makes a perfectly good substitute.

900g spring onions or salad onions, if possible a large variety with a thick bulb

40g unsalted butter

50ml olive oil, plus extra to drizzle

2 medium garlic heads, cloves peeled and halved lengthways (60g)

3 bay leaves

300g peas, fresh or frozen and defrosted

1 medium courgette, cut into 1cm dice (200g)

1.3 litres vegetable stock

80g parsley leaves, roughly chopped

60g kashk (or a mix of 40g crème fraîche and 20g finely grated Parmesan, with extra crème fraîche to serve)

20g mint leaves, chopped

finely grated zest of ½ lemon

salt and black pepper

Cut the white part of the spring onions into 1.5cm-wide slices, the green into 2.5cm-wide segments and keep the two separate.

Melt the butter in a large saucepan; add the olive oil, white spring onion slices and garlic cloves, along with ½ teaspoon of salt and some black pepper. Sauté on a medium heat for 10–15 minutes or until the vegetables are soft and have lost some of their harshness. Add the green parts of the spring onion and the bay leaves and continue cooking for about 10 minutes. Add the peas and courgette and cook for another 5 minutes.

Remove half the vegetables from the pan and set aside. Cover the remaining vegetables with the stock, bring to the boil and simmer for 3 minutes. Remove the bay leaves, add the parsley and blitz in a food processor or with a hand-held blender. Return the reserved vegetables to the pan and warm them up before stirring in the kashk (or the crème fraîche and Parmesan mix).

Transfer the soup to individual bowls, sprinkle with the chopped mint and lemon zest, and if you are not using the kashk, spoon a teaspoon of crème fraîche into each bowl. Finish with a drizzle of oil.

THAI RED LENTIL SOUP WITH AROMATIC CHILLI OIL

Fresh, creamy and loaded with flavour, this soup would be the first thing I'd make when the arrival of autumn is officially announced. If you like your soup totally smooth, with no 'interruptions', forget the sugar snaps. Thanks to the brilliant Leith's Vegetarian Cookery for the chilli oil: you'll make more than you need for the soup, but keep it in a sealed jar in the fridge for up to a month, to drizzle over other soups, salads or grilled dishes. You can also do without the oil, drizzling the soup with a good savoury chilli sauce instead.

....

First make the chilli oil. Heat 2 tablespoons of the sunflower oil in a small saucepan. Add the shallot, garlic, ginger, chilli, star anise and curry powder and fry over a low heat for 5 minutes, stirring from time to time, until the shallot is soft. Add the tomato purée and cook gently for 2 minutes. Stir in the remaining oil, along with the lemon zest, and simmer very gently for 30 minutes. Leave to cool and then strain through a muslin-lined sieve.

For the soup, bring a small pan of water to the boil and throw in the sugar snap peas. Cook for 90 seconds, drain, refresh under cold water and set aside to dry. Once cool, cut them at an angle into long, 2mm-thick slices.

Heat the sunflower oil in a large pot and add the onion. Cook on a low heat, with a lid on, for 10–15 minutes, stirring once or twice, until the onion is completely soft and sweet. Stir in the red curry paste and cook for 1 minute. Add the lemongrass stalks, lime leaves, red lentils and 700ml of water. Bring to the boil, reduce the heat to low and simmer for 15 minutes or until the lentils are completely soft.

Remove the soup from the heat, take out and discard the lemongrass and lime leaves. Use a blender to process the soup until it is completely smooth. Add the coconut milk, lime juice, soy sauce, ½ teaspoon of salt and stir. Return the soup to the stove on a medium heat and, once the soup is almost boiling, ladle into bowls. Scatter the sugar snaps on top, sprinkle over the coriander and finish with ½ teaspoon of chilli oil drizzled over each portion.

120g sugar snap peas

3 tbsp sunflower oil

1 medium onion, thinly sliced (160g)

1½ tbsp vegetarian red curry paste

2 lemongrass stalks, gently bashed with a rolling pin

4 fresh (or 12 dried) Kaffir lime leaves

250g red lentils

250ml coconut milk

1½ tbsp lime juice

1½ tbsp soy sauce

15g coriander leaves, roughly chopped

salt

Chilli-infused oil

180ml sunflower oil

1 banana shallot, roughly chopped (50g)

1 garlic clove, roughly chopped

1 tsp peeled and roughly chopped fresh root ginger

½ red chilli, roughly chopped

½ star anise

2 tsp curry powder

1 tsp tomato purée

grated zest of ½ small lemon

TOMATO AND WATERMELON GAZPACHO

2kg tomatoes (about 20),
  blanched, peeled and
  roughly chopped
5 garlic cloves, roughly
  chopped
6 celery stalks, white parts
  and leaves, finely chopped
  (450g)
1 small onion, finely
  chopped (140g)
400g watermelon flesh,
  deseeded and roughly
  chopped
100g crustless white bread,
  broken into small chunks
150ml passata (or tomato
  juice)
15g basil leaves
2 tbsp red wine vinegar
200ml olive oil, plus extra
  for drizzling
salt and black pepper
coarse sea salt, to serve

Croutons
150g crustless white bread,
  broken into 2–3cm chunks
3 tbsp olive oil
1½ tbsp red wine vinegar

I first made this during my sun-drenched days in Mallorca. The sweet, red ramallet tomatoes were out of this world, and the group of old ladies who taught me how to thread them together into a fine bunch were the most animated and amusing 70-something crew I've ever met. My offering in return was this wonderfully sweet and refreshing soup. Forgive my slipping it into the 'simmered' section; I know there is no mention of things bubbling away gently on the stove but it wanted to be with its fellow soups.

First make the croutons. Preheat the oven to 200°C/180°C Fan/Gas Mark 6. Place the bread in a medium bowl along with the oil, vinegar and ½ teaspoon of salt. Place a griddle pan on a high heat, add the croutons and cook for 2 minutes, turning until all sides are slightly charred and starting to crisp. Transfer from the pan onto a baking tray and place in the oven for about 12 minutes, until golden-brown and crispy. Set aside to cool.

Place the tomatoes, garlic, celery, onion, watermelon, bread, passata and 10g of the basil in a blender, or large bowl if using a hand blender, along with ¾ teaspoon of salt and a good grind of black pepper. Blend until smooth and then, with the blender still going, add the vinegar and olive oil. Refrigerate until needed.

To serve, pour the soup into individual bowls and top with the croutons. Scatter the remaining basil leaves over each portion, along with a final drizzle of oil. Finish with a little coarse salt and serve at once.

ALPHONSO MANGO AND CURRIED CHICKPEA SALAD

Unlike the large, often hard mangoes available year-round, the Alphonso and other Indian and Pakistani varieties (look out for Kesar, Banganpali, Langra and Chaunsa) are fibreless, fragrant, small and sublime. People get pretty evangelical about the Alphonso mango: newspaper headlines in India announce the arrival of the fruit's short season and courier companies in Mumbai advertise specialist 'mango delivery services' to transport boxes around the city. It might all seem a bit much to those who have not held out for the short but intensely sweet Alphonso mango season, which lasts through May and June. Cargo logistics mean that large supermarkets don't tend to stock them, so head to your local greengrocer's or open market stall and look out for the bright yellow boxes of the fruit, whose subcontinental labels, tissue paper and tinsel poking out make them the ready-made presents that they are.

150g dried chickpeas, soaked overnight in plenty of water with 2 tsp bicarbonate of soda
1 tsp coriander seeds
1 tsp black mustard seeds
½ tsp cumin seeds
1 tsp curry powder
½ tsp ground turmeric
1 tsp caster sugar
80ml sunflower oil
1 large onion, thinly sliced (200g)
1 small cauliflower, broken into 4cm florets (400g)
2–3 Alphonso mangoes or 1 large, ripe regular mango, peeled and cut into 2cm dice (570g)
1 medium-hot green chilli, deseeded and finely chopped
20g coriander, chopped
3 tbsp lime juice
50g baby spinach leaves
salt

Drain and rinse the chickpeas, place in a medium saucepan on a medium heat, cover with fresh water and cook on a very gentle simmer for 45 minutes to 1 hour, until the chickpeas are completely soft. Drain, transfer to a large mixing bowl and leave somewhere warm.

Place the coriander, mustard and cumin seeds in a large sauté pan and dry-roast them until they begin to pop. Use a spice grinder or pestle and mortar to crush them to a powder and then add to them the curry powder, turmeric, sugar and ½ teaspoon of salt; set aside.

In the same pan, heat up half the oil and cook the onion for 5 minutes on a high heat, stirring occasionally, so that it starts to gain some colour. Add the spice mix and keep cooking on a medium heat for another 5 minutes, until the onion is completely soft. Transfer to the bowl with the warm chickpeas and keep aside.

Bring a large pot of water to the boil, throw in the cauliflower and blanch for just 1 minute. Drain, pat dry and set aside. Once the cauliflower is completely dry, heat up the remaining oil in the same pan you cooked the onion in (you don't need to clean it), add the cauliflower, along with ¼ teaspoon of salt, and fry on a high heat for 3–4 minutes, just to give it colour.

Add the hot cauliflower and any oil from the pan to the onion and chickpeas and stir well. Leave for 5 minutes if you want the salad warm or longer for room temperature. Add the mango to the salad, along with the chilli, coriander, lime juice and spinach. Stir well and serve at once or chill and serve within 24 hours.

CANDY BEETROOT WITH LENTILS AND YUZU

750g candy beetroots, or
a variety of beetroots

225g Puy lentils

2–4 tbsp yuzu juice,
depending on intensity

3 tbsp olive oil, plus extra
to finish

½ small red onion, thinly
sliced (50g)

2 tsp maple syrup

1½ tbsp lemon juice

40g watercress

40g baby chard leaves (or
baby spinach leaves)

1 tsp yuzu powder
(optional)

salt and black pepper

The aptly named candy beetroot is as sweet as it sounds and its flesh is made up of beautiful alternating red and white rings. You can slice it thinly and use raw in salads; once cooked, it turns a uniform mellow pink. If you can't find it, search for golden beet or normal red beet. A combination of all three is stunning but just one will work absolutely fine.

Originating in East Asia, yuzu is a citrus fruit whose flavour is close to a combination of lime and mandarin. Its zest and juice are commonly used to add a fresh aroma to various Japanese dishes, including soups. As it's almost impossible to get hold of fresh yuzu, you'll have to rely on bottled juice. The intensity of one brand and the next varies considerably, though, so you'll need to check this before adding it to the dish. You can get the juice from Japanese specialists or online but, if you're not able to find it, substitute it with a bit of lime juice.

Place all but one of the beetroots in a medium saucepan and cover with plenty of water. Bring to the boil, reduce to a gentle simmer and cook for about an hour, adding more boiling water as needed, until cooked. Remove from the heat, take the beets out of the water and leave to cool down (you can now keep them refrigerated for a day or two). Peel the beetroots, halve them and cut into wedges, 1cm thick at the base.

Place the lentils in a small saucepan and cover with plenty of water. Bring to the boil and simmer for 15–20 minutes, until cooked but retaining a bite. Drain well, transfer to a mixing bowl and, whilst still hot, stir in 1 tablespoon each of yuzu juice and olive oil, along with ½ teaspoon of salt and some black pepper. Set aside to cool down (the lentils can also be kept in the fridge for a couple of days).

Peel the remaining uncooked beetroot and, using a mandoline, if you have one, cut into paper-thin slices.

To put the salad together, add the remaining yuzu juice and 2 tablespoons of oil to the lentils. Add the cooked and raw beetroot, onion, maple syrup and lemon juice and toss gently. Taste for seasoning, adding more yuzu depending on the intensity. Transfer the salad to a shallow bowl, dotting with the watercress and chard. Finish with a sprinkle of powdered yuzu, if you have it, and a final drizzle of oil.

GLOBE ARTICHOKE SALAD WITH PRESERVED LEMON MAYONNAISE

You think you know how to do something until you witness the pros at work. My summer spent filming the first series of Mediterranean Feasts *made me question my right to be calling myself a pastry chef after a day spent with kids a quarter of my age making sheets of warka pastry. My relationship with vegetables was similarly challenged upon witnessing the speed and dexterity with which artichokes were cleaned by weathered hands in the markets (without even using a chopping board; just hands up in the air). Seemingly effortless, the immaculate chokes produced within seconds by a few strikes of the knife were astounding and in a completely different league to anything I've seen before. Still, even if it costs you a good 30 minutes and a bunch of blackened fingertips, it is an effort well worth making. Fresh artichokes are heavenly!*

The mayonnaise makes more than you need but any left over will keep in a sealed jar in the fridge for a few days.

4 large globe artichokes
   (1.6kg in total)
75ml lemon juice
1 medium baking potato,
   peeled and cut into 12
   wedges, similar in size
   and proportion to the
   artichoke pieces (250g)
1 large thyme sprig, plus 1
   tbsp picked leaves
10g dill, chopped
1 tbsp tarragon, chopped
50g pea shoots
1 tbsp olive oil
salt and black pepper

Mayonnaise
1 egg yolk
¼ tsp Dijon mustard
1 small garlic clove,
   crushed
1½ tsp white wine vinegar
¼ tsp caster sugar
30g preserved lemon, flesh
   and skin chopped, seeds
   removed
75ml sunflower oil

To clean the artichokes, cut off most of the stalk and start removing the tough outer leaves by hand. Once you reach the softer leaves, trim off 2–3cm from the leaves at the top with a knife. Trim the base and around the stalk. Cut the artichoke in half lengthways so you can reach the heart and scrape it clean of all the hairs. Dip the clean heart halves in 1–2 tablespoons of lemon juice mixed with some water and cut each into 3 triangular segments.

Put the artichokes in a medium saucepan along with the potato. Add the remaining lemon juice (about 3 tablespoons), the thyme sprig and ¾ teaspoon of salt and top with enough water just to cover the artichokes, approximately 800ml. Bring to the boil, reduce the heat and simmer gently for 10–15 minutes, until a knife is easily inserted into both potatoes and artichokes. Remove from the heat and allow the vegetables to cool in the liquid.

For the mayonnaise, put all the ingredients except the oil in a small food processor bowl. With the motor running, slowly pour in the oil to get a glossy and firm mayonnaise. Refrigerate until needed.

To assemble, drain the artichokes and potatoes and mix together in a large bowl with the thyme leaves, dill, tarragon, pea shoots, olive oil, ¼ teaspoon of salt and some black pepper. Gently toss together and serve with a dollop of mayonnaise and a good grind of black pepper.

GLOBE ARTICHOKE AND MOZZARELLA WITH CANDIED LEMON

4 large globe artichokes
  (1.6kg in total)
3 lemons, halved
2 bay leaves
4 thyme sprigs
1 medium onion, quartered
  (150g)
120g Gem lettuce leaves,
  cut widthways into 1cm-
  wide strips
200g buffalo mozzarella
10g parsley, chopped
10g mint, chopped
10g basil, chopped
120ml olive oil
1 garlic clove, crushed
salt and black pepper

Candied lemon
1 lemon
35g caster sugar

As our hands are not all as adept as those mentioned on page 109, shortcuts are always possible with artichokes: instead of cleaning and cooking them, you can always use frozen or jarred artichoke hearts or bases (I do prefer frozen to jarred, though). Also, while the candied lemon looks and tastes fantastic, the juice and grated zest of a lemon will work fine instead.

Remove and discard the artichoke stems and hard outer leaves. Continue removing the leaves until you reach the heart and then cut each heart into two lengthways. Use a small serrated knife to clear the heart of all the inedible bits – tough leaves and hairs – so you are left with a clean shell. As you do this, use the juice of 1 lemon to smear the artichokes so they don't discolour.

Place the artichokes in a large saucepan, squeeze in the juice of the remaining two lemons and throw in 2 of the squeezed halves as well. Cover with water, add the bay leaves, thyme, onion and ½ teaspoon of salt and simmer for 10–15 minutes, until tender. Drain the artichokes and lemon, discarding the onions, bay and thyme and set aside to cool.

To prepare the candied lemon, use a vegetable peeler to shave off wide strips of lemon rind; avoid the white pith. Cut the strips into 1–2mm-thick slices and place them in a small saucepan. Squeeze the lemon and make up the juice to 100ml with water. Pour over the lemon skins, add the sugar and bring to a light simmer. Cook for about 15 minutes or until the syrup is reduced to about a third of its original volume. Set aside to cool down.

To assemble the dish, cut the artichoke halves into 2cm-thick wedges and arrange them on a serving platter together with the lettuce. Break the mozzarella with your hands into large, uneven chunks and dot the salad with them. Stir together the herbs, olive oil and garlic and season with ¼ teaspoon of salt; spoon this over the vegetables and cheese. Use a fork to scatter some candied zest on top and drizzle with a tiny amount of the syrup. Finish with a sprinkle of black pepper.

CURRY LAKSA

8 baby shallots, peeled
  (100g)
8 garlic cloves, roughly
  chopped
30g fresh root ginger,
  peeled and sliced
1 large lemongrass stalk,
  soft white stem only,
  sliced (20g)
2 tsp ground coriander
3 large dried red chillies
2 tbsp sambal oelek (or
  another savoury chilli
  paste)
60ml vegetable oil
40g coriander, leaves and
  stalks
1.2 litres vegetable stock
3 branches of laksa leaves
  (or fresh curry leaves, or a
  mixture of both)
2 tsp curry powder
2 tbsp caster sugar
400ml coconut milk
300g bean sprouts
150g French beans,
  trimmed and halved
100g rice vermicelli
250g fried tofu puffs
  (optional)
2 limes, halved
salt

The term laksa is used to describe two different types of spicy noodle soup: curry laksa and Assam laksa. Each has many variants but, broadly speaking, curry laksa sees its noodles served in a coconut curry soup and Assam laksa has its noodles in a sour fish version. I love the tamarind and shrimp paste often found in an Assam, but for comfort and sustenance in equal measure, you can't beat the Malaysian aromatic, coconutty, curried kind. My version is a heart-and-limb-warming soup with quite a kick, so tone down the heat if you're not a fan of chilli.

Tofu puffs are squares of bean curd that have already been deep-fried and are sold in bags in Asian markets. They're a great addition to soups and stews, absorbing tons of flavour and liquid. If you can't get tofu puffs, cut some firm tofu into large chunks, coat generously in cornflour and deep-fry. (Pictured on pages 114 and 115, top.)

Place the first seven ingredients (up to and including the sambal oelek) in the small bowl of a food processor. Add half the oil and the stalks of the coriander and process well to form a semi-smooth paste. Roughly shred the coriander leaves and keep aside for later.

Heat the remaining oil in a medium saucepan and fry the spice paste on a medium–low heat for 15–20 minutes, stirring very frequently. You want to cook it slowly without burning. Add the vegetable stock, laksa or curry leaves, curry powder, sugar, coconut milk and 1½ teaspoons of salt. Increase the heat, bring to a gentle simmer and leave to cook for 30 minutes.

Throw the bean sprouts into a pan of boiling water, drain at once and refresh under cold water. Cook the French beans in boiling water for 3 minutes, drain and refresh.

Once your broth is ready, steep the rice vermicelli in boiling water for 3 minutes and drain. Just before serving, remove the laksa branches and discard (the leaves can stay in the soup). Add the beans, noodles and half the bean sprouts to heat up in the soup. Spoon the soup into large bowls and top with the remaining bean sprouts, the tofu puffs, if using, and coriander leaves. Squeeze half a teaspoon of lime juice on top – or more, if you want – and throw one squeezed lime half into each bowl. Serve at once.

QUINOA PORRIDGE WITH GRILLED TOMATOES AND GARLIC

Quinoa as comfort food is not quite the oxymoron some might initially think. The cooking method here is opposite to the way I normally cook quinoa where, like pasta, I throw it into boiling water for 9 minutes, before draining and refreshing it under cold water. Whereas that method encourages every grain to remain separate and distinct, the porridge-like consistency of this recipe, enriched with butter and feta, is more the method you'd follow to cook polenta. The result is satisfying and comforting in a way that will appeal both to signed-up converts to the seed as well as those still in need of some convincing. You don't want the quinoa to sit once it's cooked or it will set, so make sure the tomatoes and herb oil are all ready as soon as the quinoa is done. (Pictured on page 115, bottom.)

250g quinoa
about 1.1 litres vegetable
  stock
20g unsalted butter
10g parsley, chopped
100g feta, crumbled into
  2cm chunks
1 tsp olive oil
250g baby plum tomatoes
4 garlic cloves, thinly sliced
10g mint leaves
salt

Herb oil
1 green chilli, deseeded and
  roughly chopped
15g parsley
15g mint leaves
100ml olive oil

To make the herb oil, place all the ingredients in the small bowl of a food processor, along with ½ teaspoon of salt, and process to form a smooth sauce with a thick pouring consistency.

Place the quinoa in a medium saucepan, add the stock and bring to the boil. Reduce the heat to medium and cook gently for about 25 minutes, uncovered, stirring from time to time, until a porridge-like consistency is formed. You might need to add a bit more stock if the quinoa is sticking to the pan. At the very end fold in the butter until it melts, followed by the parsley and then the feta, making sure the feta stays in chunks.

While the quinoa is cooking, place a large frying pan on a high heat with the olive oil. When the oil is hot, add the tomatoes and cook for about 5 minutes, shaking the pan once or twice so that all sides get some good charred colour. Add the garlic and cook for 30 seconds, so that it turns golden-brown without burning. Transfer to a bowl, sprinkle with ¼ teaspoon of salt and some black pepper. Chop the mint and fold through just before serving, as it will start to blacken once chopped.

Spoon the warm quinoa porridge into shallow bowls, top with the tomatoes, finish with a drizzle of the herb oil and serve at once.

IRANIAN-STYLE PASTA

3 large aubergines (1.2kg in
total)
200g kashk (or a mixture
of 140g crème fraîche and
60g grated Parmesan)
75ml olive oil, plus extra for
drizzling
1 large onion, finely
chopped (200g)
2 tsp cumin seeds
3 garlic cloves, crushed
2 tbsp lime juice
150g Greek yoghurt
2 tsp dried mint
500g reshteh noodles or
linguine pasta
½ tsp saffron threads,
soaked in ½ tbsp
lukewarm water
10g fresh mint, shredded
salt and black pepper

As in the case of pizza, I always get slightly indignant that with their pasta Italians ended up dominating a scene that includes a vast set of dishes made all over the planet. There just isn't a good alternative in English to 'pasta', as there isn't to 'pizza', even though this particular Iranian dish is about as far removed from Italian pasta as it is from pad thai. So I am just stuck with 'pasta' (though I could think of worse things to be 'stuck' with).

Kashk, the fermented Iranian yoghurt I've raved about elsewhere (see the Spring Onion Soup introduction on page 99), is a good way of giving vegetarians who don't eat Parmesan the umami-rich taste inherent in the cheese. If kashk is not available, for those who do eat Parmesan, a good alternative here can be made from mixing together crème fraîche and grated Parmesan.

For more about reshteh noodles, see page 92.

Preheat the oven to 230°C/210°C Fan/Gas Mark 8.

Pierce the aubergines in a few places with a sharp knife, place on a baking tray lined with baking parchment and roast in the oven for about 1 hour, until the flesh is completely soft. Set aside until cool enough to handle before cutting in half and spooning out the flesh into a colander to drain for at least 30 minutes. Discard the skin.

Place the kashk paste in a small saucepan with 75ml of water. Bring to a simmer on a medium heat, stir, then set aside until ready to use.

Heat 2 tablespoons of the oil in a medium sauté pan and place on a medium–high heat. Add the onion and cumin seeds and cook for 12 minutes, stirring occasionally, until soft. Add the aubergine flesh and garlic, along with 1 teaspoon of salt and some black pepper. Cook for another 2 minutes before adding the lime juice. Stir through for a final minute and then remove from the heat.

Add the yoghurt to the kashk pan and heat on a low heat for 5 minutes, stirring from time to time. Keep an eye on the mixture as you don't want the yoghurt to split.

Mix the dried mint with a tablespoon of the oil and set aside.

Bring a large pan of salted water to the boil and add the pasta. Cook for 8 minutes, or according to the packet instructions, until cooked but still retaining a bite. Stir 2 tablespoons of oil through the pasta, mix and then divide between shallow bowls or plates. Drizzle over the mint oil, followed by the aubergine. Top this with the kashk, followed by the saffron water, fresh mint and a final drizzle of oil. Serve at once.

STUFFED COURGETTES

It is not by mere coincidence that this recipe doesn't come with a picture. These courgettes, once cooked for a good two hours, are just not that handsome any more: the vibrant green turns dull grey, the firm flesh becomes limp and tired. Still, this is one of my favourite recipes so I put courgette vanity aside and forgive my green heroes their unfortunate transformation (with the help of some yoghurt foundation and some mint paste mascara).

These courgettes – stuffed with rice and cooked in a sweet and slightly sour liquor that reduces to an unctuous sauce – only get better with time. You can serve them as soon as they cool down, but I prefer to refrigerate them and have them the next day, slightly above fridge temperature. The flesh you scoop out when preparing the courgettes can be shallow-fried with garlic, diced red pepper, chilli and fresh herbs and then spooned over pasta or rice.

6 medium courgettes (1.3kg in total)
30g mint leaves
60ml olive oil
90g Greek yoghurt

Filling
1½ tbsp sunflower oil
1 small onion, finely chopped (100g)
300g short-grain rice
1 tsp ground cumin
2 tsp ground allspice
1 tbsp dried mint
1 small tomato, finely chopped (80g)
grated zest of 1 lemon
15g coriander, chopped
salt and black pepper

Cooking liquor
about 450ml vegetable stock
1 tsp ground allspice
1½ tbsp pomegranate molasses
1 tbsp caster sugar
1 tbsp dried mint
3 garlic cloves, crushed
2 tbsp lemon juice

Start with the filling. Heat the oil in a large sauté pan for which you have a tight-fitting lid. Add the onion and sauté on a medium heat for 5 minutes, stirring occasionally, before adding the rice, ground spices and mint. Continue to cook and stir for another 8 minutes. Remove from the heat and stir in the tomato, lemon zest, coriander, 1½ teaspoons of salt and some black pepper.

Cut the courgettes in half lengthways and use a teaspoon to scoop out the flesh (see the introduction, above). Fill each half generously with the rice mixture. Place the other half back on top and tie tightly with string in a few places to secure the filling inside. Wipe the sauté pan clean and place the courgettes inside, sitting snugly side by side.

For the cooking liquor, put all the ingredients in a medium saucepan, adding 1 teaspoon of salt and some black pepper. Bring to the boil and then pour over the courgettes. The juices need to come roughly 1cm up the sides of the pan; add some more stock if you need.

Place the pan on a medium heat and, as soon as the liquid comes to a simmer, press the courgettes down with a heatproof plate so they do not float when cooking. Cover the pan with a lid and cook on a gentle simmer for 1½–2 hours. At this point both the courgettes and the rice should be completely soft with about 3 tablespoons of liquid left in the pan. Remove the pan from the heat, uncover and allow the courgettes to cool down until they reach room temperature. If you are serving these the next day, refrigerate overnight but leave at room temperature for half an hour before serving, so they are not fridge-cold.

Place the fresh mint in the small bowl of a food processor, along with the olive oil and a pinch of salt. Blitz until smooth and set aside.

Place a courgette on each plate and spoon some yoghurt on top. Drizzle over the mint sauce and serve at once.

SLOW-COOKED CHICKPEAS ON TOAST WITH POACHED EGG

220g medium-sized dried
chickpeas, soaked
overnight in plenty of
cold water with 2 tsp
bicarbonate of soda

1 tbsp olive oil, plus 1 tbsp
to finish

1 medium onion, roughly
chopped (140g)

3 garlic cloves, crushed

1½ tsp tomato purée

¼ tsp cayenne pepper

¼ tsp smoked paprika

2 medium red peppers, cut
roughly into 0.5cm dice
(180g)

1 beef tomato, peeled and
roughly chopped (300g)

½ tsp caster sugar

4 slices of sourdough,
brushed with olive oil and
grilled on both sides

4 eggs, poached (see
page 210 for poaching
instructions)

2 tsp za'atar

salt and black pepper

This recipe was tested among card-carrying sceptics – '5 hours' cooking for beans on toast?!'; they couldn't see how it could possibly be justified when a variation on the theme can be made in 15 minutes (or even 15 seconds, for those inclined to open a well-known brand of beans and pop bread in the toaster). The result more than won over my fellow recipe testers – the chickpeas are impossibly soft and yielding and the flavour is rich and deep in a way that only slow-cooking can bring about. So, having won over these sceptics, I ask the reader to take a leap of faith.

Notwithstanding the cooking time, it's a very low-maintenance and highly comforting dish: one to simmer away on the stove at the weekend when you are pottering about in slippers at home. It tastes fantastic the next day and the day after that, so you might want to double the quantities and keep a batch in the fridge. A spoonful of Greek yoghurt can be served alongside each portion, if you like.

Drain and rinse the chickpeas. Place in a large saucepan, cover with plenty of cold water and set over a high heat. Bring to the boil, skim the surface, and boil for 5 minutes. Strain and set aside.

Place the oil, onion, garlic, tomato purée, cayenne, paprika and red pepper in a food processor, along with 1 teaspoon of salt and some black pepper: blitz to form a paste.

Wipe down the chickpea saucepan, return it to the stove on a medium heat and add the paste. Fry for 5 minutes (there's enough oil there to allow for this), stirring occasionally, before adding the tomato, sugar, chickpeas and 200ml of water. Bring to a low simmer, cover the pan and cook on a very low heat for 4 hours, stirring from time to time and adding more water when needed to retain a sauce-like consistency. Remove the lid and cook for a final hour: the sauce needs to thicken without the chickpeas becoming dry.

Place a piece of warm grilled sourdough on each plate and spoon over the chickpeas. Lay a poached egg on top, followed by a sprinkle of za'atar and a drizzle of oil.

QUINOA AND FENNEL SALAD

Adding freshly chopped lime or lemon flesh to a salad will be a revelation to those who haven't tried it before. Against the mild and nutty quinoa, it makes a simple salad sing. This is a small meal in its own right but can be fortified further by adding nigella or pumpkin seeds, toasted walnuts, goat's cheese and oven-dried tomatoes.

....

Pour 3 tablespoons of the olive oil into a large frying pan, place on a high heat, add the fennel and sear for 5 minutes, stirring once, to get some colour. Reduce the heat to medium and cook for another 10 minutes, stirring occasionally, until the fennel is completely soft and golden. Add the sugar and vinegar, along with ¾ teaspoon of salt, and cook for another 2 minutes. Remove from the heat and set aside.

Pour the quinoa into a pot of boiling water and cook for 9 minutes. Drain in a fine sieve and refresh under cold water. Shake well to dry and then add to the fennel, along with the skinned beans, chilli, cumin, herbs, currants, ½ teaspoon of salt and a good grind of black pepper. Stir gently and set aside.

Use a small sharp serrated knife to trim the tops and tails off the limes. Cut down their sides, following their natural curve, to remove the skin and white pith. Over a small bowl, remove the segments from the limes by slicing between the membranes. Squeeze out any remaining juice over the segments and discard the rest. Cut each segment into three and add it, along with the juice and remaining 2 tablespoons of olive oil, to the salad. Give everything a final stir and serve.

75ml olive oil
3 large fennel bulbs, trimmed and thinly sliced (700g)
1 tbsp caster sugar
3 tbsp cider vinegar
150g quinoa
300g broad beans, fresh or frozen, blanched and skinned
1 green chilli, deseeded and finely chopped
1½ tsp ground cumin
25g mint, chopped
25g coriander, chopped
25g dill, chopped
40g currants
3 limes
salt and black pepper

GREEN BEANS WITH FREEKEH AND TAHINI

70g cracked freekeh, rinsed
  and drained
700g fine green beans,
  trimmed
20g chervil leaves
50g walnuts, roughly
  chopped (optional)
½ tsp Aleppo chilli flakes
salt

Sauce
75g tahini paste
3 tbsp olive oil
2 tbsp lemon juice
1½ tsp dried mint
1 large garlic clove, crushed
1 tsp maple syrup

Scully would say that anything with freekeh shows my hand at work in the kitchen but the credit for this salad is his. When NOPI opened in 2011, there were all sorts of ways in which we thought it would be different from the existing Ottolenghi shops. Meringues and window displays would not feature. Try as we did, however, we could not resist the pull of a salad counter. Seeing the vast array of colours, textures and layers upon entering the restaurant is a treat we just couldn't keep from our customers.

The quality of the beans is important here: if they are old or overcooked, they will lose their vibrancy and the dish just won't be the same. The walnuts add another layer of texture and flavour, but there is plenty going on if you want to leave them out.

Place all the ingredients for the sauce in a medium bowl, along with ½ teaspoon of salt. Whisk until combined and set aside.

Fill a medium saucepan with plenty of water – it should be two-thirds full – and bring to the boil. Add the freekeh, along with ½ teaspoon of salt, reduce the heat to medium and simmer for 15 minutes, uncovered, until the freekeh is cooked through but still retains a bite. Drain and refresh well under cold water. Transfer the freekeh to a large bowl and set aside.

Fill a large saucepan with plenty of cold water and 2 teaspoons of salt. Place on a high heat, bring to the boil, then add the beans. Boil rapidly for 4 minutes, until the beans are just cooked, then drain and refresh under cold water. Pat dry well before adding the beans to the freekeh. Pour over the tahini sauce and mix gently so that the beans are completely coated. Just before serving, mix through the chervil and walnuts, if using, along with a sprinkle of the chilli flakes.

URAD DAL WITH COCONUT AND CORIANDER

SERVES FOUR

This is all about the texture of the urad dal. Also known as black gram or black lentil, the texture – which retains a bite even after its long cooking – is more like that of a mung bean than that of your usual lentil. The difference between black and white urad dal is that the white version has had its skin removed. I prefer to use the black – the skin helps the dal keep its shape and gives the dish a pleasing bite – but the white, which you won't need to soak overnight, works just as well. The inspiration for this I owe to Aasmah Mir, whose website, crackingcurries.com, is a treasure trove of Pakistani family cooking.

....

Drain the urad dal, rinse under cold water and set aside.

Place the butter or ghee in a large sauté pan on a medium–high heat. When it starts to sizzle, add the onion and fry for 15 minutes, stirring from time to time, until soft and golden-brown. Add the garlic, ginger, chilli and garam masala and fry for another 2 minutes, stirring constantly. Add the tomatoes and cook for a further 4 minutes. Add the dal, along with 1 litre of water and 1 teaspoon of salt. Reduce the heat to medium and simmer for 40 minutes, stirring every 5 minutes or so, until the sauce has the consistency of thick soup and the dal is cooked but still holding its shape. Bring to a rapid boil for a few minutes towards the end of cooking if the sauce needs reducing.

Turn the heat down to low then stir through the coconut cream, lime juice and black mustard seeds. Remove from the heat and serve, along with the lime wedges and toppings in three separate bowls alongside, for everyone to sprinkle on top of their portion as they like.

250g black urad dal, soaked in plenty of water overnight
60g clarified butter or ghee
1 large onion, finely chopped (200g)
3 garlic cloves, crushed
75g fresh root ginger, peeled and coarsely grated
1 green chilli, finely chopped
1 tbsp garam masala
5 medium tomatoes, peeled and roughly chopped (600g)
160g coconut cream
2 tbsp lime juice, plus 1 lime, cut into wedges, to serve
1½ tbsp black mustard seeds, toasted
salt

Toppings
100g fresh coconut, roughly grated
50g crispy fried shallots (shop-bought)
30g coriander, roughly chopped

BRAISED

LENTILS WITH MUSHROOM AND PRESERVED LEMON RAGOUT

10g dried porcini
  mushrooms
½ medium onion (100g)
4 thyme sprigs (5g)
2 bay leaves
2 medium carrots (240g in
  total), peeled; one cut in
  half widthways, the other
  cut into 1cm dice
175g Puy lentils
¼ small celeriac, peeled
  and chopped into 1cm
  dice (100g)
75ml olive oil
30g coriander, chopped
1 large leek, cut in half
  lengthways and white
  parts sliced into 5cm
  chunks (230g)
200g ceps, cut into 0.5cm
  slices
200g mixed wild
  mushrooms, cleaned
  and roughly torn
3 tbsp double cream
35g preserved lemon skin,
  finely diced
160g Greek yoghurt
salt and white pepper

I've talked previously about looking for 'drama in the mouth' when I eat. Finely chopped preserved lemon skin delivers this drama in spades in this recipe, as it does in various stews and salads. Cooking with preserved lemons spreads a mellow aroma throughout, whilst chopping and folding it in at the end gives you a more intense, yet sporadic experience. Serve this any time of the day, and that's all you'll need, really.

Soak the porcini in 200ml of boiling water for 1 hour. Strain the water – it can be gritty – into a fresh bowl through a muslin cloth and keep aside; rinse the porcini in fresh water and add them to the strained water.

Fill a medium saucepan half full with water. Place on a high heat and add the onion, thyme, bay, halved carrot and ½ teaspoon of salt. Bring to the boil and then add the lentils. Reduce the heat to medium and gently boil for 15–20 minutes, until the lentils are cooked but still retain a bite. Drain, remove and discard the vegetables and herbs and set the lentils aside.

Preheat the oven to 220°C/200°C Fan/Gas Mark 7.

Place the diced carrot and celeriac in a small bowl with 2 tablespoons of the oil, ½ teaspoon of salt and ¼ teaspoon of ground white pepper. Spread out on a baking tray and place in the oven for 30 minutes, stirring gently once during cooking, until the vegetables are cooked and starting to caramelise. Remove from the oven and transfer to a bowl, along with the lentils and 20g of the coriander. Keep warm.

Place a large sauté pan on a high heat with 1 tablespoon of the oil. Add the leek with ½ teaspoon of salt and fry for 2 minutes on each side, until soft and caramelised. Remove from the pan and add the ceps, with another tablespoon of oil and a pinch of salt, and fry for 3 minutes, until caramelised. Add these to the leeks and then repeat with the wild mushrooms, with another tablespoon of oil and a pinch of salt, before returning all the seared mushrooms and the leeks to the pan. Add the cream, preserved lemon and porcini mushrooms and strained water. Increase the heat and boil for 5 minutes, until the sauce has thickened and reduced by half.

To serve, divide the lentils between 4 plates and spoon over the mushrooms. Finish with the yoghurt, sprinkle over the remaining coriander and serve at once.

LIGHTLY STEWED BROAD BEANS, PEAS AND GEM LETTUCE WITH PARMESAN RICE

This quick stew of fresh seasonal vegetables is comfort personified, particularly when served with the cheesy rice. For those who like their comfort to be served alongside a healthy conscience then the rice can be swapped for pearl barley or spelt, boiled and mixed with olive oil and some garlic. For those of the opposite persuasion, more Parmesan than recommended can happily be added.

Place the rice, a third of the butter and ¼ teaspoon of salt in a medium saucepan on a high heat and stir as the butter melts and the rice heats up. Add 480ml of the boiling water, reduce the heat to minimum and simmer, covered, for 15 minutes. Remove from the heat and leave covered for another 10 minutes.

While the rice is cooking take a large sauté pan and pour in the oil. Add the garlic and spring onion and sauté for 4 minutes on a medium heat, stirring occasionally, until they start to take on some colour. Add the broad beans and cook for another 4 minutes. Add the peas, stock, thyme, ½ teaspoon of salt and a generous grind of black pepper. The vegetables should be well covered, so add more stock if you need. Bring to a light simmer and cook for 5 minutes. Add the lettuce and cook for another 7 minutes, stirring from time to time. The dish is ready when the lettuce hearts have softened but aren't soggy and you are left with about half of the stock.

To serve, add the Parmesan and remaining butter to the hot rice and fluff it up with a fork. Add the lemon juice before spooning the rice on to individual plates. Remove and discard the thyme from the vegetables and stir in the mint before spooning it over the rice. Finish with a drizzle of oil, a bit more black pepper and the grated lemon zest.

60ml olive oil, plus extra to finish
3 garlic cloves, sliced
10 spring onions, cut at an angle into 2cm-long slices (75g)
375g fresh or frozen broad beans, blanched and skinned
250g peas, fresh or frozen and defrosted
about 350ml vegetable stock
4 thyme sprigs
3 Little Gem lettuces, ends removed, quartered lengthways (300g)
20g mint, chopped
grated zest of 1 lemon
salt and black pepper

Rice
250g basmati rice
50g unsalted butter
80g Parmesan, grated
1½ tbsp lemon juice

BROAD BEANS WITH LEMON AND CORIANDER

60ml olive oil

1 large onion, finely diced (190g)

5 garlic cloves, crushed

50g coriander, chopped

600g broad beans, fresh or frozen and defrosted

1 tsp sweet paprika

¼ tsp ground allspice

2 tsp lemon juice

salt and black pepper

This doesn't look half as exquisite as it tastes but love really is blind with this Lebanese classic. You don't need to skin the broad beans so the temptation to fall for this low-maintenance dish is even greater. With very young beans, you could even cook and eat them in the pods, as they do in Lebanon. Serve with rice or plain quinoa, or with lots of other Middle Eastern mezze such as Courgette 'Baba Ganoush' (page 163) and Batata Harra (page 292).

Pour the oil into a large sauté pan and cook the onions on a medium heat for 8 minutes, until translucent, stirring occasionally. Add the garlic and 40g of the coriander and sauté for another minute. Add the broad beans, paprika, allspice, ½ teaspoon of salt, plenty of black pepper and 200ml of water and stir well. Cover the pan and simmer gently for about 25 minutes, stirring occasionally, until the beans are very soft. A lot of the water will have evaporated but the mixture should be wet, with the beans still immersed in liquid. Remove from the heat, take off the lid and leave to cool. Add the lemon juice, stir through the remaining coriander and serve.

BRAISED KALE WITH CRISPY SHALLOTS

If vegetables were strutting their stuff on the catwalk, kale would get the award for 'exponential surge in popularity throughout recent years'. Wherever you look it's being braised, blitzed, blanched and seared. I have even seen a kale ice lolly. The combination of it being exceptionally tasty and obscenely healthy might have something to do with it. For a non-vegetarian option, oyster sauce can be used instead of the kecap manis, which is an Indonesian sweet soy sauce, now easily available in many supermarkets; if you do this, you'll need to add a tablespoon more. With thanks to Sarah Joseph for this recipe.

550g kale, stems removed
  and leaves roughly
  shredded
1 tbsp olive oil
3 garlic cloves, thinly sliced
1½ tbsp kecap manis
1 tsp sesame oil
1 tbsp sesame seeds,
  toasted
2 tbsp plain flour
8 shallots, thinly sliced
  (140g)
120ml sunflower oil
salt

Bring a large pan of water to the boil with 2 teaspoons of salt and add the kale. Blanch for 4 minutes, strain and set aside to dry.

Heat the olive oil in a large sauté pan. Add the garlic and cook for 2 minutes on a medium heat, until golden and crispy. Add the cooked kale and stir well. Pour in the kecap manis and sesame oil and cook for a couple of minutes until the kale has softened and any liquid reduced. Remove from the heat and stir through the sesame seeds, along with ¼ teaspoon of salt. Cover the pan and set aside somewhere warm.

Place the flour and shallots in a medium bowl and mix well so that the onions are evenly coated. Heat the sunflower oil in a small saucepan on a medium–high heat. When hot, add a third of the onions and cook for 5 minutes, until golden and crispy. Use a slotted spoon to remove them from the oil and transfer to a plate lined with kitchen paper. Sprinkle with ⅛ teaspoon of salt and repeat with the remaining onions.

To serve, either arrange the warm kale on a serving dish and scatter over the crispy shallots or mix the kale and onions and serve at once.

SWEET AND SOUR LEEKS WITH GOAT'S CURD AND CURRANTS

I have done it before, and I am doing it again here – that is, placing leek right in the centre of a substantial stand-alone dish. This is not trivial for a vegetable that is normally given the side job of flavouring other things, like stocks and soups. I find the creaminess of leeks and their sweet oniony flavour very satisfying. This dish makes an elegant starter, with its jewel-like currants. Use long, relatively thin leeks if you can find them; otherwise, just halve their number.

8 small leeks, green parts discarded
2 bay leaves
2 garlic cloves, thinly sliced
200ml dry white wine
3 tbsp olive oil
1 small red onion, finely chopped (100g)
20g currants
1 tbsp cider vinegar
2 tsp caster sugar
2 tbsp sunflower oil
100g goat's curd or a creamy goat's cheese
1 tbsp chervil leaves (or parsley, as an alternative)
salt and black pepper

Cut the leeks widthways into two segments, each about 10cm long, and wash well. Lay all of the leeks on the bottom of a large shallow pan and add the bay leaves, garlic, wine, olive oil and about 250ml of water, so that the leeks are half covered in liquid. Add ¾ teaspoon of salt and some black pepper, place on a medium heat and simmer gently for about 30 minutes or until a knife can be inserted into the leeks without any resistance. Turn the leeks over once or twice during cooking so that they are cooked evenly.

Use a slotted spoon to remove the leeks from the pan and place on a plate to one side. Strain the remaining cooking liquid into a small saucepan and reduce over a high heat until you are left with just 3 tablespoons. This should take between 12 and 15 minutes. Remove from the heat and add the onion, currants, vinegar, sugar, ¼ teaspoon of salt and some black pepper. Set aside to soften and marinate.

Heat the sunflower oil in a large frying pan on a medium–high heat. Carefully add the leeks and fry for 2 minutes on each side, until lightly golden. Transfer to a plate and set aside to cool.

To serve, divide the leeks between four plates. Dot with the cheese, spoon over the onion and currant dressing and finish with the chervil.

BUTTERNUT SQUASH WITH BUCKWHEAT POLENTA AND TEMPURA LEMON

Butternut squash

1 large butternut squash
 (1.3kg in total)
3 tbsp olive oil
25g unsalted butter, diced
300ml vegetable stock
3 whole oregano sprigs
 (10g)
15 black peppercorns
8 allspice berries (pimento)
6 cardamom pods, lightly
 crushed
6 bay leaves
6 thyme sprigs
long shaved strips of 1
 large orange
8 garlic cloves, lightly
 cracked with the skin on
salt

Polenta

30g kasha (roasted
 buckwheat), or buckwheat
 groats
150ml full-fat milk
900ml vegetable stock
10g oregano leaves, roughly
 chopped
1 bay leaf
1 tbsp thyme leaves
shaved skin of ½ lemon
120g traditional polenta
60g unsalted butter
white pepper

Tempura lemon

35g plain flour
25g cornflour
75ml cold soda water
ice
sunflower oil, for frying
1 medium lemon, cut
 widthways into 6 round
 slices each 3mm thick

Karl and I spent a few months in Boston working our way, amongst other things, around the city's eateries. One of our top five memories is the tempura meyer lemon skin we had at restaurant Toro on Washington Street. It was sublime. A squeeze of fresh lemon can be used as an alternative but, for those with the time and inclination, it turns the dish into something rather special.

Preheat the oven to 200°C/180°C Fan/Gas Mark 6.

Trim the top and bottom off the butternut and cut it in half lengthways. Scoop out and discard the seeds and cut each half into 3 long wedges, skin on. Place these in a large roasting tin along with the other butternut ingredients and ¾ teaspoon of salt. Coat the butternut well with all the aromatics and place in the oven. Bake for 50 minutes, turning the butternut pieces every 10 minutes or so and spooning the juices over them, until the squash is cooked, golden-brown and starting to crisp on top. Add a little stock throughout the cooking if the pan is drying out.

Meanwhile, put the kasha on a small oven tray and toast in the oven at the same time as the squash for 5 minutes, or 10 minutes for plain groats. Remove and lightly crush with a pestle and mortar.

In a large saucepan mix the milk, stock, herbs and lemon strips, along with ¾ teaspoon of salt and a pinch of white pepper. Bring to the boil and then turn the heat to low and whisk in the polenta and buckwheat. Use a wooden spoon to stir every few minutes until the polenta is thick and cooked – 35–40 minutes. If it is getting too thick add a little water. At the end of the cooking time, add the butter and stir through until melted. The polenta should be thick but runny enough to fall off the spoon easily, like a runny mash. Cover the top of the polenta with cling film to stop a skin forming and leave somewhere warm.

To make the tempura, mix the flours together and whisk in the soda water until the mixture is smooth and runny. Sit the bowl over ice for 45 minutes.

Heat enough oil to come 3cm up the side of a medium saucepan. To test whether it is the right temperature (approximately 160°C) put some drops of batter into the oil. If they sink to the bottom and then bounce straight back up with large bubbles, the oil is ready.

Dip the lemon slices into the batter and fry for 2–3 minutes, until crispy. Remove with a slotted spoon and sprinkle immediately with a little salt.

Serve a spoonful of warm polenta on each plate and place a piece of butternut across it, adding a mix of the baked aromatics on top. Finish with a lemon tempura slice and serve at once.

LENTILS, RADICCHIO AND WALNUTS WITH MANUKA HONEY

200g Puy lentils

2 bay leaves

3 tbsp red wine vinegar

90ml olive oil

100g manuka honey

¼ tsp chilli flakes

½ tsp ground turmeric

100g walnuts

½ medium radicchio, or 2
  red endives, quartered
  lengthways (120g)

60g pecorino fiore sardo, or
  another mature ewe's or
  goat's cheese, shaved

20g basil, roughly chopped

20g dill, roughly chopped

20g parsley, roughly
  chopped

salt and black pepper

I got a thorough introduction to manuka honey on a trip to New Zealand, where it appears repeatedly on restaurant menus and cocktail lists. Aside from its famous healing properties, manuka has a strong, woody flavour that colours a whole dish with a unique aroma. Still, manuka is expensive and not available everywhere, so you can substitute it with Scottish heather honey or another good strong variety. Radicchio's bitterness offers the right balance to the rich sweetness of honey, but if this isn't to your taste you can leave it out or replace it with red endive, if you like.

Preheat the oven to 170°C/150°C Fan/Gas Mark 3½.

Place the lentils in a medium saucepan, cover with plenty of water, add the bay leaves and simmer for 20 minutes or until tender. Drain well and return to the pan.

Whisk together the vinegar, half the oil, half the honey, ¾ teaspoon of salt and some black pepper until the honey dissolves. Stir into the lentils, while they are still hot, and leave to cool down a little, discarding the bay leaves.

While you are cooking the lentils, prepare the walnuts. Put the remaining honey, chilli flakes, turmeric and ¼ teaspoon of salt in a small bowl. Mix well, adding just enough water – about 1 teaspoon – to create a thick paste. Add the walnuts and stir until well coated. Spread them out on a baking sheet lined with baking parchment and roast in the oven for about 20 minutes, stirring once, until golden and crunchy but still a little sticky. Remove from the oven and set aside, removing the walnuts from the baking parchment as soon as they are cool enough to touch.

To cook the radicchio, pour the remaining oil into a medium frying pan and place on a high heat. Cut the radicchio into 8 long wedges and place them in the hot oil. Cook them for about a minute on each side and transfer to a large mixing bowl. Add the lentils, walnuts, pecorino and herbs. Stir gently and serve warmish or at room temperature.

INDIAN RATATOUILLE

about 120ml sunflower oil,
  for frying

2 medium red onions, cut
  into 3cm dice (300g)

1kg Charlotte potatoes,
  peeled and cut into 3cm
  dice

3 large red peppers, cut into
  3cm dice (300g)

1½ tbsp panch phoran

¼ tsp ground turmeric

5 cardamom pods

450g okra, trimmed, or
  French beans if you
  remain unconvinced

2 tomatoes, peeled and
  chopped (160g)

3 green chillies, deseeded
  and finely chopped

about 24 fresh curry leaves

2 tsp caster sugar

1–3 tbsp tamarind paste,
  depending on acidity

50g pumpkin seeds, lightly
  toasted

1 tbsp chopped coriander,
  to serve

salt

Okra is to grown adults what Brussels sprouts are to 10-year-olds: those subjected to the over-cooked, soggy or slimy version will just never, point-blank, try them again. Having done my bit for Brussels in the form of advocating roasting over boiling every time, I now urge all okra-phobes to give them one more go in this version of a ratatouille, based on a Bengali vegetable curry. Panch phoran is a whole-seed mix from eastern India. It can be bought or made by mixing equal amounts of fenugreek, fennel, black mustard, nigella and cumin seeds. Making your own tamarind paste from pulp is ideal but ready-made pastes are widely available. The difference between one brand and the next is great so you'll need to taste and assess – the vinegar levels can be high – before adding it to the pot. Remember, you can always add more. For more on tamarind, see page 244. Serve this with white or brown rice with a dollop of yoghurt, if you like.

....

Preheat the oven to 220°C/200°C Fan/Gas Mark 7.

Heat the oil in an extra-large sauté pan. Add the onions and potatoes and fry on a medium–high heat for 10 minutes, stirring occasionally. Lift the vegetables out with a slotted spoon and set aside.

Top up the oil, if needed, so you have 2 tablespoons in the pan. Add the pepper and spices and fry on a high heat for 3 minutes, stirring often. Add the okra or beans, tomatoes, chilli and curry leaves and fry for 5 minutes on a high heat.

Return the onions and potatoes to the pan. Add the sugar, tamarind paste, 200ml of water and ¾ teaspoon of salt and simmer for 5 minutes.

Spread the vegetables out on a large baking tray, sprinkle over the pumpkin seeds and bake in the oven for 12 minutes. Serve warm, sprinkled with coriander.

FENNEL WITH CAPERS AND OLIVES

SERVES FOUR

as a starter

If there were one ingredient I could 'magic' on to all supermarket and grocers' shelves it would be verjuice. Common in Australia thanks, largely, to Maggie Beer's championing of the product, it's a mystery to me why it hasn't yet taken hold here. Made from the juice of semi-ripe wine grapes, it has the mildly sweet tartness of lemon juice and acidity of vinegar without the harshness of either. It's used, as you would both of these more common ingredients, to heighten other flavours and as a base for sauces and dressings. If you can't get hold of it, a mixture of two-thirds lemon juice and one-third red wine vinegar works well as an alternative. And, no, '15 garlic cloves' isn't a typo: once scorched they add a mellowing sweetness to an otherwise sharp dressing. The ricotta isn't essential, if you'd rather keep this dairy-free, but it helps to balance the acidity.

....

Cut the trimmed fennel from top to bottom along the longest side into 2cm slices.

Place 2 tablespoons of the olive oil in a large sauté pan for which you have a lid and place on a medium–high heat. Add half of the fennel along with a pinch of salt and a good grind of black pepper. Cook for 5–6 minutes, turning once, so that both sides are nice and browned. Remove from the pan and repeat with the remaining fennel, adding more oil, if needed, and seasoning as you go.

Once all the fennel is seared and removed from the pan, add the garlic cloves and a tiny bit of oil, if needed (about 1mm of oil is enough here), and fry for about 3 minutes, tossing occasionally, so that the garlic skin gets scorched all over. Reduce the heat to medium before carefully (it spits!) adding the verjuice. Let it reduce for a couple of minutes to about 2 tablespoons of liquid. Add the tomato, 100ml of the stock, the capers, olives, thyme, sugar, ¼ teaspoon of salt and some black pepper. Bring to a simmer for 2 minutes before returning the fennel to the pan. Add the remainder of the stock, cover the pan and simmer for about 12 minutes, turning once during the cooking, until the fennel is completely soft and the sauce has thickened. You might need to remove the lid and increase the heat for the final 2 or 3 minutes of cooking, to reduce and thicken the sauce.

Place 2 slices of fennel on each plate, spoon over the sauce and serve with a spoonful of ricotta, if using, and some freshly grated lemon zest. Finish with a drizzle of olive oil and serve warm or at room temperature.

4 medium fennel bulbs, roots trimmed (750g)

about 3 tbsp olive oil, plus extra for drizzling

15 large garlic cloves, skin on (75g in total)

60ml verjuice or a mixture of 60ml lemon juice and 2 tbsp red wine vinegar

1 small tomato, cut into 1cm dice (70g)

250ml vegetable stock

20g capers, drained

30g black wrinkly olives, pitted and chopped in half

1 tbsp chopped thyme leaves

2½ tsp caster sugar

100g ricotta (optional)

1 tsp grated lemon zest

salt and black pepper

MUSHROOMS, GARLIC AND SHALLOTS WITH LEMON RICOTTA

If you are not put off by peeling lots of shallots and garlic cloves, you are in for a winter treat: hearty, oniony mushroom stew, topped with fresh ricotta. You don't need much more, though a chunk of sourdough will not go amiss. To help with the peeling, soak the shallots and garlic in water for half an hour.

Put the olive oil in a large sauté pan with 40g of the butter. Place on a medium heat, add the shallots, garlic, thyme and cinnamon and sauté gently for about 12 minutes, until the onions are beginning to soften. Increase the temperature to medium–high, add the Portobello and chestnut mushrooms, mix well and cook for 2 more minutes. Add the remaining mushrooms and chilli flakes and cook for another minute. Pour over the vegetable stock and simmer rapidly for 8–10 minutes, stirring gently once or twice, until the liquid has almost disappeared and the shallots and garlic are cooked through. Pour in the Pernod, along with 1¼ teaspoons of salt and a good grind of black pepper. Cook for 1–2 minutes to allow the alcohol to evaporate, before stirring through the remaining butter and chopped herbs.

Mix the ricotta and lemon zest in a small bowl. Divide the warm mushrooms between four plates and top each with a quarter of the ricotta mixture. Finish with a drizzle of oil and serve.

2 tbsp olive oil, plus extra to finish
60g unsalted butter
470g peeled baby shallots (about 35)
80g peeled garlic cloves (about 24)
2 thyme sprigs
2 cinnamon sticks
200g Portobello mushrooms, quartered
250g chestnut mushrooms, halved
100g buna-shimeji mushrooms, divided into small clumps or wild mushrooms
¼ tsp chilli flakes
200ml vegetable stock
100ml Pernod
5g tarragon leaves, chopped
10g parsley leaves, chopped
10g mint leaves, chopped
250g ricotta
grated zest of 1 lemon
salt and black pepper

IRANIAN VEGETABLE STEW WITH DRIED LIME

50g clarified butter

1 large onion, finely diced
(220g)

½ tsp ground turmeric

1½ tsp cumin seeds

1 tbsp tomato purée

20g coriander

10g tarragon

10g dill

1kg Charlotte potatoes (or
another waxy variety),
peeled and chopped into
4cm chunks

1 medium butternut squash,
peeled, deseeded and
chopped into 4cm chunks
(760g)

3 Iranian limes, pierced 2–3
times

1 green chilli, slit on one
side from stem to tip

4 medium tomatoes,
quartered (400g)

150g spinach leaves

15g barberries

300g Greek yoghurt
(optional)

salt

Small dried limes (or lemons) are a regular feature in Iranian cooking, adding a sharp tang and sweetish aroma to marinades, stews and salads. They are rock hard and not easy to grind (although you can do so, in a coffee or spice grinder) so puncture them a couple of times and then put them in whole. You can also buy them in powdered form although this isn't as pungent. Sumac or grated lemon zest can be used as an alternative but if you are passing a Middle Eastern grocer's or if you shop online, they are well worth seeking out. Serve this sweet and sharp stew with steamed rice – that's all.

Preheat the oven to 200°C/180°C Fan/Gas Mark 6.

Place a large casserole on a medium heat and sauté the butter, onion, turmeric and cumin for 10 minutes. Add the tomato purée and cook, stirring, for another 2 minutes. Bundle the herbs together and use some string to tie them into a bunch. Add these to the dish along with the potatoes, squash, limes, chilli, 1½ teaspoons of salt and 1 litre of water and bring to the boil. Reduce the heat and boil gently for 15 minutes, until the potatoes are semi-cooked. Stir through the tomatoes, spinach and barberries, crushing the limes gently to release some of the juice inside, and transfer everything to a large roasting tray. Bake uncovered for 20 minutes, or until the sauce has thickened a little and the vegetables are soft. Remove from the oven and allow to sit for 5 minutes before serving with a dollop of yoghurt on the side, if you choose.

GRILLED

GRILLED LETTUCE WITH FARRO AND LEMON

SERVES TWO TO FOUR

You want to serve this salad quite soon after the Romaine hearts are char-grilled so they retain their fresh colour and texture. The farro has a great texture – like, but not to be confused with, spelt – and the mixture of lemon, Parmesan, tarragon and the smoky Romaine is a twist on a Caesar salad.

Preheat the oven to 240°C/220°C Fan/Gas Mark 9.

Bring a small saucepan with plenty of water to the boil, add the farro and simmer on a medium heat for 14 minutes or until the farro is cooked but still has a little bit of bite. Drain, refresh under cold water and leave aside to dry.

While the farro is cooking, make the dressing. Use a small sharp serrated knife to trim the top and tail off the fresh lemon. Cut down its sides and along its natural curves, to remove the skin and white pith. Over a medium bowl, remove the segments from the lemon by slicing between the membranes. Chop the segments roughly and return to the bowl, along with any juices left in the lemon or on your chopping board. Next, add the preserved lemon, garlic, shallot, 2 tablespoons of the olive oil, the Pernod, maple syrup, ¼ teaspoon of salt and a generous grind of black pepper. Gently whisk and keep to one side.

Brush the slices of bread with 2 tablespoons of olive oil, place on a small baking tray and put in the oven for 8–10 minutes, turning over halfway. Remove from the oven once they have started to brown and are completely crisp, and allow to cool down, before breaking into rough 3cm croutons.

When you are ready to serve, place a ridged griddle pan on a high heat. Whilst you wait for it to heat up, put the Romaine quarters in a large bowl with the remaining tablespoon of olive oil and ¼ teaspoon of salt. Gently mix and when the pan is smoking hot, place the lettuce wedges in the pan for approximately 30 seconds, turning over once, so they get char marks all over. Return to the bowl and add the cooked farro, tarragon and dressing. Gently mix with your hands and then finally add the croutons and Parmesan, giving the salad a final toss before serving.

Ingredients

75g farro dicocco

1 medium lemon

45g preserved lemon, halved and sliced thinly, seeds discarded

1 small garlic clove, crushed

1 shallot, finely chopped (15g)

75ml olive oil

2 tsp Pernod or another aniseedy liqueur, such as raki or pastis

¾ tsp maple syrup

2 slices crusty white bread (60g)

2 Romaine hearts, outer leaves removed, quartered lengthways (250g)

15g tarragon leaves, roughly chopped

50g Parmesan, shaved

salt and black pepper

COURGETTE AND FENNEL WITH SAFFRON CRUMBS

¼ tsp saffron strands

120g ciabatta bread, crust removed (60g)

sunflower oil, for frying

3 garlic cloves, thinly sliced

2 medium courgettes, cut lengthways into 0.5cm slices (350g)

2 tbsp olive oil

2 small fennel bulbs, trimmed and cut lengthways into 0.5cm slices (250g)

2 tbsp lemon juice

10g dill, chopped

salt and black pepper

Something resembling a crumb obsession took hold of the test kitchen at one point, where few soups, salads or grilled dishes escaped the additional crunch and layer of taste brought about by flavoured crumbs. Mustard or chilli croutons, saffron crumbs, sumac-sprinkled fried pitta: they are a great and versatile way of bringing colour and luxury to otherwise simple dishes. Cook more crumbs than you need here, omitting the garlic, and keep them in an airtight jar for a week or so, to elevate midweek meals.

Preheat the oven to 170°C/150°C Fan/Gas Mark 3½.

Pour 80ml of boiling water over the saffron and leave to infuse for 10 minutes. Tear the ciabatta into small but not uniformly sized pieces, up to 2cm long. Place them in a small bowl then pour the saffron water over slowly, as you stir the bread with your other hand, so that all the pieces evenly soak up the liquid. Spread the bread out on a baking tray lined with baking parchment and toast in the oven for 10–15 minutes, until the bread has dried out completely, then remove.

Pour enough sunflower oil into a medium pan so it comes 1cm up the sides. Place on a medium heat and, once the oil is hot, carefully drop in the saffron 'crumbs' and garlic. Fry for just 30 seconds, until the garlic is golden. Remove with a slotted spoon on to kitchen paper and sprinkle with ⅛ teaspoon of salt.

Place a ridged griddle pan on a high heat and leave for a few minutes. Mix the courgette with ½ tablespoon of the olive oil and ¼ teaspoon of salt and char-grill lightly, about 1 minute on each side. Repeat with the fennel, again mixing it with ½ tablespoon of olive oil and ¼ teaspoon of salt before char-grilling on both sides. Place all the vegetables in a bowl and pour over the lemon juice and remaining tablespoon of olive oil and a good grind of black pepper. Mix gently and leave to marinate for 15–20 minutes.

Spread the vegetables out on a platter, sprinkle over the dill followed by the breadcrumbs and garlic and serve at once.

SQUASH WITH LABNEH AND PICKLED WALNUT SALSA

100g pickled walnuts

½ medium red onion, cut into 0.5cm dice (80g)

1½ tbsp cider vinegar

1 tsp caster sugar

1 mild red chilli, deseeded and finely chopped

¼ tsp ground allspice

3 tbsp olive oil, plus extra to finish

1 crown prince squash or another variety of squash or pumpkin, (about 1.1kg in total)

30g rocket

150g labneh (or goat's curd or a very fresh goat's cheese)

10g dill leaves

salt and black pepper

A few years ago I went to visit Opie's pickle factory in Kent, where I was shown the process of pickling fresh, green walnuts. If I am completely frank, I had more than a doubt or two about the idea of pickling walnuts, a process exclusive to Britain and New Zealand, I hear. It seemed pretty esoteric. Well, I still think they are somewhat of an oddity but I do love pickled walnuts now and use them regularly in various salsas and sauces. If you can't get pickled walnuts try making the salsa for the roasted Red Onions (see page 176) and using it here instead of the pickled walnut salsa.

Labneh, thick strained yoghurt, is available from many Arab grocers, as small white balls marinated in olive oil. You can make your own by hanging natural yoghurt in muslin cloth for a couple of days. Alternatively, use goat's curd or a very fresh goat's cheese.

....

Start by making the salsa. Rinse the walnuts briefly to remove the outer black skin, pat dry and cut into 0.5cm dice. Place in a small bowl and add the red onion, vinegar, sugar, chilli, allspice, 1 tablespoon of the oil and ⅛ teaspoon of salt. Mix and set aside.

Preheat the oven to 220°C/200°C Fan/Gas Mark 7.

Cut the squash in half lengthways (there is no need to peel it), remove the seeds and cut the flesh widthways into 1.5cm slices. Place in a large bowl, add the remaining oil, ¼ teaspoon of salt and a good grind of black pepper. Mix with your hands to coat in the oil.

Place a ridged griddle pan on a high heat and let it turn red-hot. Cook the squash pieces in batches, for 2–3 minutes on each side, to get good grill marks all over.

Transfer to a baking sheet lined with baking parchment and place in the oven for 15 minutes or until tender. Remove from the oven and leave to cool.

To assemble, arrange the squash wedges and rocket leaves on a serving plate, dotting with dollops of labneh as you go. Spoon over the walnut salsa and sprinkle with dill. Finish with a drizzle of olive oil and serve.

GRILLED ZITI WITH FETA

3 tbsp olive oil, plus extra
   for drizzling
1½ tbsp cumin seeds
1 tbsp caraway seeds
2 tsp dried oregano
2 small onions, chopped
   into 1cm dice (210g)
2 celery stalks, chopped
   into 1cm dice (110g)
1½ tsp caster sugar
2 tbsp tomato purée
8 large ripe tomatoes,
   roughly chopped (800g)
1 red chilli, finely chopped
15g basil, chopped
10g oregano leaves,
   chopped
2 garlic cloves, crushed
500g long ziti (broken into
   uneven smaller segments)
   or penne rigate
150g Parmesan, coarsely
   grated
150g mature Cheddar,
   coarsely grated
150g feta, broken into 2cm
   chunks
salt and black pepper

I always preferred my father's pasta the next day, when it was thrown into the oven with heaps of cheese and ended up slightly burnt and completely crisp on top. To maximise this effect make sure your baking dish's surface is large enough to accommodate the pasta in a shallow layer. This is a wonderful main course, no matter what age you are.

Place the oil in a medium saucepan and on a medium–high heat. Add the cumin and caraway seeds, dried oregano, onion and celery and cook for 6 minutes, stirring from time to time, until the onion is soft but not coloured. Add the sugar and tomato purée and cook for another minute before adding the tomatoes, chilli, 1½ teaspoons of salt and a good grind of black pepper. Reduce the heat to medium and let the sauce simmer for 20 minutes, stirring occasionally. Add the basil, fresh oregano and garlic: stir and set aside.

Bring a large pan of water to the boil with 1 tablespoon of salt, add the pasta and cook for 10–12 minutes, or according to the packet instructions, until al dente. Drain and add to the tomato sauce, along with a third of the Parmesan and a third of the Cheddar. Stir and then transfer into a shallow ovenproof dish, roughly 30cm x 30cm. Dot the feta on top, sprinkle over the remaining Parmesan and Cheddar and place under a medium-hot grill for anywhere between 8 and 15 minutes (oven grills tend to vary a lot), until the cheese melts and the top layer of pasta dries out and turns crisp.

Allow to sit for 5 minutes, to cool a little, before serving with a final drizzle of oil.

SWEETCORN SLAW

Most sweet things will benefit from a bit of smoke here and there. For this you can set up your kitchen with some seriously geeky and expensive kit; you can smoke casually in a wok or a saucepan (see Smoked Beetroot with Yoghurt and Caramelised Macadamias on page 185), or you can use my preferred method and just cook whatever it is you are smoking on a hot ridged griddle pan, with a bit of oil. Sweetcorn on the cob is ideal this way because the kernels are protected on one side so don't dry out.

This slaw was originally made to go with my southern fried chicken but it is also a welcome addition alongside anything cooked on the barbecue, under the grill or roasted in the oven. (Pictured on page 159.)

100ml white wine vinegar

¼ white cabbage, shredded (300g)

3 small carrots, peeled and cut into fine strips (175g)

1 medium red onion, thinly sliced (140g)

4 corn cobs, lightly brushed with olive oil (600g)

2 red chillies, finely chopped

20g coriander leaves

20g mint leaves

olive oil

salt and black pepper

Dressing

50g mayonnaise

2 tsp Dijon mustard

1½ tsp sunflower oil

1 tbsp lemon juice

1 garlic clove, crushed

Place the vinegar and 200 ml of water in a small saucepan along with 1 tablespoon of salt. Bring to the boil and then remove from the heat. Place the cabbage and carrot in a bowl, pour over two-thirds of the salty liquid and set aside to soften for 20 minutes. Pour the remaining liquid over the onion and, again, set aside for 20 minutes. Rinse the vegetables and onion well, pat dry, place together in a large bowl and set aside.

Place a ridged griddle pan on a high heat and, when it starts to smoke, lay the corn over it. Char-grill for 10–12 minutes, turning so that all sides get some colour (this will create quite a lot of smoke so put on the extractor fan, if you have one). Remove from the heat and, when cool enough to handle, use a large knife to shave off the corn in clumps and add to the salad bowl.

Whisk together all the dressing ingredients, pour over the salad and stir gently. Add the chilli, coriander and mint, along with a grind of black pepper, give everything another gentle stir and serve.

BUTTERNUT TATAKI AND UDON NOODLE SALAD

120ml rice vinegar

1½ tbsp caster sugar

25g fresh root ginger, peeled and cut into very fine matchsticks

1 small butternut squash, peeled, deseeded and cut into 5cm x 0.5cm x 0.5cm batons (600g)

2½ tbsp groundnut oil

160g dried udon noodles

7 radishes, thinly sliced (75g)

50g mangetout, cut into very fine matchsticks

3 baby or Lebanese cucumbers, unpeeled and cut into very fine strips (300g)

2 mild red chillies, cut into long thin strips

20g baby shiso leaves (or 5 normal shiso leaves, chopped) or any baby cress

½ tsp sesame oil

1½ tsp black sesame seeds (or white, if unavailable)

10g coriander leaves

salt

Somewhere between a pickle and a salad – there's a lot of vinegar and sugar here – this concoction is one of my all-time favourites. Thanks to the char-grilling, the butternut squash tastes both fresh and smoky at the same time and hence makes this dish feel like a complete and complex meal-in-a-bowl. You can add crushed salted cashew nuts here, if you like, to enrich this even further. (Pictured on page 158.)

Gently heat the vinegar, sugar, ginger and ¾ teaspoon of salt in a small saucepan, stirring so that the sugar dissolves. Remove from the heat and set aside.

Place a ridged griddle pan on a high heat and wait until it is red-hot. Toss the butternut in the groundnut oil and sear in batches for 3 minutes, turning once so that both sides get charred. You might need to do this in four batches as you don't want to overcrowd the pan. Transfer the batons to a large mixing bowl, pour over half the ginger dressing and set aside to cool, stirring gently once or twice.

Bring a large pan of water to the boil. Add the noodles and cook for 6–7 minutes or according to the packet instructions. Drain, refresh under cold water and set aside to dry.

Add the noodles to the butternut, followed by all the remaining ingredients. Stir gently, transfer to a serving plate, spoon over the remaining dressing and serve.

COURGETTE 'BABA GANOUSH'

SERVES FOUR

as a starter or as part of
a mezze selection

*This looks rather like a volcanic eruption, in the best possible sense. There is
none of the tahini you'd associate with baba ganoush: it's the garlic, smokiness
and texture of the mashed courgette flesh that calls its purple friend to mind.
I don't know why we don't roast courgettes more. Getting some smokiness into
the naturally bland flesh is a real revelation. Served with bread, this is a delicate
and delightful way to whet the appetite at the beginning of a meal. (Also
pictured overleaf.)*

5 large courgettes (about
   1.2kg in total)
80g goat's yoghurt
15g Roquefort, coarsely
   grated
1 egg, lightly beaten
15g unsalted butter
20g pine nuts
½ tsp Urfa chilli flakes, or
   a pinch of normal chilli
   flakes if unavailable
1 tsp lemon juice
1 garlic clove, crushed
½ tsp za'atar, to finish
salt and black pepper

Preheat the grill to its highest setting. Place the courgettes on a baking
parchment-lined baking tray and grill for 45 minutes, turning once or
twice during the cooking, until the skin crisps and browns nicely. Remove
from the grill and, once cool enough to handle, peel off the courgette skin,
discard it and set the flesh aside in a colander to drain; you can also scoop
out the flesh with a spoon. The courgettes can be served warm or at room
temperature.

Place the goat's yoghurt in a small saucepan with the Roquefort and egg.
Heat very gently for about 3 minutes, stirring often. You want the
yoghurt to heat through but not quite reach simmering point. Set aside
and keep warm.

Melt the butter in a small frying pan with the pine nuts on a gentle heat
for 3–4 minutes. Cook until the nuts turn golden-brown, stirring often. Stir
in the chilli flakes and lemon juice and set aside.

To serve, put the courgette in a mixing bowl and add the garlic, ⅓ teaspoon
of salt and a good grind of black pepper. Gently mash everything together
with a fork and then spread the mixture out on a large serving platter. Spoon
the warm yoghurt sauce on top, followed by a drizzle of the warm chilli
butter and pine nuts. Finish with a sprinkle of za'atar and serve at once.

CORN ON THE COB WITH MISO MAYONNAISE

4 corn cobs, husks
  removed, cut into 5cm
  segments (600g)
3 tbsp olive oil
2 tbsp finely chopped
  parsley
salt

Mayonnaise
1 egg yolk
1 tbsp Dijon mustard
3 garlic cloves, crushed
½ tbsp cider vinegar
2 tbsp tamarind paste
250ml sunflower oil
80g white miso paste (not a
  sweet variety)
1 green chilli, deseeded and
  finely chopped

Fresh corn on the cob, or just shaved off the cob, is a delicacy that isn't celebrated enough – the awful sweet stuff that comes out of a tin has a lot to answer for – but there isn't really anything like good fresh corn, lightly grilled or simmered, paired with butter, oil or something else that's rich and savoury. Here I smother it with sharp miso mayo, but a mixture of mayonnaise with feta or Parmesan will also taste great. The mayonnaise will make more than you need but it will keep in the fridge for up to a week in a sealed container. Use it with grilled oily fish or to dress root vegetables such as celeriac or potato.

First make the mayonnaise. Place the egg yolk, mustard, garlic, vinegar and tamarind in the small bowl of a food processor. Turn it on and slowly start adding the sunflower oil, continually pouring in a light stream until half the oil is incorporated. With the machine still running, add the miso and continue with the last of the oil until the mayonnaise is thick. Add the chilli and mix until combined.

Bring a large pan of water to the boil. Add the corn and blanch for 3 minutes. Drain, pat dry and mix with the olive oil and ¼ teaspoon of salt. Place a ridged griddle pan on a very high heat. When it starts to smoke, add the corn and char-grill, turning often so that all sides get coloured – about 8 minutes. As soon as the corn comes off the pan, brush a layer of the mayonnaise all over the cob, so that it gets a light glaze, about 2 tablespoons for all the corn. Sprinkle with parsley and serve straight away, dipping the corn in the remaining mayonnaise as you go, or spreading on more with a knife.

MARROW WITH TOMATO AND FETA

SERVES FOUR

generously

It's easy to dismiss marrows as the plain cousin to the sweeter, finer courgette, but their mild flavour and meatiness make a great blank canvas upon which to load other, more intense flavours. I like adding them to spicy curries or filling them with rich meat or cheese stuffings. When buying this summer squash, choose the smallest you can find: oversized marrows tend to taste bitter and have watery flesh; a small one should be firm and heavy for its size. Not everyone likes fennel seeds so omit them if you prefer.

1 marrow, skin on, cut
   widthways into 1.5cm
   slices (810g)
5 garlic cloves
100ml olive oil, plus extra
   for drizzling
2 tsp fennel seeds
400g peeled and chopped
   tomatoes (tinned are fine)
½ tsp caster sugar
50g feta, crumbled
10g basil leaves, roughly
   shredded
salt and black pepper

Place each disc of marrow flat on a chopping board and use a small serrated knife to cut out and discard the central seeds and fibre. Place the discs in a large mixing bowl and add 2 crushed garlic cloves, 85ml of the olive oil, ¼ teaspoon of salt and some black pepper. Mix well and set aside for 30 minutes.

Slice the remaining garlic cloves and place in a small frying pan with the fennel seeds and 2 teaspoons of the oil. Cook for 2 minutes on a medium heat. Add the tomatoes before the garlic starts to brown, along with the sugar, ¼ teaspoon of salt and some black pepper. Bring the sauce to a simmer and cook for about 7 minutes, until thick. Transfer to a small food processor bowl and blitz until silky smooth.

Put a large frying pan on a medium–high heat and add the remaining teaspoon of olive oil. Fry the marrow in batches for about 8 minutes each, turning once, until golden. Whilst still warm, spread the slices out in a single layer on a large serving dish, pour over the tomato sauce and leave to cool. Just before serving, sprinkle over the feta, followed by the basil and a final drizzle of olive oil.

ROASTED

AUBERGINE WITH BLACK GARLIC

3 medium aubergines,
  sliced widthways into
  1.5cm rounds (900g)
200ml olive oil
8 large or 16 small black
  garlic cloves (35g)
200g Greek yoghurt
1½ tsp lemon juice
7 large garlic cloves, thinly
  sliced (30g)
3 red chillies, sliced on the
  diagonal into 3mm rounds
5g dill leaves
5g basil leaves
5g tarragon leaves
salt and black pepper

Slices of roast aubergine have been through many incarnations and have been a constant feature on the Ottolenghi menu since we first set up shop in 2002. Every now and then a new kid on the block will appear to shake up the old-timers and our latest bright young thing is this black garlic sauce. I'd love black garlic to be more widely available: its taste is reminiscent of molasses and tamarind and it gives an unexpected depth of flavour to dishes. You can simply slice a few thin slivers and add these to crunchy salads or creamy risottos – it's mellow enough not to dominate – or use it in sauces, dips and purées, as here, to enliven (and challenge) old favourites.

Preheat the oven to 250°C/230°C Fan/Gas Mark 9 (or to its highest setting).

Place the aubergine rounds in a large bowl with 60ml of the olive oil, ½ teaspoon of salt and a good grind of black pepper. Mix well and spread out on 2 large baking trays lined with greaseproof paper. Roast in the oven until golden-brown and completely soft – about 30 minutes. Remove from the oven and set aside to cool.

Place the black garlic cloves in the small bowl of a food processor with ⅓ teaspoon of salt, 2 tablespoons of oil, 2 tablespoons of yoghurt and the lemon juice. Blitz for a minute, to form a rough paste, and then transfer to a medium bowl. Mix through the rest of the yoghurt and keep in the fridge until needed.

Heat the remaining 110ml of oil in a small saucepan on a high heat. Add the garlic and chilli slices, reduce the heat to medium and fry for about 5 minutes, stirring from time to time, until the garlic is golden-brown and the chilli is crispy. Use a slotted spoon to transfer the garlic and chilli on to a kitchen paper-lined plate.

Arrange the aubergine slices, overlapping, on a platter. Spoon the yoghurt sauce on top, sprinkle over the chilli and garlic and finish with the herbs.

SQUASH WITH CARDAMOM AND NIGELLA SEEDS

20g unsalted butter

1 tbsp olive oil

1 large red onion, thinly sliced (170g)

1 large butternut squash, peeled and cut into 3cm chunks (1kg)

30g pumpkin seeds

1¼ tsp nigella seeds

½ tsp ground cumin

½ tsp ground coriander

¼ tsp ground turmeric

4 cardamom pods, lightly crushed

1 large cinnamon stick

1 green chilli, halved lengthways

1 tbsp caster sugar

200ml vegetable stock

150g Greek yoghurt

1 tbsp coriander, chopped

salt

Getting the number of roasted squash recipes down to just two for this chapter involved much debate and much eating. The squash-off, judged in our test kitchen with discriminating web-store colleagues Maria and Saga, saw this uncommon pairing of the sweet squash with the clear and citrus note of the cardamom win out. Serve it with the Lemon and Curry Leaf Rice (see page 57) for a striking vegetarian main course.

Preheat the oven to 220°C/200°C Fan/Gas Mark 7.

Place the butter and oil in a large sauté pan on a medium heat. Add the onion and fry for about 8 minutes, until soft. Add the squash, increase the heat to medium–high and cook for a further 10 minutes, stirring occasionally, until it starts to colour. Remove from the heat and add the pumpkin seeds, 1 teaspoon of the nigella seeds, the cumin, coriander, turmeric, cardamom, cinnamon, chilli, sugar and ¾ teaspoon of salt. Mix well and transfer to a baking tray large enough to hold the vegetables in a single but snug layer, about 25cm x 30cm. Pour over the stock and bake in the oven for 30 minutes, until the squash is tender. Set aside for about 10 minutes: the liquid in the tray will continue to be absorbed.

Serve warm, with the yoghurt spooned on top or on the side, along with a sprinkling of the coriander and the remaining nigella seeds.

HONEY-ROASTED CARROTS WITH TAHINI YOGHURT

SERVES FOUR

The inspiration for this was Sarah's 'nan', Dulcie, in Tasmania, who always used to add some honey to the tray before roasting her carrots. I'm not sure what Dulcie would have thought about a tahini yoghurt sauce served alongside, but the sweetness of the carrots certainly welcomes it. Make this extra-vibrant by using different-coloured carrots and serve alongside the Broad Bean Spread with Roasted Garlic Ricotta (see page 234) and Aubergine Kuku (see page 253).

Preheat the oven to 220°C/200°C Fan/Gas Mark 7.

Place all the ingredients for the tahini sauce in a medium bowl with a pinch of salt. Whisk together and set aside.

Place the honey, oil, coriander and cumin seeds and thyme in a large mixing bowl with 1 teaspoon of salt and a good grind of black pepper. Add the carrots and mix well until coated then spread them out on a large baking tray and roast in the oven for 40 minutes, stirring gently once or twice, until cooked through and glazed.

Transfer the carrots to a large serving platter or individual plates. Serve warm or at room temperature, with a spoonful of sauce on top, scattered with the coriander.

60g clear honey

2 tbsp olive oil

1 tbsp coriander seeds, toasted and lightly crushed

1½ tsp cumin seeds, toasted and lightly crushed

3 thyme sprigs

1.3kg carrots, peeled and cut into 2cm x 6cm batons

1½ tbsp coriander leaves, roughly chopped

salt and black pepper

Tahini yoghurt sauce

40g tahini paste

130g Greek yoghurt

2 tbsp lemon juice

1 garlic clove, crushed

RED ONIONS WITH WALNUT SALSA

4 medium red onions (600g
in total)

1½ tbsp olive oil

20g rocket

15g picked parsley leaves

60g soft goat's cheese,
broken into 2cm chunks

salt and black pepper

Salsa

65g walnuts, roughly
chopped

1 red chilli, deseeded and
finely chopped

1 garlic clove, crushed

3 tbsp red wine vinegar

1 tbsp olive oil

When Tara moved to Clapham and was in the process of making friends, she had some mums over for lunch one day when their children were at school. The friendships endure to this day and Tara's pretty sure that it was the secret handing over of this roasted onion recipe that sealed the deal. The natural sweetness of red onions is accentuated when they are grilled or baked and gives them enough individual character to take centre stage. They also work well in a sandwich or alongside other dishes as a mezze. A few pomegranate seeds sprinkled on top of each portion would add special vibrancy and a nice sweet crunch.

Preheat the oven to 220°C/200°C Fan/Gas Mark 7.

Peel the onions and remove the tops and the tails. Cut each widthways into 3 slices, about 2cm thick, and place on a baking tray. Brush the slices with the olive oil, sprinkle over ¼ teaspoon of salt and some black pepper and roast in the oven for about 40 minutes, until the onions are cooked and golden-brown on top. If they haven't taken on much colour, place under a hot grill for a few minutes. Set aside to cool slightly.

While the onions are cooking, put all of the salsa ingredients in a small bowl, add ¼ teaspoon of salt, stir and set aside.

To serve, put the rocket and parsley in a large mixing bowl. Add the warm onions, the cheese and half the salsa and toss carefully so the onions don't fall apart. Divide between shallow plates, spoon over the remaining salsa and serve.

CAULIFLOWER, GRAPE AND CHEDDAR SALAD

1 large cauliflower head,
   broken into bite-size
   florets (900g)
90ml rapeseed oil
2 tbsp sherry vinegar
1 tsp Dijon mustard
½ tsp clear honey
30g raisins
40g hazelnuts, toasted and
   roughly crushed
100g red grapes, halved and
   deseeded
80g creamy, mature
   Cheddar, roughly
   crumbled
20g parsley, roughly
   chopped
salt and black pepper

This dish – a fantastic autumnal starter – was inspired by one I had at NoMad, a great restaurant in New York run by the brilliant Daniel Humm of Eleven Madison Park. Sami, who has eaten a lot of good meals and is not a man prone to hyperbole, tweeted after a recent meal at NoMad that he'd just had 'one of the best meals of my life'.

Preheat the oven to 220°C/200°C Fan/Gas Mark 7.

Toss the cauliflower florets with half the oil, ½ teaspoon of salt and some black pepper. Spread out on a baking tray and roast for 20–25 minutes, stirring once or twice, until golden-brown. Remove from the oven and set aside to cool.

To make the dressing, whisk together the remaining oil with the vinegar, mustard, honey and ¼ teaspoon of salt. Add the raisins and let them marinate for at least 10 minutes.

Just before serving, transfer the cauliflower to a large mixing bowl along with the remaining ingredients. Pour over the raisins and dressing, toss together, transfer to a large platter and serve.

AUBERGINES WITH CRUSHED CHICKPEAS AND HERB YOGHURT

SERVES FOUR
as a starter

3 large aubergines, cut widthways into 2cm-thick slices (1.2kg)
120ml olive oil
240g soft cooked chickpeas (see introduction), plus some of their cooking liquid
1½ tsp cumin seeds, toasted and lightly crushed
1 small lemon, skin, pith and seeds removed, flesh roughly chopped (35g)
100g Greek yoghurt
10g mint, roughly chopped
15g parsley, roughly chopped
salt and black pepper

Every single time I try an old recipe I want to change it. I have no idea why that is; all I know is that what tasted perfect two years ago seems 'slightly unbalanced' this year, or 'too savoury', 'lacking oomph', 'a little stodgy' or 'a bit predictable'. This is why recipes evolve. This recipe had a slow-cooked red pepper and tomato sauce with vinegar and smoky paprika, instead of herb yoghurt, spooned over the aubergines and chickpeas. I felt I needed to freshen things up a little, but you could definitely reinstate the old red sauce for a vegan alternative: simply sauté some chopped onion, garlic and red pepper in plenty of olive oil for a good 30 minutes; add tinned tomatoes and cook slowly for another hour, adding some sherry vinegar and smoked paprika towards the end. Leave to cool before using.

The chickpeas should be very soft here. If cooking with dried chickpeas you'll need to start with 100g to yield the 240g of cooked and make sure you boil them to the stage when they just start to fall apart. If using tinned, cook them in their liquid, plus some extra water, for about 30 minutes.

When roasting aubergines (and not just for this recipe), I recommend placing a tray with water at the bottom of the oven to give out steam and prevent the aubergines from drying out.

....

Preheat the oven to 250°C/230°C Fan/Gas Mark 9 (or to its highest setting).

Place the aubergines in a large mixing bowl with 4 tablespoons of the oil, ¾ teaspoon of salt and a good grind of black pepper. Mix well and then spread out in a single layer on one or two baking trays lined with baking parchment and roast in the oven for about 40 minutes, until golden-brown and cooked through. Remove and set aside to cool.

Meanwhile, put the chickpeas in a mixing bowl with the cumin seeds, lemon flesh, 3 tablespoons of the oil, 2 tablespoons of the cooking liquid, ½ teaspoon of salt and a good grind of black pepper. Mash roughly using a fork or potato masher, adding a bit more of the cooking liquid if needed to get a thick, spreadable paste.

Place the yoghurt in the small bowl of a food processor along with the remaining tablespoon of olive oil, 2 tablespoons of water, the herbs, ¼ teaspoon of salt and some black pepper. Blitz until well combined. You need to be able to drizzle the yoghurt so add a tablespoon or two of water or oil if you need to.

To arrange, spread the aubergine slices out on a platter or individual plates. Spoon the crushed chickpeas on top, followed by a drizzle of the yoghurt, and serve.

CARROT AND MUNG BEAN SALAD

Mung beans are the ABBA of the food world: hearty and healthy but intrinsically bland and forever stuck in the 1970s. I'll leave ABBA fans to fight the band's corner but the reputation of mung beans I can help to redress. Used right, mung beans soak up loads of flavour, pack a real punch and just taste fantastic. To keep this dairy-free, omit the feta.

140g dried green mung beans

60ml olive oil, plus extra for drizzling

1 tsp cumin seeds

1 tsp caraway seeds

1 tsp fennel seeds

2 garlic cloves, crushed

2 tbsp white wine vinegar

½ tsp chilli flakes

3 large carrots, peeled and cut into 5cm x 1cm batons (320g)

½ tsp caster sugar

20g coriander, chopped

grated zest of 1 lemon

140g feta, broken into 2cm chunks

salt

Bring a medium saucepan of water to the boil, add the mung beans and simmer for 20–25 minutes, until the beans are cooked but still retain a bite. Drain, shake well and transfer to a large mixing bowl. About 3 minutes before the beans are cooked, heat 2 tablespoons of the olive oil in a small frying pan and add the cumin, caraway and fennel seeds. Cook on a medium heat, stirring often, until the seeds start to pop – about 3 minutes. Pour the oil and seeds over the hot beans, and add the garlic, vinegar, chilli flakes and ½ teaspoon of salt. Set aside to cool.

While the beans are cooking, place the carrots in a pan large enough so that they form a shallow layer. Pour over about 150ml of water – they need to be nearly submerged – along with the remaining oil, the sugar and ½ teaspoon of salt. Bring the water to a rapid boil and keep on a high heat for 10–12 minutes, by which time all the water should have evaporated and the carrots should have become slightly caramelised whilst still retaining a crunch. Drain some liquid, if needed. Add the carrots to the mung beans along with the coriander, and stir gently. Transfer to a large platter, sprinkle over the lemon zest, dot with feta, finish with a final drizzle of oil and serve.

ROASTED BRUSSELS SPROUTS WITH POMELO AND STAR ANISE

100g caster sugar
2 cinnamon sticks
5 star anise
3 tbsp lemon juice
1 pomelo (900g in total; 300g after peeling and segmenting)
600g Brussels sprouts, trimmed
250g shallots, peeled
75ml olive oil
10g coriander leaves
salt and black pepper

Why anyone ever thought that boiling Brussels sprouts was a good idea when there is the option of roasting them, is one of life's great mysteries. For those who have tried the oven version, there is no turning back. All sprout-doubters, I urge you to give them one more chance: like the Brussels, you'll never be bitter again. If you can't get pomelo (see more in the Pomelo Salad introduction on page 31), use grapefruit segments, but not as much lemon juice. Don't throw out the leftover sugar syrup: you can add it to fruit salads.

Place the sugar, cinnamon and star anise in a small saucepan with 100ml of water and bring to a light simmer. Cook for a minute, stirring until the sugar dissolves, then remove from the heat, add 1 tablespoon of the lemon juice and set aside to cool.

Peel the thick skin off the pomelo and discard. Divide into segments, release the flesh from the membrane, then break into bite-sized pieces and put in a shallow bowl, taking care to remove all of the bitter white membrane. Once the syrup has cooled a little, pour it over the pomelo. Leave to marinate for at least an hour, stirring occasionally.

Preheat the oven to 220°C/200°C Fan/Gas Mark 7.

Bring a large pan of salted water to the boil, add the sprouts and shallots and blanch for 2 minutes. Drain, refresh under cold water and pat dry. Cut the sprouts in two, lengthways, and halve or quarter the shallots (so that they are a similar size to the sprouts). Place everything in a bowl with 3 tablespoons of oil, ½ teaspoon of salt and some black pepper. Spread out on a baking tray and roast in the oven for about 20 minutes, until the sprouts are golden-brown but still retain a bite. Set aside to cool.

Before assembling the salad, remove the cinnamon and star anise from the bowl, strain the pomelo and keep the juices. Just before serving, put the shallots, sprouts, pomelo and coriander in a large mixing bowl. Add the remaining 2 tablespoons of olive oil, lemon juice, 1 tablespoon of the pomelo marinade juices and ¼ teaspoon of salt. Gently mix, then check the seasoning – you might need to add another tablespoon of the marinade – and serve.

SMOKED BEETROOT WITH YOGHURT AND CARAMELISED MACADAMIAS

With plain beetroot already divisive as an ingredient, a debating society will need to be set up to discuss the smoked version. Either way, constructing your own smoker requires no more than a big wok or pan for which you have a lid and a roll of tin foil. A timer is essential (as the flavour becomes too intense if smoked for too long) and an extractor fan recommended. This is a stunner of a salad – both in flavour and looks – and a fantastic way to open a fancy meal.

250g long-grain rice

shaved rind of 1 lemon

5 thyme sprigs

12 medium beetroots, skin on (1.2kg)

1 tsp maple syrup

2 tbsp olive oil, plus extra for drizzling

50g macadamia nuts

35g caster sugar

150g Greek yoghurt

½ tsp Aleppo chilli flakes (or regular chilli flakes, if unavailable)

5g picked coriander leaves

salt and black pepper

....

Preheat the oven to 270°C/250°C Fan/Gas Mark 9 (or its highest setting).

Line a large frying pan or wok with two large sheets of tin foil, with the edges generously overhanging the sides of the pan. Add the rice, lemon rind and thyme and stir through 2 tablespoons of water. Sit the beetroots on top of the rice and seal the pan with a large lid. Draw up the tin foil and fold it back over the lid to completely seal the lid in the foil; gaps will hamper the smoking process. Place on a very high heat on the stove and, once you see a little bit of smoke coming through, after 3 or 4 minutes, leave to smoke for exactly 8 minutes. Remove from the heat.

Discard the rice, lemon peel and thyme, transfer the beetroots to a baking tray and roast for a further 45 or 50 minutes in the oven, or until a knife inserted into a beetroot goes in easily. Set aside to cool and then peel the charred skin off the beetroots. Cut the beets into 2mm slices and place in a large bowl with the maple syrup, 1 tablespoon of the olive oil, ½ teaspoon of salt and some black pepper. Mix together and set aside.

Reduce the oven temperature to 160°C/140°C Fan/Gas Mark 2.

To caramelise the nuts, place them on a baking tray and bake for 15 minutes. Remove from the oven. Place the sugar in a small saucepan and cook on a gentle heat. Don't stir as the sugar melts and starts to caramelise and turns golden. Carefully add the nuts, stir gently until they are coated, then pour them out on to a baking parchment-lined tray to cool. Chop up the nuts and set aside. Mix the yoghurt with the remaining olive oil and set aside.

To serve, spread out the beetroot slices on a large platter, slightly overlapping. Drizzle over the yoghurt before sprinkling the chopped nuts on top. Finish with the chilli flakes, coriander and a final drizzle of olive oil.

SWEET POTATOES WITH ORANGE BITTERS

350ml freshly squeezed
   orange juice (the juice of
   4–5 oranges)
80g soft brown sugar
60ml red wine vinegar
60ml Angostura bitters
1½ tbsp olive oil
4–5 sweet potatoes,
   unpeeled, halved
   widthways, each half cut
   into 2.5cm-wide wedges
   (1.5kg)
2 red chillies, slit open
   along the centre
3 sage stems (15g)
10 thyme sprigs (10g)
2 heads of garlic, unpeeled
   and halved horizontally
90g chèvre (goat's cheese)
   log, broken into pieces
salt and black pepper

One of my greatest idols is Ruth Reichl, a clever writer who delightfully manages to approach food with just the right balance of weightiness and sense of humour, the latter often a rare commodity among 'serious' authors. I love Reichl's recipes, I love her storytelling and I always benefit from her vast knowledge. This recipe – a rhapsody for sweet, bitter and salty – is based on one of hers, published in Gourmet Today, *a selection from the sadly defunct* Gourmet *magazine, which Reichl edited for many years.*

Preheat the oven to 220°C/200°C Fan/Gas Mark 7.

Place the orange juice in a medium saucepan with the sugar and vinegar. Bring to the boil over a high heat, then reduce the heat to medium–high and simmer fairly rapidly for about 20 minutes, until the liquid has thickened and reduced to 200ml (about the amount in a large glass of wine). Add the bitters and olive oil, along with 1½ teaspoons of salt.

Place the potatoes in a large bowl, along with the chillies, sage, thyme and garlic, and then pour over the reduced sauce. Toss well so that everything is coated and then spread out on a baking tray that is snug-fitting but large enough for the potatoes to form a single layer, about 30cm x 40cm.

Place in the oven and roast for 50–60 minutes, turning and basting the potatoes every 15 minutes or so. They need to remain coated in the liquid in order to caramelise, so add some more orange juice if they are drying out. At the end the potatoes should be dark and sticky. Remove from the oven and leave to cool slightly before arranging on a platter and dotting with the goat's cheese. Serve warm or at room temperature.

CURRY ROASTED ROOT VEGETABLES WITH LIME LEAVES AND JUICE

Supermarkets are beginning to stock fresh curry leaves, which is very good news. The flavour they impart to a dish is worlds apart from the dried varieties. For the curry powder, I tend to use the 'Rajah' or 'East End' packets of mild madras curry but if you want an extra kick, the ante is there to be upped. Once you've stocked your freezer with plenty of lime and curry leaves – both freeze very well – this simple and quick dish can easily become a staple. All you need is some freshly steamed rice to serve alongside.

3 large carrots, peeled and cut into 6cm x 2cm batons (350g)

2 large parsnips, peeled and cut into 6cm x 2cm batons (400g)

1 small swede, peeled and cut into 6cm x 2cm batons (400g)

60ml olive oil

3 tbsp lime juice

2 tsp curry powder

6 Kaffir lime leaves, fresh or frozen, very finely shredded

2 stems of curry leaves (about 30 leaves), kept on the stem

6 spring onions, cut widthways into 6cm segments (85g)

3 tbsp chopped coriander

salt and black pepper

Preheat the oven to 240°C/220°C Fan/Gas Mark 9.

Place the carrots, parsnip and swede in a large roasting tray, about 30cm x 40cm. Add the olive oil, half the lime juice, the curry powder, 1¼ teaspoons of salt and a good grind of black pepper. Mix well and place in the oven to roast for 30 minutes, turning the vegetables once or twice during the cooking. Add the lime leaves, curry leaves and spring onions and roast for a further 10 minutes. The vegetables should have taken on a nice golden-brown colour and the spring onions should have softened. Remove from the oven, pour over the remaining lime juice, sprinkle over the coriander and serve warm or at room temperature.

BEETROOT AND RHUBARB SALAD

beetroots of various kinds (or, if you can't get them, one type is fine)

300g trimmed rhubarb, cut at an angle into 2.5cm pieces

30g caster sugar

2 tsp sherry vinegar

¾ tbsp pomegranate molasses

2 tbsp maple syrup

2 tbsp olive oil

½ tsp ground allspice

1 small red onion, thinly sliced (75g)

20g parsley leaves

100g creamy Gorgonzola or similar blue cheese, torn into small chunks

salt and black pepper

For someone who didn't grow up with rhubarb, this vegetable (or stalk?) is a bit of an oddity. I guess the same could be said of artichoke, a thistle, but for me, eating a thick, greenish, reddish branch will always seem much weirder than scoffing a thorny flower. Each to their own, I say.

One of my sweetest rhubarb memories dates from the early years of Ottolenghi, when one of our sales assistants, the lovely Alexandra from Mexico, used to come down to the kitchen on her breaks with a cappuccino cup full of caster sugar and a raw rhubarb stalk to dip in the sugar as dessert. Slightly unusual but, as I said, each to their own.

During the beet season the different varieties around offer a great opportunity to play with colours and subtlety of flavour. If you can get some golden, red, white and some candy beets, you can mix them up; otherwise, one variety is absolutely fine.

Preheat the oven to 220°C/200°C Fan/Gas Mark 7.

Wrap the beetroots individually in foil, place on a baking tray and roast in the oven for anywhere between 40 and 70 minutes, depending on their size, until cooked through. Set aside to cool before peeling and cutting roughly into 2cm dice.

Toss the rhubarb with the sugar, spread out on a small roasting tray lined with foil and bake for about 12 minutes, until the pieces have softened without becoming mushy. Set aside to cool.

Place the vinegar, molasses, maple syrup, oil and allspice in a bowl with ½ teaspoon of salt and a good grind of black pepper. Add the onion and set aside for a few minutes to soften. Add the parsley and beetroot and stir well. Just before serving, add the Gorgonzola and the rhubarb, along with its juices. Give everything a very gentle mix and serve at once.

SQUASH WITH CHILLI YOGHURT AND CORIANDER SAUCE

Sweet chilli sauce has been making its way into dressings and dipping sauces for a while, but the rise in demand for the hot savoury Sriracha sauce – originating from eastern Thailand and made from sun-ripened chilli peppers and garlic, ground into a smooth paste – points to an increasing demand for the hot stuff. Recent threats of shortages have created a small panic among those addicted to the stuff. Mixing Sriracha with Greek yoghurt and drizzling it over a dish like this is a fast-track way to reach a sweet-sharp depth of flavour. The fresh herb paste brings in another layer of freshness, along with a visual 'wow'. This is perhaps the simplest recipe in the book and, if I were a betting man, destined to become a favourite.

1 small coquina or 1 large butternut squash (1.4kg in total)
1 tsp ground cinnamon
90ml olive oil
50g coriander, leaves and stalks, plus extra leaves to garnish
1 small garlic clove, crushed
20g pumpkin seeds
200g Greek yoghurt
1½ tsp Sriracha (or another savoury chilli sauce)
salt and black pepper

Preheat the oven to 220°C/200°C Fan/Gas Mark 7.

Cut the squash in half lengthways, remove and discard the seeds, and then cut into 2cm-thick wedges, about 7cm long, leaving the skin on. Place in a large bowl with the cinnamon, 2 tablespoons of the olive oil, ¾ teaspoon of salt and a good grind of pepper. Mix well so that the squash is evenly coated. Place the squash on two baking trays, skin side down, and roast for 35–40 minutes, until soft and starting to colour on top. Remove from the oven and set aside to cool.

To make the herb paste, place the coriander, garlic, the remaining 4 tablespoons of oil and a generous pinch of salt in a small food processor, blitz to form a fine paste and set aside.

Reduce the oven temperature to 180°C/160°C Fan/Gas Mark 4. Lay the pumpkin seeds out on a baking tray and roast in the oven for 6–8 minutes. The outer skin will pop open and they will become light and crispy. Remove from the oven and allow to cool.

When you are ready to serve, swirl together the yoghurt and Sriracha sauce. Lay the squash wedges on a platter, drizzle over the spicy yoghurt sauce and then the herb paste (you can also swirl the yoghurt sauce and herb paste together, if you like). Scatter the pumpkin seeds on top, followed by the extra coriander leaves, and serve.

FRIED

3 tbsp olive oil

6 banana shallots, finely
  chopped (300g)

1 tbsp white wine vinegar

700g frozen and defrosted
  peas

20g mint leaves, finely
  shredded

1 garlic clove, crushed

4 eggs

100g plain flour

150g panko breadcrumbs

sunflower oil, for frying

salt and black pepper

Sauce

1 tsp dried mint

120g soured cream

1 tbsp olive oil

PEA AND MINT CROQUETTES

For a while we had a pretty wicked trio running the evening service at Ottolenghi in Islington. Tom, Sam and Myles were notorious for working hard and playing hard – in so many senses – but unfortunately the whiteness of this page prevents me from disclosing any details. All three had two things in common: a cheeky, irresistible grin, and an unusual passion for what they cooked. These croquettes are their creation and worth a little effort. They can be made well in advance and taken up to the stage where they are covered in panko breadcrumbs and frozen. You can then partially defrost and fry them as you need.

The recipe makes 16 generously sized patties, ample for four people. To feed more, or to serve as a snack or starter, make them into smaller croquettes, weighing about 40g each. (Also pictured on previous page.)

To make the sauce, place all the ingredients in a bowl with ¼ teaspoon of salt and a grind of black pepper. Mix well and refrigerate until ready to use.

Place the olive oil in a medium sauté pan on a medium heat. Add the shallots and sauté for 15–20 minutes, stirring often, until soft. Add the vinegar, cook for a further 2 minutes and then remove from the heat.

Place the peas in a food processor and briefly blitz. They need to break down without turning into a mushy paste. Transfer to a mixing bowl and stir in the shallots, mint, garlic, 1 egg, ½ teaspoon of salt and plenty of black pepper.

Line a tray that will fit in your freezer with baking parchment and shape the pea mixture into 16 patties (around 60g each), about 7cm across and 2cm thick. Freeze for a couple of hours to firm up.

Place the remaining eggs in a bowl and gently beat. Place the flour in a separate bowl and the breadcrumbs in a third. Remove the croquettes from the freezer and, one at a time, roll them in the flour, dip them in the egg, then coat in the crumbs. You can then either return them to the freezer at this point or leave them at room temperature for about 1 hour, until partly defrosted. Whatever you do, it's important, when it comes to frying, that the patties are not entirely frozen: you want them to cook through without burning the crust.

Preheat the oven to 220°C/200°C Fan/Gas Mark 7.

Fill a medium frying pan with enough sunflower oil so that it comes 2.5cm up the sides. Place on a medium–high heat and leave for 5 minutes for the oil to get hot. Reduce the heat to medium and fry the croquettes in batches for about 4 minutes, turning once, until both sides are golden-brown.

Transfer to a baking tray and place in the oven for 5 minutes, to warm through. Serve at once, with the sauce spooned on top or served alongside.

POLENTA CRISPS WITH AVOCADO AND YOGHURT

SERVES SIX TO EIGHT

as a snack

For all of its versatility, polenta is one of those ingredients that spends too much of its time at the back of the kitchen cupboard, on the 'no one knows quite what to do with me' shelf. Quick-cook polenta puts an end to tennis-elbow accusations so there really isn't any reason to keep it abandoned and disused. These crisps aren't quick 'n' easy like many polenta dishes, but they are fun and worth a little effort. Still, if you are after a quicker result, stop after you have boiled the polenta, before it's time to spread it on a board; spoon into a big bowl and top with soft-boiled egg and some pesto.

750ml vegetable stock
160g quick-cook polenta
10g chives, chopped
30g Parmesan, finely grated
100g coarse semolina
about 300ml sunflower oil, for frying
salt and white pepper

Avocado dipping sauce
2 small avocados, halved and flesh scooped out (180g)
100g Greek yoghurt
1½ tbsp lime juice
1 tsp grated lime zest
1 tsp hazelnut (or olive) oil

Place all the ingredients for the dipping sauce in the small bowl of a food processor, along with ⅓ teaspoon of salt and some white pepper. Blitz to form a smooth paste and set aside.

Pour the stock into a medium saucepan and bring to the boil. Add the polenta and cook on a high heat for about 5 minutes, stirring constantly, until all the liquid has been absorbed and the mixture is thick. Add the chives and Parmesan, stir for another 30 seconds and then transfer the mixture on to 2 large chopping boards or trays, measuring about 25cm x 40cm. Use a palette knife to spread out the polenta very thinly. Don't worry about the surface being slightly uneven: ideally the thickness should range from 1 to 3mm. Leave to set for about 20 minutes and then use a palette knife or spatula to remove the polenta from the board in odd pieces of roughly 5cm x 7cm. Dip each piece in the semolina – turning so that both sides are covered – and set aside. If they are fragile and tending to break, sprinkle the pieces on both sides whilst on the board.

Pour enough oil into a large frying pan so that it comes 1cm up the sides. Place on a medium–high heat and fry the crisps in batches, each for about 5 minutes, turning once so that both sides become golden-brown; the edges will crisp up and brown while the centre remains soft to the touch and golden in places. Transfer to a plate lined with kitchen paper to drain and sprinkle with a little salt. Serve hot, with the dipping sauce on the side.

SEARED GIROLLES WITH BLACK GLUTINOUS RICE

2½ tbsp olive oil, plus extra
to finish
6 shallots, chopped (100g)
2 lemons, rind shaved in
long strips from one, ½
tsp finely grated zest from
the other, plus extra to
finish
4 thyme sprigs
1 bay leaf
200g black glutinous rice,
soaked overnight in water
600g girolle mushrooms,
brushed clean
1½ tsp truffle oil
1 tsp unsalted butter
2 tsp lemon juice
2 tbsp chopped tarragon
120g goat's curd or a soft
and mild goat's cheese
(optional)
salt and black pepper

I love all rice but I really, really love this rice. Striking to look at, it is, like other short-grained rice, nutty and chewy, soft and starchy. Each grain retains its integrity when cooked so it's slightly al dente too. You can use the Italian nerone rice if that's what you find, but for the real deal seek out ketan hitam rice from Asian stores or online. Black glutinous rice is a hugely popular rice in South East Asia where it's cooked in coconut milk for pudding and served with diced mango or banana, or in a range of savoury dishes. Remember to soak the rice overnight, or it will take a very long time to cook. If you want to keep this dairy-free, just do without the goat's curd. Girolles, which aren't always easy to find, can easily be substituted with oyster mushrooms.

Pour 1 tablespoon of the olive oil into a medium saucepan. Add the shallots, lemon rind, thyme, bay leaf, ½ teaspoon of salt and some black pepper and place on a medium–low heat. Cook for 5–6 minutes, until the shallots are soft. Drain the black rice and add to the pan. Pour over 400ml of water, bring to the boil, reduce to a gentle simmer, cover the pan and cook for 35–40 minutes, stirring from time to time, until the rice is well cooked and has a starchy consistency. Remove the lemon, thyme and bay and keep the rice somewhere warm until serving.

Place the remaining olive oil in a large sauté pan and add the girolles along with ¼ teaspoon of salt and some black pepper. Sauté for about 5 minutes, stirring so that all sides get a bit of colour. Remove from the heat and add the truffle oil, butter, grated lemon zest, lemon juice and tarragon.

Spoon the black rice on to individual plates. Top with the mushrooms followed by the goat's curd, if using. Drizzle with a little olive oil and some more grated lemon zest and serve.

MIXED VEGETABLES AND YOGHURT WITH GREEN CHILLI OIL

SERVES FOUR

This is a dish I picked up on a visit to Istanbul. I had it in a kebab restaurant, but for me it was actually the vegetables that were the highlight. Try to overlook the fact the vegetables are fried; the dish is still extremely fresh-tasting thanks to the yoghurt and all the herbs. Serve it with Fava (see page 233) and Crushed Carrots with Harissa and Pistachios (see page 242) as a perfectly balanced mezze trio, with some fresh bread to pile the stuff on.

....

Preheat the oven to 170°C/150°C Fan/Gas Mark 3½.

Spread out the tomatoes on a baking tray, sprinkle with ¼ teaspoon of salt and place in the oven for 40 minutes to dry out a little. Remove and set aside to cool.

To make the herb oil, place all the ingredients in a small food processor with a pinch of salt and process to a smooth, thick sauce.

Pour enough sunflower oil into a medium saucepan to come 5cm up the sides of the pan and place on a medium–high heat. Once the oil is hot, reduce the heat to medium. Pat dry the courgette and aubergine and deep-fry them and the red pepper in batches, between 12 and 15 minutes for each batch. The aubergine might take a little longer than the other vegetables: you want it to be golden-brown. Drain in a colander, sprinkle with salt and set aside to cool.

Finally, stir the yoghurt in a medium bowl with the garlic, fresh and dried mint, lemon juice and plenty of black pepper. Add the vegetables and tomatoes and stir very gently. Spoon the herb oil on top and serve.

3 large plum tomatoes, each
   cut into 6 wedges (300g)
sunflower oil, for frying
2 medium courgettes, cut
   into 2cm chunks (400g)
1 large aubergine, cut into
   2cm chunks (450g)
2 large red peppers, cut into
   2cm chunks (420g)
150g Greek yoghurt
1 large garlic clove, crushed
1 tbsp shredded fresh mint
1½ tsp dried mint
1½ tsp lemon juice
salt and black pepper

Chilli and herb oil
1 green chilli, roughly
   chopped
20g parsley
1 tbsp chopped mint
1 tsp ground cumin
60ml olive oil

SMOKY POLENTA CHIPS

375ml vegetable stock

60g quick-cook polenta

20g unsalted butter

60g scamorza affumicata,
   coarsely grated

3 large plum tomatoes
   (320g)

2 tbsp olive oil

½ medium onion, thinly
   sliced (100g)

2 garlic cloves, crushed

⅛ tsp chilli flakes

1 tsp tomato purée

¾ tsp caster sugar

vegetable oil, for frying

50g plain flour

salt and black pepper

Smoky, crisp and cheesy with a rich tomato sauce: my version of fries with ketchup but, possibly, even more moreish. I use a smoked Italian cheese, scamorza affumicata, to give these chips a deep flavour and a gorgeous melting texture, but you can happily substitute with another cheese with substantial flavour such as Italian provolone or Applewood smoked Cheddar.

Bring the stock to the boil in a small saucepan. Slowly add the polenta while stirring with a wooden spoon. Cook on a gentle heat for 5–7 minutes, stirring all the time. Remove the pan from the heat and mix in the butter, cheese, ½ teaspoon of salt and a good grind of black pepper. Once the cheese and butter have both melted into the mix, transfer to a small shallow tray, about 22cm square and 3cm deep, lined with cling film. Use a wet spatula to smooth out and level the polenta to an even layer of about 1.5cm. Cover the surface with more cling film, so that a skin does not form, and leave to cool completely, before chilling for at least 30 minutes.

Meanwhile, make a tomato sauce. Place a large non-stick frying pan on a high heat and turn on the extractor fan, if you have one. Once hot, put the tomatoes inside and leave on a high heat for about 15 minutes, stirring occasionally. The tomato skins need to blacken well; don't be tempted to remove them from the heat too early. Transfer the hot tomatoes to a mixing bowl and break them with a spoon. When cool enough to handle, pick out the skins and discard.

Heat the olive oil in a small pan, add the onion and cook on a medium heat for 5–6 minutes. Add the garlic and cook for another 4 minutes before transferring the mixture to the tomatoes, along with the chilli flakes, tomato purée, sugar and ½ teaspoon of salt. Use a hand-held blender or the small bowl of a food processor to blitz to a rough paste. Set aside until the sauce comes to room temperature.

Once the polenta is chilled and properly set, remove it from the tray and cut into chips, roughly 1.5cm thick and 6cm long. Fill a medium saucepan with enough vegetable oil to come 2cm up its sides and place on a medium-high heat.

Toss the chips in the flour until well coated, shake off the excess and carefully place in the hot oil. Fry for about 6 minutes to a golden-brown colour and transfer to kitchen paper to drain. Don't fry too many chips at a time: if the pan is overcrowded the temperature of the oil will drop and the chips won't crisp.

Serve hot, with the tomato sauce spooned on top or in a bowl alongside.

BUTTERMILK-CRUSTED OKRA WITH TOMATO AND BREAD SAUCE

One shouldn't really have favourites but, as with children in the eyes of their doting parents, some just do shine a bit more brightly on particular days. This meal-in-a-bowl was, for me, a revelation. I was inspired to make the batter after a trip to the iconic Californian restaurant Chez Panisse, where chef Cal Peternell used a similar batter with some young spring onions. You'll get more basil oil than you need here: keep what remains in the fridge to drizzle over roasted vegetables or grilled white meat.

75g plain flour

25g fine polenta

¼ tsp caster sugar

200ml buttermilk

3 tbsp sparkling water

about 350ml sunflower oil, for frying

250g okra, trimmed

4 tbsp soured cream

salt and black pepper

Tomato sauce

2 tbsp olive oil

1 garlic clove, sliced

200g fresh tomatoes, blanched, peeled and roughly chopped

200g tinned Italian tomatoes

12 large basil leaves, roughly shredded

1 small slice of sourdough or another good white bread, crusts removed (25g)

Basil oil

25g basil

3 tbsp olive oil

1 large garlic clove, crushed

You can make the tomato sauce and the basil oil in advance. Heat the olive oil for the sauce in a large frying pan and add the garlic. Let it soften for 2 minutes before adding both types of tomato and 300ml of water. Simmer gently for 30 minutes to thicken. Stir in the basil, ⅓ teaspoon of salt, some black pepper and the bread; add a little water, if needed, to allow the bread to soak up the sauce and break up as you stir. The sauce should be thick and hearty, yet runny enough to spoon.

Place all the ingredients for the basil oil in a food processor, along with a pinch of salt, and blitz until smooth.

Shortly before serving, make the batter. Place the flour, polenta, sugar, ¼ teaspoon of salt and some pepper in a large mixing bowl. Add the buttermilk and water and whisk until smooth. Pour the sunflower oil into a medium saucepan, making sure you have enough oil to deep-fry the okra. To hasten the process, double the quantity of oil and use 2 pans simultaneously. Heat the oil over a medium–high heat, then reduce the heat to medium so the okra doesn't fry too quickly. Dip a few okra pods in the batter, shake off the excess and fry for 2 minutes, turning once, until golden-brown. Place on kitchen paper, sprinkle with salt and keep warm, in a low oven, as you continue with the rest.

Warm the sauce and spoon it on to plates. Pile okra on top and finish with the soured cream and the basil oil. Serve at once.

FRIED UPMA WITH POACHED EGG

100g chana dhal

1½ tbsp sunflower oil, plus
  extra for greasing the tray

1 small onion, chopped
  (90g)

2 tsp cumin seeds

30g fresh root ginger,
  peeled and finely chopped

1 small green chilli,
  deseeded and finely
  chopped

20 fresh curry leaves (about
  3 stems)

2 tsp black mustard seeds,
  toasted

⅓ tsp curry powder

¼ tsp ground turmeric

30g unsalted peanuts,
  toasted and roughly
  chopped

200g coarse semolina

about 60g ghee or clarified
  butter

4 eggs

1 tbsp white wine vinegar

100g Indian lime pickle
  (Patak's or another shop-
  bought variety), optional

120g Greek yoghurt

salt

Upma, a thick semolina-based porridge, is a popular south Indian breakfast dish or tiffin-box staple. The spices are not as they might be if you were eating this later on in the day but, if your taste buds have woken up, you might want to increase the spices accordingly. The lime pickle is optional because it tends to slightly mask the wonderful flavour of the humble upma. Still, I love it so much that I can't help but adding a little. I have a bit of a reputation in the test kitchen for the non-return of Tupperware when leftovers have been taken home the night before. Entirely undeserved, of course, but the Indian way makes me think that designated tiffin boxes might be the way forward.

Bring a small pan of water to the boil and add the chana dhal. Cook for 30 minutes, or until just cooked. Drain, refresh under cold water and set aside.

Heat the oil in a large sauté pan on a medium heat. Add the onion and cumin and cook for 4 minutes. Add the ginger, chilli, curry leaves, black mustard seeds, curry powder and turmeric and cook for 2 minutes more, stirring often. Add the peanuts, cooked dhal and 1 teaspoon of salt and fry for another minute, stirring from time to time. Add the semolina, pour over 400ml of water and cook for a final 2 minutes, stirring continuously.

Lightly oil a 20cm x 20cm tray and spread out the semolina mix. Use a palette knife to flatten it down before setting aside for about 20 minutes, to cool and set. Wipe down the frying pan, add the ghee or butter and place on a high heat. Use a knife to cut the upma into four squares and then cut each square in half on the diagonal. Add the triangles to the pan and fry for about 6 minutes, turning once, so that both sides turn golden and crispy. You will need to do this in 2 batches so keep them warm, in a low oven, whilst you continue with the second batch, adding more ghee or butter if you need to.

Finally, poach the eggs. Fill a shallow saucepan with enough water for a whole egg to cook in. Add the vinegar and bring to a rapid boil. To poach each egg, carefully break it into a cup, then gently pour into the boiling water. Immediately remove the pan from the heat and set it aside. After about 4 minutes the egg should be poached to perfection. Using a slotted spoon, carefully transfer the poached egg to a bowl of warm water to keep it from cooling down. Once all the eggs are done, dry them on kitchen paper.

Put two triangles on each plate, leaning one up against the other. Spoon a poached egg alongside, with some pickle, if you like, along with some yoghurt. Serve at once.

FRIED CAULIFLOWER WITH MINT AND TAMARIND DIPPING SAUCE

120g panko breadcrumbs
1 small garlic clove,
  crushed
1 tsp ground ginger
1¼ tsp ground cumin
2 tsp curry powder
1½ tsp coriander seeds
1½ tsp black mustard seeds
1 tsp chilli flakes
1½ tsp caster sugar
3 eggs, beaten
90g plain flour
1 medium cauliflower,
  broken into 3cm florets
  (600g)
about 1 litre sunflower oil,
  for frying
salt

Sauce
40g parsley leaves
25g coriander leaves
10g mint leaves
1 tbsp tamarind paste
1 tsp maple syrup
1 tbsp olive oil
2 tsp lime juice

To me, fried cauliflower is up there as the best of all comfort foods. It possibly has to do with my childhood – when my dad simply dipped cauliflower in egg and breadcrumbs, fried and served it to us with homemade mayonnaise – or, perhaps, it's just because fried cauliflower is so damn delicious.

The dipping sauce is not essential here – a squeeze of lime is perfectly fine – but it is fantastically fresh. Somehow I just know that you will find yourself making this sauce again and again and spooning it over everything, from grilled meat to various curries and stews.

Place all the ingredients for the sauce, apart from the lime juice, in the small bowl of a food processor along with ½ teaspoon of salt and 2 tablespoons of water. Process until completely smooth and set aside.

Place the breadcrumbs, garlic, ground spices, seeds, chilli flakes and sugar in the small bowl of a food processor with ½ teaspoon of salt. Blitz a few times until the spices are mixed and the breadcrumbs are slightly broken down: you don't want the texture to be completely fine. Transfer to a bowl.

Place the eggs in a separate bowl and the flour in a third, along with ½ teaspoon of salt. Dip a cauliflower floret into the flour so that it's completely covered. Next, dip it into the egg and then, finally, into the spicy breadcrumbs, turning so that all sides get covered. Set aside on a large plate whilst you continue dipping the remaining cauliflower.

Pour enough oil into a medium saucepan so that it comes 3–4cm up the sides. Place on a medium–high heat and, once hot, carefully lower in about 8 pieces of cauliflower. Fry for 2–3 minutes, until golden-brown. Use a slotted spoon to transfer them to a plate lined with kitchen paper and keep somewhere warm whilst you continue with the remaining cauliflower. (The oil can be strained and reused.) Stir the lime juice into the dipping sauce just before serving alongside the fried cauliflower.

BRUSSELS SPROUTS WITH CARAMELISED GARLIC AND LEMON PEEL

There are a number of dishes in Plenty *that I keep hearing about from people who cook from the book. I call them the 'Top 10'. One of them is my caramelised garlic tart, which seems to have been a revelation to many a garlic lover. A similar surprising transformation of the garlic cloves, from harsh and abrasive to mild and sweet, occurs here, allowing you to use tons of garlic without any risk of harming yourself or your loved ones.*

There are a couple of elements in this Christmassy affair that will come in handy elsewhere. The caramelised garlic makes a great condiment to lentils and roasted vegetables and the candied lemon can be used to garnish creamy desserts or leafy salads. Pan-frying sprouts is a great way to cook them: the flavour is enhanced and a healthy texture is retained.

200g garlic (5 regular heads or 3 large heads), cloves removed and peeled
about 120ml olive oil
2 tsp balsamic vinegar
3 tbsp caster sugar
1 medium lemon
600g Brussels sprouts
1 red chilli, deseeded and finely chopped
20g basil leaves, coarsely shredded
salt and black pepper

Start with the garlic. Bring a medium saucepan of water to the boil, add the garlic and blanch for 3 minutes. Drain the garlic, dry the pan and pour in 2 tablespoons of the olive oil. Return the garlic to the pan and fry on a high heat for 2 minutes, stirring all the time, until golden on all sides. Add the vinegar, 1 tablespoon of the sugar, 90ml of water and ¼ teaspoon of salt. Bring to the boil and simmer gently on a medium heat for 10–15 minutes, or until hardly any liquid is left, the garlic cloves have caramelised and the syrup is thick. Set the pan aside.

To prepare the lemon peel, use a vegetable peeler to shave off wide strips of lemon skin; avoid the white pith. Cut the strips widthways into slices 1–2mm thick and place them in a small saucepan. Squeeze the lemon and make the juice up to 100ml with water. Pour over the lemon skins, add the remaining 2 tablespoons of sugar and bring to a light simmer. Cook for 12–15 minutes, or until the syrup is reduced to about a third. Set aside to cool down and then strain the lemon, discarding the syrup.

Meanwhile, trim the sprouts and cut them in half lengthways. Place about 3 tablespoons of olive oil in a large heavy-based pan and heat up well. Add half the sprouts, ⅛ teaspoon of salt and a good grind of black pepper. Cook on a high heat for about 5 minutes, stirring once or twice, so that they char well without breaking up; add more oil if needed. The sprouts will have softened but still retain a bite. Transfer to a mixing bowl and continue with your remaining oil and sprouts.

Once the sprouts are cooked, mix them with the chilli, along with the garlic and its syrup. Stir and leave aside for about 10 minutes. Stir in the basil and candied lemon peel and serve warm or at room temperature.

QUINOA AND WILD GARLIC CAKES WITH SALBITXADA SAUCE

SERVES FOUR
makes 16 cakes

As anyone who reads her 101cookbooks blog will know, Heidi Swanson is the very lovely champion of all things vegetarian. She is also the source of inspiration for these quinoa patties, which are great with just a squeeze of lemon but work like a dream with the salbitxada sauce. Tara, who steers away from breadcrumbs whenever she can, makes the cakes with ground flaxseed instead, for those who want a gluten-free option. Make more than you need of the wonderfully versatile salbitxada – a Catalan sauce similar to romesco. Store it in the fridge for up to a week to have ready to serve alongside any rice-based dish or grilled vegetables, meat or fish.

Preheat the oven to 220°C/200°C Fan/Gas Mark 7.

First make the sauce. Place the red pepper, chillies and garlic cloves on a baking tray and roast for 10 minutes. Remove the chillies and garlic, turn the red pepper and continue cooking for another 20 minutes. Once the skin is blistered and the pepper roasted, remove it and place in a bowl covered with cling film. When cool, peel and deseed the pepper. Do the same with the chillies and also peel the garlic.

Reduce the oven temperature to 200°C/180°C Fan/Gas Mark 6.

Place the almonds in the small bowl of a food processor and grind to a coarse powder. Add the cooked pepper, chilli, garlic and the tomatoes and continue to process to a paste. Add the sherry vinegar, along with ¼ teaspoon of salt, and then slowly pour in the oil until you have a thick sauce.

Throw the quinoa into a medium saucepan with plenty of boiling water and simmer for 9 minutes, until tender but still with a bite. Strain in a fine sieve, refresh under cold water and set aside until completely dry.

Place all the remaining ingredients, apart from the oil and lemon, in a large bowl with 1 teaspoon of salt and a good grind of black pepper. Add the quinoa, stir well and form the mixture into 60g patties, about 6cm wide and 2cm thick.

Place a medium non-stick pan on a medium heat and add half the oil. Fry the patties in batches for 3 minutes on each side, until golden, adding more oil as needed. Transfer to a baking tray and finish off in the oven for about 8 minutes. Serve hot with a squeeze of lemon juice, if using, or with the salbitxada sauce spooned on top or alongside.

250g quinoa
40g wild garlic leaves, thinly sliced (or 6 thinly sliced spring onions, as an alternative)
1 small red onion, finely diced (100g)
2 eggs, lightly whisked
2 green chillies, deseeded and finely diced
120g cottage cheese
30g mature Cheddar, coarsely grated
60g dried breadcrumbs
2 tsp ground cumin
60ml olive oil, for frying
1 large lemon, cut into wedges (optional)
salt and black pepper

Salbitxada sauce
1 medium red pepper (150g in total)
2 red chillies
5 garlic cloves, unpeeled
40g flaked almonds, toasted
4 ripe tomatoes, blanched, peeled, deseeded and roughly chopped (250g)
2 tsp sherry vinegar
100ml olive oil

UDON NOODLES WITH FRIED AUBERGINE, WALNUT AND MISO

SERVES FOUR

as a main course; more
as a starter or side

3 spring onions
25g fresh root ginger,
   peeled and cut into very
   fine matchsticks
2 small aubergines (500g in
   total)
250ml sunflower oil, for
   deep frying, plus 1 extra
   tablespoon
6 shallots, thinly sliced
   (100g)
2 garlic cloves, crushed
120g walnuts, lightly
   toasted and roughly
   chopped
50g sweet white miso paste
150ml vegetarian dashi or
   vegetable stock from a
   cube
3 tbsp mirin
2 tbsp soy sauce
1 tbsp caster sugar
1 tbsp sake (optional)
250g dried udon noodles
½ cucumber, unpeeled,
   cored and cut into very
   fine strips (150g)
salt

Miso has become a cupboard staple of mine since I wrote Plenty. *It's a fantastic way of getting tons of umami-rich flavour into vegetarian dishes, whether added to a marinade, sauce, soup or dressing.*

A decent vegetarian dashi can be made by boiling kombu, an edible kelp often used in Asian cooking, for just five minutes. Kombu is available at health food shops and some oriental grocers'.

Cut each spring onion into 5cm lengths. Slice each length in two, from top to bottom, and then cut each half into long strips, as thin as you can. Place the onions and 10g of the ginger into a bowl of iced water and put in the fridge.

Use a potato peeler to peel off 4–5 strips of skin from the aubergines, from top to bottom, so you are left with a stripy pattern. Slice the aubergines into 2.5cm-thick discs and then cut each disc into quarters. Pour 250ml of sunflower oil into a medium saucepan and place on a medium–high heat. Once hot, add the aubergine in small batches and deep-fry for about 4 minutes, until they turn golden and cook through. Transfer to a colander to drain and sprinkle with a little salt.

Place the shallots and the tablespoon of sunflower oil in a sauté pan and sauté on a medium heat. Once the shallots soften, after about 2 minutes, add the remaining ginger and the garlic and cook on a low heat for 5 minutes. Add the walnuts and fried aubergine and set aside.

Whisk all the remaining ingredients, bar the noodles and cucumber, in a bowl and add them to the pan with the walnuts and aubergines.

Cook the noodles as instructed on the packet. While you do this, heat up the sauce and aubergine, allowing some evaporation so the sauce thickens a little but not much. Serve individual portions of hot noodles, topped in the centre with walnut sauce. Drain and pat dry the spring onion and ginger and sprinkle these on top, along with the cucumber.

CRISPY SAFFRON COUSCOUS CAKES

SERVES FOUR
makes 20 patties

This was inspired by Ana Sortun, a friend and the owner of the legendary Oleana restaurant in Cambridge, Massachusetts. Ana's original cakes are made to have the texture of tah-dig, the crispy, lightly fried base of Iranian rice. My version – busier, of course – replaces the rice with couscous and has a sweet and salty edge, which makes them very popular with little people. It is the yoghurt and the egg that make these so nice and crunchy. For an adult main, serve the patties with tomato chutney or relish and a green salad. If you want, add fresh herbs such as dill, parsley or mint to the mix.

Currants soaked for 20 minutes in lemon juice can be used instead of barberries, if you can't get hold of them.

½ tsp saffron threads
275g couscous
30g barberries
50g caster sugar
140g Greek yoghurt
2 eggs, lightly beaten
20g chives, chopped
100g feta, crumbled into 1cm chunks
about 4 tbsp clarified butter or ghee
salt and black pepper

Place the saffron in a large mixing bowl and pour over 500ml of boiling water. Leave to infuse for a minute or two, then add the couscous. Stir with a fork, cover the bowl with cling film and let stand for 15 minutes.

Put the barberries and sugar in a small saucepan. Add 120ml of water, bring to a light simmer, stir to dissolve the sugar, and remove from the heat. Once cool, drain the barberries and dry on kitchen paper.

Fluff up the couscous with a fork and then add the yoghurt, eggs, chives, feta, barberries, 1¼ teaspoons of salt and some black pepper. Mix well and then use your hands to shape the couscous into firm round patties, about 1.5cm thick and weighing 55g each; press and compact them well so they don't disintegrate during cooking.

Heat 2 tablespoons of the butter or ghee in a large frying pan placed on a medium–high heat. Reduce the heat to medium and fry the patties in batches, adding more butter if needed. Cook each batch for 5 minutes, turning once, until crisp and golden-brown. Transfer to kitchen paper and keep somewhere warm whilst you continue cooking the remainder. Serve at once.

I tried to think of a more inspired title for this recipe. It all got too long, with fried potatoes, spicy tomatoes and poached eggs all trying to get a mention. Reverting back to basics, I tell it like it is.

For all you shakshuka lovers, this is another dish to cherish for a late weekend breakfast, though it takes longer to make because the different components need to be prepared separately. You can prepare them in advance, though, and just put everything together at the last minute. This can be served straight out of the skillet or frying pan. I recommend always stirring the tahini in the tub before using it.

....

Place the tomatoes in a colander for 30 minutes to drain. Transfer to a medium bowl and add the onion, vinegar, parsley, Sriracha and ¼ teaspoon of salt. Mix gently and set aside.

Mix the aubergine with 1½ teaspoons of salt, place in a colander and set aside over a bowl for half an hour, to remove any excess liquid. Transfer to a plate lined with kitchen paper and pat dry. Place 200ml of the olive oil in a 26cm frying pan, along with all of the sunflower oil: it needs to come 1cm up the sides of the pan, so add more if you need to. Place on a high heat and, once hot, add the aubergine in batches. Fry for 3–4 minutes, until golden-brown. Remove with a slotted spoon, transfer to a plate lined with kitchen paper and set aside somewhere warm whilst you continue with the remaining batches. Leave the oil to cool, pour it away into a jar – you'll be able to use it for future frying – and wipe down the pan.

Bring a medium pan of water to the boil, add the potatoes and cook for 3 minutes. Drain, refresh under cold water and set aside to dry. Add 2 tablespoons of fresh olive oil to the frying pan and place on a medium–high heat. Add the potatoes and fry for 10 minutes with ¼ teaspoon of salt and a grind of black pepper, until they are cooked through and golden-brown, shaking the pan from time to time. Remove the pan from the heat and set aside.

Place the tahini, 60ml of water, 1½ tablespoons of lemon juice, garlic and a pinch of salt in a medium bowl and whisk until you have a thick, pourable consistency. Spoon half of the sauce over the potatoes and spread the aubergines on top. Follow this with the remaining tahini and then spoon over the tomatoes. Poach the eggs just before you are ready to serve and then lay these on top of the tomatoes, along with a drizzle of the remaining olive oil, a sprinkle of the sumac and coriander and the last of the lemon juice. Bring to the table in the pan.

4 medium tomatoes, cut into 1cm dice (400g)
½ small red onion, finely chopped (40g)
2 tsp white wine vinegar
15g parsley, chopped
1 tbsp Sriracha sauce (or another hot savoury chilli sauce)
2 medium aubergines, cut into 3cm chunks (600g)
250ml olive oil, for frying
about 300ml sunflower oil
600g Charlotte potatoes (or another waxy variety), peeled and cut into 3mm slices
80g tahini paste
2½ tbsp lemon juice
1 small garlic clove, crushed
6 eggs, freshly poached (see page 210 for poaching instructions)
1 tsp sumac
1 tbsp coriander, chopped
salt and black pepper

COATED OLIVES WITH SPICY YOGHURT

1 green chilli, roughly
   chopped
¼ tsp ground cardamom
⅛ tsp ground cloves
¾ tsp caster sugar
20g coriander, roughly
   chopped
20g parsley, roughly
   chopped
45g preserved lemon
   (skin and flesh), roughly
   chopped
60ml olive oil
80g panko breadcrumbs,
   blitzed to a very fine
   crumb
50g plain flour
2 eggs, beaten
160g pitted green olives
sunflower oil, for frying
300g Greek yoghurt

This recipe is more or less nicked from the fantastic cookbook of the even more fantastic restaurant, Balaboosta, in New York's SoHo. The talented chef, Einat Admoni, is the local face of the increasingly popular Israeli food scene. Coating and frying individual olives may seem, at first, a little painstaking, but they can be prepared in advance, at leisure; the resulting pre-dinner nibble is, for those who can't face yet another smoked salmon blini, really very special.

Place the chilli, spices, sugar, coriander, parsley, preserved lemon and olive oil in a small blender and blitz to a rough paste. Pour into a small bowl and set aside until required.

Place the breadcrumbs, flour and eggs in three separate small bowls.

Drain the olives from their preserving juices and pat dry with kitchen paper. Once dry, take one olive and dip in the flour, then the egg and finally coat well in panko. Place on a plate to one side. Repeat with the rest of the olives.

Pour enough sunflower oil into a small saucepan so that it comes 3cm up the sides and place on a medium–high heat. Once the oil is hot, add a couple of the olives. They should take 1 minute to go golden-brown and need to be turned over during the process. If they brown too quickly, turn the heat down. Remove the olives from the oil and transfer on to kitchen paper. Repeat with the rest of the olives until they are all cooked.

Spoon the yoghurt into a shallow bowl, then swirl the green paste into it (don't mix them completely). Pile the olives, warm or at room temperature, into the centre and serve.

POT BARLEY AND LENTILS WITH MUSHROOMS AND SWEET SPICES

SERVES FOUR

I've always tended to cook with pearl barley, so pot barley was a real revelation after Diana Henry suggested I use it instead of rice for a take on lentil mejadra. Unlike pearl barley – whose hulled, polished and tender nature makes it very happy to take on more robust flavours – pot barley's inherent nuttiness and bite allows it to sing more independently in a dish. With more to get through before the grain is cooked, pot barley takes longer to cook than the pearled version but soaking it in cold water the night before will speed things along. It's a robust and versatile grain that can be used instead of pasta, rice, couscous or bulgar. I'm finding all sorts of excuses to eat it with every meal at the moment – savoury and sweet (see Pot Barley Orange and Sesame Pudding, page 337). (Also pictured overleaf.)

20g dried porcini mushrooms

120g pot barley, covered with cold water and soaked overnight

170g brown lentils

2 medium onions (240g in total), 1 peeled, halved and thinly sliced; the other peeled, halved and cut into 2cm-wide wedges

2 tbsp plain flour

about 600ml sunflower oil, for frying

2 tbsp olive oil

1½ tsp ground cumin

1 tsp ground allspice

1 tsp ground cinnamon

3 large Portobello mushrooms, sliced into 1cm strips (250g)

1 lemon, rind shaved into long strips

½ tsp caster sugar

1 tbsp dried mint

1 tbsp lemon juice

10g dill, roughly chopped

10g parsley, roughly chopped

60g soured cream (optional)

salt and black pepper

Place the dried porcini in a bowl, cover with 400ml of boiling water and leave to stand for 1 hour. Once cool, lift out the mushrooms and strain the liquid through a fine sieve lined with a clean J-cloth, to remove any grit. Return the mushrooms to the liquid.

Drain the pot barley, rinse under cold water and place in a large saucepan with the lentils. Pour over plenty of cold water – it should come 5cm above the barley and lentils – place on a high heat and bring to the boil. Reduce the heat to medium–high and cook for 15–20 minutes, until the lentils and barley are cooked but still hold their shape. Drain, and transfer to a medium bowl to cool down.

Place the onion slices in a small bowl, add the flour and shake gently. Pour the sunflower oil into a medium saucepan so that it comes 2cm up the sides. Place on a high heat and, once hot, add half of the onion and fry for 3–4 minutes, until golden-brown. Use a slotted spoon to remove them from the oil and place them on a plate lined with kitchen paper. Repeat with the remaining slices and set aside to cool.

Place the onion wedges in a large sauté pan on a high heat with the olive oil and fry for 5 minutes, stirring frequently, until the onion is charred and soft. Add the ground spices and continue to cook for 30 seconds before adding the Portobello mushrooms, lemon strips, sugar and ½ teaspoon of salt. Fry for 3 minutes, until the mushrooms are starting to soften and gain some colour, stirring from time to time. Add the porcini, along with all of their soaking liquid, and boil rapidly for 5 minutes, until you have about 6 tablespoons of liquid left in the pan. Reduce the heat to low and add the lentils and barley to the pan, along with the dried mint, ¾ teaspoon of salt and a generous grind of black pepper. Stir to combine and cook for a final minute. Remove from the heat and add the lemon juice, dill, parsley and crispy onion. Transfer to a large serving platter or individual plates and serve warm, with a spoonful of soured cream on top, if using.

AUBERGINE PAHI

about 400ml grapeseed or
sunflower oil, for frying
2 large aubergines, halved
lengthways, each half cut
into 2.5cm x 5cm wedges
(750g)
1 tsp ground turmeric
3 medium onions, peeled
and each cut into 8
wedges (420g)
4 Romano (or Ramiro)
peppers, halved
lengthways, deseeded and
cut widthways into 2cm-
wide strips (480g)
1 mild red chilli, deseeded
and quartered
10g fresh root ginger, peeled
and roughly chopped
4 garlic cloves, roughly
chopped
1½ tsp curry powder
¼ tsp ground cloves
¼ tsp ground cardamom
1 tsp ground cinnamon
2 tsp mustard seeds
10cm pandan leaf, roughly
chopped (optional)
3cm piece of lemongrass,
roughly chopped
about 12 fresh curry leaves
60ml cider vinegar
2½ tsp caster sugar
salt

This Sri Lankan dry curry makes a thrilling accompaniment to rice, roasted vegetables or plainly cooked chicken. It can be served warm but is even better the next day, at room temperature. Don't be afraid of it looking oily: any rice or bread will be grateful to soak it up. Jennifer Gomes, an Australian architect originating from Sri Lanka, who gave me the recipe, says she loves it best in a baguette with roasted beef. I couldn't agree more. It's also lovely with a drizzle of tahini or with Greek yoghurt. Kept in a sealed jar it will last in the fridge for two weeks.

Pour the oil into a very large sauté pan or casserole and place on a medium–high heat. Meanwhile, toss the aubergines with the turmeric in a bowl. Add to the oil and fry in batches for about 8 minutes, turning once, until light golden. Use a slotted spoon to transfer to a colander layered with kitchen paper, sprinkle with ¼ teaspoon of salt and leave to drain.

Add the onions to the oil and fry them for about 8 minutes, turning once, until golden brown, then add them to the aubergines, along with another ¼ teaspoon of salt. Next, fry the peppers and chilli for 5 minutes, until the edges begin to brown, and add to the rest, along with ¼ teaspoon of salt. You should now have about 1 tablespoon of oil in the pan. Add or remove some if you need to.

Place the ginger, garlic, spices, pandan leaf (if using), lemongrass and curry leaves in the small bowl of a food processor or spice grinder and blitz to form a paste. Fry this paste in the pan with the oil, on a medium heat, for 2–3 minutes, until it begins to colour. Return all of the vegetables to the pan, along with the vinegar, 60ml of boiling water and the sugar. Stir gently and simmer for 8 minutes, until most of the liquid has boiled away, before serving warm or at room temperature.

MASHED

ROOT MASH WITH WINE BRAISED SHALLOTS

80g Puy lentils

½ large head of celeriac, peeled and cut into chunks (300g)

2 large carrots, peeled and cut into chunks (300g)

½ kabocha squash, or another type, peeled and cut into chunks (300g)

2 sweet potatoes, peeled and cut into chunks (600g)

70g unsalted butter, diced

2 tbsp maple syrup

1½ tsp ground cumin

salt and black pepper

Braised shallots

2 tbsp olive oil

600g shallots, peeled

400ml red wine

200ml vegetable stock

2 bay leaves

1 tsp whole black peppercorns

4 thyme sprigs

1 tbsp caster sugar

30g unsalted butter

It would be almost sacrilegious to serve this without a roasted bird alongside but, thanks to the hefty lentils and the slow-cooked shallots, it could easily be served as a vegetarian main course to feed a hungry crowd.

Start with the shallots. Pour the oil into a medium pan and place on a high heat. Add the shallots and fry for about 5 minutes, stirring occasionally, until coloured all over. Add the wine, stock, bay, peppercorns, thyme, sugar and ¾ teaspoon of salt. Cover, reduce the heat to low and simmer gently for 1 hour. Remove the lid, increase the heat and boil for about 8 minutes, until the remaining liquid is reduced by half. Use a slotted spoon to remove the shallots from the pan and keep them somewhere warm. Stir the butter into the sauce and set aside until ready to use.

Bring a pan of water to the boil, add the lentils, reduce the heat to medium and simmer for about 25 minutes, until tender. Drain and set aside.

For the mash, half fill a medium pan with water and bring to the boil. Add the celeriac and carrot and cook for about 10 minutes. Add the squash and sweet potato and cook for a further 10–15 minutes, until all the vegetables are cooked.

Drain the vegetables, shaking off as much liquid as possible, and mash well with a potato masher. Add the butter, maple syrup, cumin, cooked lentils, 1 teaspoon of salt and plenty of black pepper. Mix well and then divide the warm mash between individual plates. Top with the shallots, spoon over the sauce and serve at once.

FAVA

I thought I knew everything there was to know about pastes made of various legumes until a couple of summers ago, when I was holidaying on the charming Greek island of Kea (or Tzia) in the Cyclades and came across this variation, which is nothing like hummus or similar pastes. Fava is crushed-up split peas, eaten warm, topped with capers and caramelised onion, and served alongside meat or fish or as a starter dip. It is soothing yet exciting and got me licking many plates during this break. In Greece fava is made with yellow split peas. When it is made with dried fava beans (i.e. broad beans) it is called koukofava. A minefield!

3 large onions (600g in total)
300g yellow split peas
2 bay leaves
¼ tsp ground turmeric
100ml olive oil, plus extra for drizzling
2 garlic cloves, crushed
2 tbsp lemon juice
35g capers, roughly chopped
10g chives, finely chopped
salt and white pepper

Peel and quarter one of the onions and place it in a medium saucepan. Add the split peas, bay leaves and turmeric and cover generously with water. Bring to the boil and reduce to a simmer, cooking for 50 minutes to 1 hour, until the peas are soft and just about holding their shape. Top up the water as they cook, if needed. Strain the peas, keeping the cooking juices, and discard the bay leaves, leaving the onion in. Leave to cool down just a little.

While the peas are cooking, peel and slice the 2 remaining onions 0.5cm thick. Place a large sauté pan on a medium–high heat and add 1 tablespoon of the oil. Add the onions and cook for 15–20 minutes, until golden-brown, sweet and caramelised. Remove from the heat and set aside.

Remove 100g of the cooked split peas and set aside. Put the rest in a food processor bowl, adding the garlic, lemon juice, remaining olive oil, ¾ teaspoon of salt, ⅛ teaspoon of white pepper and 3 tablespoons of the cooking juices. Blitz until almost completely smooth, transfer to a large bowl and fold through the reserved split peas, half the chives and half the caramelised onion. Put in a shallow bowl and use a palette knife to swirl the mixture. Top with the rest of the onions, the capers and remaining chives and finish with a drizzle of olive oil.

BROAD BEAN SPREAD WITH ROASTED GARLIC RICOTTA

1 head of garlic (10 cloves),
  cloves separated, skin on
125ml olive oil
240g ricotta
3 tbsp soured cream
2 lemons, rind shaved in
  long strips from one; 2 tsp
  finely grated zest from the
  other
600g broad beans (400g
  if starting with skinned
  beans)
1½ tbsp lemon juice
15g mint leaves, chopped,
  plus 1 tbsp shredded mint
  leaves to garnish
salt and black pepper

An extra portion for all bean-sheller helpers here! Don't be put off by the need to start with skinned beans: buy them already skinned (I have seen them in a few Middle Eastern grocers') or else it's a fun and therapeutic task to delegate to helpers – little or big. This is a favourite with Tara's twins, Scarlett and Theo, who race to see who can catapult the beans out first and, crucially, fly them into the designated bowl. Serve with toasted sourdough as a starter. (Also pictured overleaf.)

Preheat the oven to 220°C/200°C Fan/Gas Mark 7.

Mix the garlic cloves with 1 teaspoon of the olive oil, place on a baking tray and cook for 15 minutes, until soft. Remove from the oven and when cool enough to handle, squash each garlic clove out of its skin using the back of a fork. Discard the skin and place the flesh in a small bowl, along with the ricotta, soured cream, ¼ teaspoon of salt and some black pepper: use a whisk to mix everything together well and set aside.

Place the remaining olive oil in a small saucepan with the shaved lemon skin. Place on a medium heat, bring to a gentle simmer, then remove from the heat to cool and infuse.

Bring a large pan of water to the boil. Add the broad beans, blanch for 1 minute, drain and then remove them from their skins. Crush the beans with a fork, add all but 1 tablespoon of the lemon-infused oil (removing the skin first), lemon juice, chopped mint, ½ teaspoon of salt and some black pepper and mix together.

Spread the ricotta mix in a thin layer on to the base of each individual plate or one larger platter. Spoon the broad bean mixture on top, lightly spreading it out to cover most of the ricotta. Sprinkle over the shredded mint and grated lemon zest and finish with a drizzle of the lemon-infused oil.

CRUSHED PUY LENTILS WITH TAHINI AND CUMIN

200g Puy lentils

30g unsalted butter

2 tbsp olive oil, plus extra
   for drizzling

3 garlic cloves, crushed

1 tsp ground cumin

4 medium tomatoes,
   blanched, skinned and cut
   into 1cm dice (330g)

25g coriander, chopped

60g tahini paste

2 tbsp lemon juice

1/3 small red onion, thinly
   sliced (25g)

2 hard-boiled eggs,
   quartered

½ tsp paprika, to garnish
   (optional)

salt and black pepper

This recipe has been through various incarnations before ending up uncannily similar to one of the typical Arab hummus variations I am used to from my childhood: warm hummus, topped with whole soft chickpeas and served with raw onion and hard-boiled egg. Here it is made with lentils and tomatoes but, essentially, we are talking about a similar set of hearty flavours that can set you up nicely for a busy day, or be served as an early supper. For a dairy-free option, substitute the butter with more olive oil. Serve this with a pitta and nothing else.

Bring a medium pan of water to the boil. Add the lentils and cook for 20–30 minutes or until completely cooked. Drain and set aside.

Put the butter and oil in a large sauté pan and place on a medium–high heat. Once the butter melts, add the garlic and cumin and cook for about a minute. Add the tomatoes, 20g of the coriander and the cooked lentils. Continue to cook and stir for a couple of minutes before adding the tahini, lemon juice and 70ml of water, along with 1 teaspoon of salt and a good grind of black pepper. Lower to a medium heat and continue to stir and cook gently for about 5 minutes, until hot and thickened. Using a potato masher, roughly mash the lentils a little so that some are broken up and you get a thick porridge consistency.

Spread the lentils on a flat serving plate and sprinkle with the onion, remaining coriander and a final drizzle of olive oil. Serve warm with the hard-boiled eggs alongside and a sprinkle of paprika, if using.

CANNELLINI BEAN PURÉE WITH PICKLED MUSHROOMS AND PITTA CROUTONS

SERVES FOUR

as a starter

This needs to be started a day in advance, both for the beans to soak and for the onions and mushrooms to pickle, but it is well worth the wait as it is one of the most glorious mezze dishes, both in flavour and look. The pickle works just as well without the miso, so don't worry if you can't get hold of it; just add an extra tablespoon of sugar to the pickling liquid.

Prepare the pickle a day before serving. Place the sugar, vinegar, miso and 180ml water in a medium saucepan with 1 teaspoon of salt. Bring to the boil and then pour into a heatproof, non-reactive bowl containing the mushrooms, onion, both types of peppercorn, allspice and bay leaves. Leave to cool, cover and refrigerate overnight. Take out of the fridge at least an hour before using.

The next day, drain and rinse the beans, put them in a large saucepan and cover with plenty of water. Bring to the boil and then simmer gently for 30–60 minutes (beans vary greatly in cooking time), topping up the water if needed, until completely soft: you'll need to skim the surface a few times during cooking. Drain, keeping some of the cooking liquid, and transfer to a food processor, along with the tahini, 4 tablespoons of the olive oil, the garlic, lemon juice, ¾ teaspoon of salt and ½ teaspoon of white pepper. Blitz well, until a very smooth paste has formed, and set aside. Once ready to serve, add a little cooking liquid if you need to get a soft and fluffy consistency (like a runny mash).

Pour the remaining 40ml of olive oil and all of the sunflower oil into a frying pan and place on a high heat. When hot, add the pitta and fry for about 3 minutes, shaking the pan from time to time, until golden and crisp all over. Transfer to a colander lined with kitchen paper and sprinkle with a pinch of salt.

When ready to serve, spread the purée out on a large platter. Spoon over the mushrooms and onions along with a few tablespoons of the pickling liquid and a teaspoon or two of the aromatics. Dot with some of the pitta croutons (the rest served on the side), sprinkle over the parsley and serve at once.

250g dried cannellini beans, soaked overnight in water with 2 tsp bicarbonate of soda
50g tahini paste
100ml olive oil
1 garlic clove, crushed
2 tbsp lemon juice
3 tbsp sunflower oil
2 pitta breads, torn into 3cm pieces (120g)
1 tbsp chopped parsley, to garnish
salt and white pepper

Pickled mushrooms
2 tbsp caster sugar
160ml cider vinegar
1 tbsp brown miso
80g button mushrooms, cut into 0.5cm slices
½ medium red onion, very thinly sliced into pinwheels (60g)
½ tsp black peppercorns
½ tsp red peppercorns
½ tsp allspice berries (pimento)
3 bay leaves

CRUSHED CARROTS WITH HARISSA AND PISTACHIOS

SERVES FOUR

as a starter

The sweetness of carrots makes them a bestselling vegetable in North Africa, where the combination of sweet with sour and spicy is used to make some unusually harmonious creations: tagines blending hearty meats and dried fruit, a colourful spread of salads to open a hefty meal, and a bunch of savoury fillings encased in paper-thin pastry. Carrots are the ideal candidates for all these, as they are for various syrupy desserts. Here, cooked carrots are crushed to make a sharp and hot spread that you can bring to the table as a starter, on a large platter, with a pile of warm pittas. You are welcome to increase the harissa if you like this very hot.

1 tbsp olive oil, plus extra for drizzling
15g unsalted butter
1kg carrots, peeled and cut into 2cm slices
200ml vegetable stock
grated zest of 1 orange
1 garlic clove, crushed
2 tsp harissa paste
grated zest of 1 lemon
200g Greek yoghurt
1 tbsp lemon juice
25g shelled unsalted pistachios, roughly chopped
salt and black pepper

Place the olive oil and butter in a large sauté pan on a medium–high heat. Add the carrots and sauté for 6 minutes, stirring often; they need to soften and take on a bit of colour. Add the stock, reduce the heat to medium–low, cover the pan and cook for another 25 minutes, until the carrots are completely soft and there is hardly any liquid left. Transfer the carrots to a food processor, add ¾ teaspoon of salt and blitz briefly to form a coarse paste. Leave to cool and then add the orange zest, garlic, harissa, half the lemon zest and some black pepper. Stir to combine.

Mix together the yoghurt, lemon juice, remaining lemon zest and ¼ teaspoon of salt.

Spread the yoghurt out on a serving platter and spoon the carrot mixture on top. Sprinkle with the pistachios, drizzle with a little olive oil and serve.

SPICE-STUFFED POTATO CAKES

1kg Maris Piper potatoes
  (or another waxy variety),
  peeled and halved
1 tsp ground turmeric
1 tbsp black mustard seeds,
  toasted
60g coriander
40g mint leaves
2 green chillies, roughly
  chopped
2 tbsp tamarind paste
2 garlic cloves
½ tsp caster sugar
sunflower oil, to fry
1 lemon, cut into wedges, or
  a sweet chutney, to serve
salt

Fried patties of pretty much anything are generally a winner in my book, but smooth mashed potato running high on the spice and fresh herb front is both hard to beat and, delightfully, impossible to stop eating. Tamarind, like miso paste and Parmesan, has a strong and pungent taste which can impart a real depth of flavour to vegetarian dishes. Ready-made tamarind paste is widely available if you can't get hold of the pulp to make your own. It can lack the fruity depth and sweet-sour-salty balance of the real deal but it is an adequate substitute. Acidity levels vary widely from one brand to the next, so be sure to taste and assess these before adding the amount a recipe calls for, and adjust accordingly.

Bring a large pan of salted water to the boil. Add the potatoes and cook for 15 minutes, until soft. Drain well and transfer to a mixing bowl with the turmeric, mustard seeds and ¼ teaspoon of salt. Mash well and leave to cool.

Place the coriander, mint, chillies, tamarind, garlic, sugar and ¼ teaspoon of salt in a food processor and blitz to form a smooth, dry paste.

Shape a small handful of the potato mixture – weighing about 40g – into a ball. Place the ball in the palm of one hand and use the thumb of the other to create a dent large enough to fill with 1 teaspoon of the spice mixture. Once the mixture is added, shape the potato back into a ball, with the stuffing sealed inside, and then flatten it between both hands so that the cakes are 1.5cm thick. Continue with the rest of the potato and spice mixture until you have about 20 cakes and then place them in the fridge for 20 minutes.

Smear the base of a large non-stick frying pan with sunflower oil. Place on a medium heat and fry the cakes for 5–8 minutes, turning once, until they are light, golden and crisp on the outside. Serve at once, with a wedge of lemon or some sweet chutney on the side.

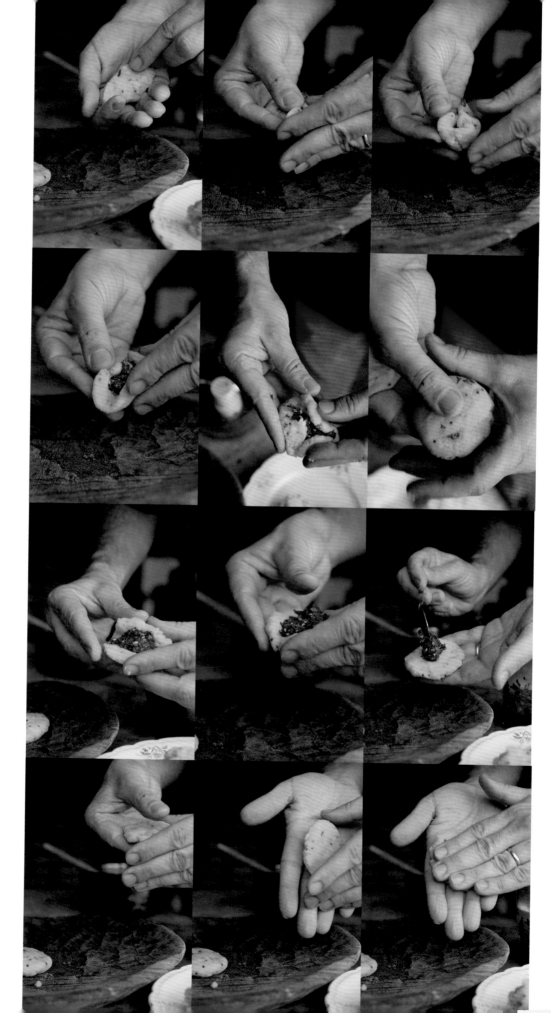

YOGHURT AND KAFFIR LIME LEAF SPREAD

1 small courgette, grated
  (150g)
½ cucumber, grated (150g)
4 large fresh (or 12 dried)
  Kaffir lime leaves, roughly
  chopped
250g Greek yoghurt
20g unsalted butter
1½ tsp lime juice
1 tbsp shredded mint leaves
1 garlic clove, crushed
salt

Were there to be an alternative word for 'dip' or 'spread', I would patent it as my own. In the meantime, we have to transcend the dodgy connotations and embrace this dish, which, along with a few slices of sourdough bread and some olive oil, is perhaps the perfect way to open a meal. Thanks to Gena Deligianni, one of our cooks in the early days of NOPI, for this dish.

Mix the courgette and cucumber in a colander with ½ teaspoon of salt. Leave to drain for about 20 minutes and then squeeze with your hands to remove as much liquid as you can. Transfer to a large mixing bowl.

Process the lime leaves in a spice grinder to a fine powder (you can also chop them up finely with a knife or crush using a pestle and mortar) and add most of it to the courgette and cucumber, along with the yoghurt.

Melt the butter in a small saucepan and cook until it goes a light brown colour and smells a little nutty, about 3–4 minutes. Add most of the butter to the dip, along with all the remaining ingredients, mix well and spread on a plate. Drizzle over the reserved butter, sprinkle with the reserved lime leaves and serve.

CRACKED

CRESPÉOU

15 eggs, lightly beaten
   (about 900g)
200g feta, crumbled
80ml double cream
2 tsp olive oil
salt and black pepper

Red mix
60ml olive oil
1 small red onion, thinly
   sliced (100g)
2 tsp tomato purée
2 large red peppers, sliced
   into 0.5cm strips (300g)
¾ tsp ground coriander
¾ tsp caster sugar

Yellow mix
60ml olive oil
1 large onion, thinly sliced
   (180g)
2 tsp ground turmeric

Green mix
4 spring onions, trimmed
   and thinly sliced (60g)
25g basil leaves, shredded
15g tarragon, finely
   chopped
¾ tsp ground cumin
1 green chilli, deseeded and
   thinly sliced

If I was going to sum up my cooking style in five words, 70s-style-retro-picnic-bling would not be them. And if there is one recipe that might make me cringe in the years to come, it will, for sure, be this one. Still, I'm keeping my head held high enough to peer over the top layer of this savoury cake, which is, I will have you know, absolutely delicious and does make a perfect picnic dish.

Mix together the eggs, feta and cream and set aside. Start with the red mix. Place the oil in a medium non-stick sauté pan on a medium heat. Add the onion and sauté for 10 minutes, until soft. Add the tomato purée, peppers, coriander, sugar, ¼ teaspoon of salt and some black pepper and continue to cook for another 5–7 minutes, stirring from time to time. Transfer to a bowl and leave to cool before pouring over a third of the egg, cream and feta mix and stirring.

For the yellow mix, clean the pan, pour in the oil and place on a high heat. Add the onion and sauté for 5 minutes, until parts of the onion are dark brown and crisp. Reduce the temperature to low, add ¼ teaspoon of salt, some black pepper and the turmeric and continue to cook for about 5 minutes. Transfer to a bowl and leave to cool before whisking in the second third of the egg, cream and feta mix. Clean out the pan.

Place all the ingredients for the green mix in a bowl with ¼ teaspoon of salt and the remaining egg, cream and feta.

Preheat the oven to 170°C/150°C Fan/Gas Mark 3½.

Return the clean pan to a medium heat. Add about ¼ teaspoon of the olive oil before pouring in half of the red mix and making a shallow omelette. Just before it sets completely on top – about 4–5 minutes – transfer it to a baking tray lined with greaseproof paper. Repeat the process with the yellow mix and then the green mix – these need a slightly shorter cooking time, about 3 minutes – building the omelettes up one on top of the other, alternating in colour. You should aim for a neat pile of 6. Place in the oven and cook for 12 minutes. Remove from the oven and leave to cool down a little.

Once warmish, place an inverted plate over the pile of omelettes and flip it over. Keep as is or use a sharp knife to trim the edge to get a nice round cake with distinct layers. Serve warm or at room temperature.

AUBERGINE KUKU

Looking back on the ingredients I relied upon for Plenty, *there is a handful that has been resolutely pushed to the back of the cupboard in favour of the new. The dried sour cherries, for example, now mostly languish in the shadows of some new staples, barberries being one of them. These tiny sweet-and-sour Iranian berries have a dramatic sharpness that magically accentuates other flavours in a dish. There is a reason they look like little gems. Currants soaked in lemon juice or the old dried sour cherries, chopped up, can be used as alternatives but barberries are worth seeking out in Middle Eastern grocers' if you can. Don't be surprised by the slightly 'wet' nature of my kuku: this is how it's meant to be, so serve it with a good hunk of bread.*

120ml sunflower oil, plus extra to brush the baking tin

4 small onions, thinly sliced (400g)

3 small aubergines, tops removed, peeled (580g)

5 eggs, lightly beaten

25g plain flour

1½ tsp baking powder

35g fresh breadcrumbs

25g parsley, finely chopped

½ tsp saffron strands, soaked in 1 tbsp hot water

3 garlic cloves, crushed

20g barberries

salt and black pepper

Preheat the oven to 210°C/190°C Fan/Gas Mark 6½.

Pour the oil into a large heavy-based sauté pan and heat well. Add the onions and sauté on a medium heat for 7 minutes or until they soften but don't brown.

While the onions are cooking, cut the aubergines in half widthways, and then cut each half into 1cm-thick slices; cut the slices into 1cm-thick strips so that you end up with batons that are 7–8cm long and 1cm wide. Add these to the cooking onion, with ½ teaspoon of salt, and continue to cook on a medium–high heat, stirring occasionally and gently, so that the aubergine does not break up, for 12–14 minutes or until the aubergine is completely soft. Leave aside to cool down.

In a large bowl, whisk together the eggs, flour, baking powder, breadcrumbs, parsley, saffron-infused water, garlic, ½ teaspoon of salt and a good grind of black pepper. Once smooth, fold in the barberries, aubergine and onion.

Line the base and the sides of a 20cm cake tin with greaseproof paper and brush the paper lightly with oil. Pour the egg mix into the tin and bake in the oven for about 35 minutes, or until golden-brown and completely cooked. Insert a skewer in the middle of the cake to make sure the egg has set.

Remove from the oven and leave to cool down. Serve warm or at room temperature, sprinkled with chopped parsley, if you like. The kuku will keep in the fridge for 2 days.

AUBERGINE CHEESECAKE

65ml olive oil, plus extra for
  brushing
2 medium aubergines, cut
  widthways into 2cm-thick
  slices (700g)
150g feta, crumbled into
  large chunks
150g cream cheese
3 eggs
60ml double cream
150g baby plum tomatoes,
  halved lengthways
10g oregano leaves, torn
1½ tsp za'atar
salt and black pepper

We weren't sure we'd have space to include this as well as the Aubergine Kuku (see page 253). The process of elimination was totally unsuccessful, however, so we just had to find room for both. Heaven as a large square for lunch, it also works well cut down to smaller pieces for nibbles before supper.

Preheat the oven to 210°C/190°C Fan/Gas Mark 6½. Line the base and sides of a deep, 19cm square baking tin (or a round ovenproof dish, 20cm in diameter) with a sheet of foil and brush with a little olive oil.

Lay out the aubergines on a baking tray lined with greaseproof paper and brush with 60ml of olive oil, making sure that plenty of oil is absorbed. Sprinkle with ¼ teaspoon of salt and a generous grind of black pepper, and roast in the oven for 40 minutes, until the aubergines are soft and golden. Set aside to cool. Reduce the oven temperature to 170°C/150°C Fan/Gas Mark 3½.

Place the feta, cream cheese, eggs, cream and some black pepper in a bowl and blend with an electric whisk until smooth and thick.

Arrange the aubergine slices in the baking tin; they should fill up the tray as they lean against each other, almost standing on their sides. Fill the gaps between the pieces with tomatoes and sprinkle with half the oregano.

Pour the cream mix into the tin, just enough to leave some aubergine and tomatoes exposed, sprinkle with the remaining oregano and cook in the oven for 35–40 minutes or until the custard sets and turns golden. Remove from the oven and allow to come to room temperature.

Remove the cake from the tin and cut into four squares (or into wedges, if using a round dish). Mix the za'atar with the remaining teaspoon of olive oil, brush this gently over the top and sides of the cake and serve.

FRITTER ROULETTE

*The stakes were considerably lowered once I changed the whole green chillies –
initially planned to be dropped in the centre of each of these sweetish pancakes
– to the less fiery option of padrón peppers. An air of excitement still lingers
when a plate of these peppers is being devoured: rumour has it that, once in
a while, a really hot one will come along – but I've never seen anyone reach for
the fire extinguisher yet. These are wonderful for a weekend brunch or a light
supper, with just a simple salad alongside. Padrón peppers are not as widely
available as they should be, but you'll often see them in packets on delicatessen
counters, in some butchers' and fishmongers' or any Spanish grocers' or
market stalls. If you can't get hold of any, don't worry: the fritters are still great
without them.*

3 eggs

120ml coconut milk

75g self-raising flour

30g cornflour

¾ tsp ground cumin

1½ tsp ground coriander

½ tsp ground turmeric

3 tbsp coriander seeds,
   toasted and lightly
   crushed

½ butternut squash, peeled
   and coarsely grated (225g)

300g corn kernels, frozen or
   fresh (2 large corn cobs, if
   using fresh)

3 spring onions, thinly
   sliced (30g)

15g coriander, chopped

½ red chilli, deseeded and
   finely chopped, or more
   for extra heat

about 250ml sunflower oil,
   for frying

150g padrón peppers

3 limes, cut into wedges

salt and black pepper

Place the first eight ingredients (up to and including the coriander seeds)
in a large mixing bowl, along with 1½ teaspoons of salt and a good grind
of black pepper. Whisk to form a smooth batter. Add the butternut, corn,
spring onion, coriander and chilli and stir well.

Pour enough sunflower oil into a medium frying pan to come 1cm up
the sides and place on a high heat. Scoop three tablespoons of the batter
into the oil and cook for about 2 minutes. Using your hands, carefully
push 1–3 peppers (depending on size) into the surface of the fritter and
fry for another minute. Flip the fritter over and fry for another 3 minutes,
until golden-brown. Transfer to a plate lined with kitchen paper and keep
somewhere warm while you continue with the remaining batter. Serve
warm, with a wedge of lime alongside.

CAULIFLOWER CAKE

1 small cauliflower, outer
  leaves removed, broken
  into 3cm florets (450g)
1 medium red onion (170g)
75ml olive oil
½ tsp finely chopped
  rosemary
7 eggs
15g basil, chopped
120g plain flour, sifted
1½ tsp baking powder
⅓ tsp ground turmeric
150g coarsely grated
  Parmesan, or another
  mature cheese
melted butter, to line the tin
1 tbsp white sesame seeds
1 tsp nigella seeds
salt and black pepper

Having lived in Britain for more than sixteen years, there are certain names and phrases with which I am perfectly familiar: Doctor Who, *Ring a Ring o' Roses,* Curly Wurlies, Blue Peter *and cauliflower cheese, to name just a few; but I have no clue as to their significance. This is mostly a disadvantage because I miss out on all sorts of innuendos and references, but occasionally it works pretty well for me. When it comes to cauliflower cheese, for example, what to me sounds like the most indulgent and comforting of dishes has to an alumnus of the British school system a stomach-turning echo of drearily soft florets swimming in a puddle of greasy water. So when it comes to cauliflower and particularly when cheese is involved, I need to work extra hard to convince my readers that this is something they might want to eat. Well, I think I've got a winner here.*

Serve this cake as a light supper alongside a makeshift salad of sliced cucumber, dill, mint, dressed with a little sugar, cider vinegar and rapeseed oil. Kept well wrapped, it will taste even better the next day.

Preheat the oven to 200°C/180°C/Gas Mark 4.

Place the cauliflower florets in a saucepan and add 1 teaspoon of salt. Cover with water and simmer for 15 minutes, until the florets are quite soft: they should break when pressed with a spoon. Strain and set aside in a colander to dry.

Cut 4 round slices, each 0.5cm thick, off one end of the onion and set aside. Coarsely chop the rest of the onion and place this in a small pan, with the oil and rosemary. Cook for 10 minutes on a medium heat, stirring from time to time, until soft. Remove from the heat and set aside to cool. Transfer the cooked onion to a large bowl, add the eggs and basil, whisk well and then add the flour, baking powder, turmeric, Parmesan, 1 teaspoon of salt and plenty of pepper. Whisk until smooth before adding the cauliflower and stirring gently, trying not to break up all the florets.

Line the base and sides of a 24cm springform cake tin with baking parchment. Brush the sides with melted butter, mix together the sesame and nigella seeds and toss them around the inside of the tin so that they stick to the sides. Tip in the cauliflower mix and arrange the reserved onion rings on top. Place in the centre of the oven and bake for 45 minutes, until golden-brown and set: a knife inserted into the centre of the cake should come out clean. Remove from the oven and leave for at least 20 minutes before serving: it needs to be served just warm, rather than hot, or at room temperature.

MEMBRILLO AND STILTON QUICHE

This quiche, in canapé form, was one of the most popular items on our catering menu at Ottolenghi a couple of years ago. The combination of a sharp blue cheese alongside the intense sweetness of membrillo creates a wonderfully satisfying excitement in the mouth. It's the one-stop answer to Christmas meals for vegetarians. Membrillo can be bought in many cheese shops and supermarkets.

1 medium butternut squash, peeled and cut into 2cm cubes (700g)

1½ tbsp olive oil

250g best-quality shortcrust pastry

plain flour, for dusting

200g Stilton, crumbled

75g membrillo (quince paste), cut into 1cm dice

3 eggs

150ml double cream

150ml crème fraîche

salt and black pepper

Preheat the oven to 220°C/200°C Fan/Gas Mark 7.

Toss the butternut in the oil with ¼ teaspoon of salt and some black pepper and spread out on a baking tray. Roast for 30 minutes, turning once, until golden-brown. Set aside to cool and reduce the oven temperature to 190°C/170°C Fan/Gas Mark 5.

Roll out the pastry on a floured work surface, roughly 3mm thick, and transfer it to a 24cm quiche or flan tin. When lining, leave some pastry hanging over the edge. Prick the base of the pastry with a fork and chill for 20 minutes in the fridge. Line the pastry case with baking parchment, fill it with baking beans and cook in the oven for 30 minutes. Remove the beans and paper and continue to cook for 10 minutes, until the pastry is golden-brown. Remove and leave to cool.

Spread the roasted butternut out on the base of the quiche, dot the Stilton between and sprinkle the membrillo all over. Place the eggs, cream and crème fraîche in a mixing bowl with ¼ teaspoon of salt and some black pepper. Whisk together and then pour this over the butternut, leaving some of the filling exposed. Place in the oven for about 40 minutes, until the custard has set. Remove from the oven and allow to rest before removing from the tin and breaking off the hanging pastry. Serve warm or at room temperature.

CORN AND SPRING ONION PANCAKES

6 corn cobs, husks removed
  (900g)
½ tbsp olive oil
5 spring onions, finely
  chopped (70g)
1 green chilli, roughly
  chopped
1 tsp ground cumin
1½ tsp soft brown sugar
2 eggs
100g plain flour
120g clarified butter
2 limes, cut into wedges
salt and black pepper

I'm not sure something that has been around for as long as corn fritters can claim to have a modern-day father but credit is due to Bill Granger for getting these on to people's breakfast radar. Of all the corn pancakes I've tried over the years, these are certainly the most successful: fluffy and spongy but with nothing soft in terms of flavour.

Place a ridged griddle pan on a high heat until smoking. Brush one cob with oil and char-grill for 5 minutes. Turn regularly until charred all over. Set aside.

Remove the kernels from the remaining five cobs by holding them upright on a work surface and running a sharp knife down each side. Place these kernels in a food processor with half the spring onion, the chilli, cumin, sugar, 1 egg, ¾ teaspoon of salt and a good grind of black pepper. Blitz for a minute until smooth and then transfer to a mixing bowl. Separate the last egg and add the yolk to the mix, along with the flour and remaining spring onion. Cut the smoky corn off the griddled cob and gently stir in. Whisk the egg white to soft peaks and then fold this into the mix.

Place a large sauté pan on a medium–high heat and add half the butter. Add 2 heaped tablespoons of batter and fry for about 2 minutes on each side, until golden-brown. Cook them in batches of three or four – you don't want to overcrowd the pan – and remove and keep warm as you cook the rest, adding more butter as necessary. Serve warm, alongside the lime wedges.

SPICY SCRAMBLED EGGS

Many of my brunch dishes were devised BC (before children), so food-meets-the-need-to-soothe was often in mind when cooking on a Sunday morning. A few dishes have remained part of the weekend breakfast repertoire since we started turning in early on a Saturday night: this is one of them.

Put a large, preferably non-stick, frying pan on a medium heat and add the oil, cumin, caraway, onion, ginger and chilli. Cook for 8 minutes, stirring occasionally, until the onion is soft. Add the ground spices, tomato purée and ¾ teaspoon of salt and cook and stir for 2 minutes. Add the tomatoes and cook for a further 8–10 minutes, until most of the liquid has evaporated. Add the eggs, reduce the heat to medium–low and continuously, but very gently, scrape the base of the pan with a wooden spatula. You want to get large, curd-like folds and for the eggs to be soft and very moist, cooking it for a total of about 3 minutes. Sprinkle with the spring onion, coriander and chilli flakes and serve at once.

2 tbsp sunflower oil
¾ tsp cumin seeds
½ tsp caraway seeds
1 small onion, finely diced (100g)
10g fresh root ginger, peeled and finely chopped
1 medium red chilli, deseeded and finely chopped
¼ tsp ground turmeric
¼ tsp ground cardamom
½ tsp tomato purée
4 medium tomatoes, peeled and cut into 2cm dice (300g)
8 eggs, beaten
3 spring onions, finely sliced (50g)
10g coriander, chopped
½ tsp Urfa chilli flakes or ¼ tsp regular chilli flakes
salt

KALE AND CHEESE PIKELETS

50g kale leaves, tough
  stalks removed, thinly
  sliced
170g self-raising flour
1 tsp finely grated lemon
  zest
1 egg yolk
150ml full-fat milk
80g unsalted butter, melted
150g cottage cheese
50g Stilton, broken into 1cm
  chunks
15g dill, roughly chopped
2 egg whites, whisked to
  soft peaks
salt

Sauce
1 tbsp olive oil
¼ tsp chilli flakes
100g soured cream

Pancake Day always rather takes me by surprise each year. I'm not one to abstain from food and definitely don't practise any sort of religious self-denial – but it's always a joy to have an excuse to fill batter with all sorts of things one is meant to give up for the month ahead. Pikelets, drop scones, Scotch pancakes: what these are called depends on who's cooking. In any case, they are soft and fluffy and reheat very well, whatever time of the year it happens to be.

Preheat the oven to 200°C/180°C Fan/Gas Mark 6.

Bring a medium pan of water to the boil. Add the kale and blanch for a minute. Drain well, making sure all the water is squeezed out, and set aside.

For the sauce, place the olive oil in a small saucepan with the chilli flakes. Cook on a medium–high heat for just 1 minute before transferring to a small bowl. Leave to cool before mixing in the soured cream and ⅛ teaspoon of salt. Keep in the fridge until needed.

Place the flour and lemon zest in a large bowl with ⅓ teaspoon of salt. Make a well in the centre and add the egg yolk and milk. Use a wooden spoon to combine the ingredients, starting from the centre and working your way towards the edge, until you get a thick batter, almost like dough. Add the kale, half the butter, the cottage cheese, Stilton and dill. Mix together before, finally, using a spatula to gently fold in the whisked egg whites.

Heat a large non-stick frying pan on a medium heat with half of the remaining butter. When it starts to foam, use half of the batter to make 4 round pikelets, each about 9cm wide and 1.5cm thick. Fry for about 5 minutes on a low heat, turning once, until both sides are golden-brown. Transfer to a large baking tray and repeat with the remaining butter and batter. Place in the oven for 10 minutes, until cooked through. Place two pikelets on each plate and serve warm, with a generous spoon of the sauce on top or alongside.

BAKED

CORSICAN PIE WITH COURGETTE FLOWERS

½ small red onion, thinly
  sliced (85g)
3 celery stalks with leaves,
  thinly sliced (220g)
8 large Swiss chard leaves,
  white stalks discarded,
  roughly chopped (175g)
2 garlic cloves, thinly sliced
2 tbsp torn mint leaves
2 tbsp chopped parsley
2 tsp chopped sage
2 tbsp olive oil, plus extra
  for brushing
75g feta, crumbled
50g pecorino, finely grated
15g pine nuts, lightly
  toasted
grated zest of 1 lemon
350g all-butter puff pastry
plain flour, for dusting
100g brocciu cheese or
  ricotta
4–6 courgette flowers,
  cut in half lengthways if
  large, or 6 long, shaved
  strips of raw courgette
  (optional)
1 egg, lightly beaten
salt and black pepper

Cooking on location is a very lengthy process. It often takes an hour or two, sometimes much more, to get the cooking station ready, the lighting right, the camera angles and the sound. By the time we're ready to shoot, everybody is hungry and tired, so our generous hosts often spoil us with snacks and drinks. Setting up for the Swiss chard scene when shooting my Mediterranean Island Feast *programme took even longer than usual because we had to wait for the restaurant's guests to finish their lunch and leave before we could even start getting ready. In the meantime, Monique, the chef and owner of the legendary Chez Seraphin, buttered us up with tremendous local charcuterie and lots and lots of red wine. By the time we were ready to start everybody was pretty beat and completely unfocused. The result was utter lethargy and the shoot being dragged almost until sunset, when, of course… it was time to eat again.*

You can use a wide range of wild, cultivated or supermarket greens in this recipe. Consider nettles, beetroot tops, turnip tops, spinach or watercress in place of the chard. The combination is up to you so choose the ones you like most. The courgette flowers look wonderful but you can leave them out or substitute them with some long shaved strips of courgette, if you prefer. Brocciu, produced on the island of Corsica and considered a national food, is a fresh young white cheese made with goat's or ewe's milk. I couldn't omit it from the ingredients – Monique would never forgive me! – but the easier-to-find Italian ricotta can be used just as well instead. (Pictured on previous page.)

Place a large sauté pan on medium–high heat and sauté the onion, celery, chard, garlic, mint, parsley and sage in the olive oil. Cook, stirring continuously, for 15 minutes or until the greens have wilted and the celery has softened completely. Remove from the heat and stir through the feta, pecorino, pine nuts, lemon zest, ¼ teaspoon of salt and a hearty grind of black pepper. Leave aside to cool.

Preheat the oven to 220°C/200°C Fan/Gas Mark 7.

Roll out the pastry on a floured work surface until 3mm thick, then cut it into a circle, approximately 30cm in diameter. Place on an oven tray lined with baking parchment. Spread the filling out on the pastry leaving a 3cm border all the way around. Dot the filling with large chunks of brocciu or ricotta and top with courgette flowers or courgette strips, if using. Bring the pastry up around the sides of the filling and pinch the edges together firmly to form a secure, decorative lip over the edge of the tart. Alternatively, press with the end of a fork. Brush the pastry with egg and refrigerate for 10 minutes.

Bake the tart for 30 minutes, until the pastry is golden and cooked on the base. Remove from the oven and brush with a little olive oil. Serve warm or at room temperature.

AUBERGINE KADAIFI NESTS

*Kadaifi – which you can get online or in Greek, Arab or Turkish grocers' –
is a type of shredded filo pastry; you can think of it as a bit like shredded wheat,
only ten times tastier. The pepper salsa is not essential but tastes great. Use
it sparingly, so as to not mask the flavour of the aubergine and cheese, and
keep any extra in the fridge for up to five days to spoon over roasted vegetables.
If you don't make the salsa, a lemon wedge is an essential condiment.
(Pictured overleaf.)*

4 medium aubergines
  (1.2kg in total)
200g ricotta
65g mature pecorino
  cheese, coarsely grated
25g parsley, chopped
1 egg, lightly beaten
110g unsalted butter,
  melted, plus extra for
  greasing the baking tray
80ml sunflower oil
240g kadaifi pastry
salt and black pepper

Preheat the oven to 250°C/230°C Fan/Gas Mark 9. Pierce the aubergines
in a few places with a sharp knife. Place on a tray in the top shelf of the
oven for 1½ hours, turning occasionally, to blacken all sides. Remove from
the oven and, when cool enough to handle, scoop the flesh into a colander,
discard the skin and leave the flesh to drain for at least 30 minutes.

*Red pepper and tomato
salsa*
1 medium red pepper (160g
  in total)
1 red chilli
3 garlic cloves, unpeeled
4 tomatoes, blanched and
  peeled (400g)
2 tsp sherry vinegar
50ml olive oil
¼ medium red onion, very
  finely diced (30g)

While the aubergines are roasting, prepare the salsa. Put the pepper, chilli
and garlic on an oven tray and place on the shelf beneath the aubergines
in the oven for 10 minutes. Remove the chilli and garlic, turn the pepper
and roast for another 20 minutes. Once the skin is blistered, put the pepper
in a bowl and cover with cling film. When cool, peel and deseed both the
pepper and chillies and peel the garlic.

Cut half of the tomatoes into 1cm dice and set aside. Deseed the remaining
tomatoes and place in the small bowl of a food processor along with the
pepper, chilli and garlic. Whizz to a paste, add the vinegar and ¾ teaspoon
of salt then slowly add the oil to make a thick sauce. Transfer to a bowl,
add the diced tomatoes and onion, stir gently and set aside.

Mix the drained aubergine in a bowl with the ricotta, pecorino, parsley,
egg, ¾ teaspoon of salt and a good grind of black pepper.

Reduce the oven temperature to 220°C/200°C Fan/Gas Mark 7.

Now make the kadaifi nests. Mix together the melted butter and sunflower
oil. Remove a 20g bundle of pastry from the pack and place in a small
bowl. Add 1 tablespoon of the melted butter and oil and toss together
so the pastry soaks it up. Take the bundle and spread it flat on a work
surface to a rectangle, roughly 15cm x 5cm. Spoon 1½ tablespoons of the
aubergine mixture on to one end of the pastry and then roll the pastry
very loosely around the filling into an airy ball so all the filling is covered.
Repeat with the remaining pastry and filling and arrange all 12 stuffed
balls inside a buttered ovenproof dish or baking tray, 31cm x 23cm, so that
they are touching each other snugly. Drizzle over all the remaining butter
and oil. Bake for 25–30 minutes, until the top of the nests are golden and
crunchy. Serve at once, with the tomato salsa on the side.

BREAD AND PUMPKIN 'FONDUE'

350g sourdough bread, cut
 into 1.5cm-thick pieces
1 medium pumpkin, peeled
 and cut into 2cm chunks
 (800g)
2 small turnips, peeled
 and cut into 2cm chunks
 (200g)
170g Gruyère, coarsely
 grated
170g Emmental, coarsely
 grated
2½ tsp English mustard
 powder
400ml double cream
350ml dry white wine
1 large garlic clove, crushed
½ tsp freshly grated nutmeg
10g sage leaves, roughly
 chopped
salt and white pepper

This was inspired by Ruth Reichl's (learn more about her in the Sweet Potatoes introduction on page 186) brilliant, pot-saving trick, where she uses a whole pumpkin to house the pumpkin flesh, creamy cheese and crusty bread that is layered inside. Though my version uses a dish, it shares with the original the advantage of being a kind of cheese fondue that will not necessitate fishing about in a pool of melted cheese for lost chunks of bread.

Preheat the oven to 210°C/190°C Fan/Gas Mark 6½. Lay the sourdough out on a baking tray and cook for 10 minutes, until lightly toasted. Remove and set aside.

In a large mixing bowl, mix together the vegetables with 120g of the Gruyère, 120g of the Emmental and 1 teaspoon of the mustard powder. Spread the mixture into a deep gratin dish, roughly 23cm x 33cm.

Place the cream and wine in a saucepan on a medium heat. Whisk gently as you add the remainder of the mustard powder, along with the garlic, nutmeg, sage, ½ teaspoon of salt and ¼ teaspoon of white pepper. Warm through before pouring over the gratin.

Cover the dish with foil, place in the oven and bake for 45 minutes.

Remove the foil and layer the toasted bread on top, each piece slightly overlapping with the next. Press the bread down and turn it over so that it soaks up some of the liquid. Sprinkle the remaining cheese on top, cover again with foil and cook for a further 15 minutes. Remove the foil and cook for a final 15 minutes, until the top is golden and crispy. Remove from the oven and set aside for 10 minutes before serving.

MUSHROOM AND TARRAGON PITHIVIER

300ml vegetable stock
50g dried porcini
  mushrooms
3 tbsp olive oil
45g unsalted butter
400g small shallots, peeled
  and left whole
200g chestnut mushrooms,
  quartered
150g shiitake mushrooms,
  halved
150g oyster mushrooms,
  quartered
150g buna-shimeji
  mushrooms, divided into
  clusters
200g crème fraîche
2 tbsp ouzo or Pernod
15g tarragon, chopped
15g parsley, chopped
900g all-butter puff pastry
plain flour, for dusting
1 egg, beaten
salt and black pepper

Many people refuse to believe that, of all places, I got my basic training at Le Cordon Bleu cookery school. There really is nothing French about my cooking. As a matter of fact, I often describe it as anti-French, or at least anti-classical French. This has probably to do with the fact that I am not too big on stocks, I don't do brunoise and I use less meat and more vegetables in my cooking and tend to be more concerned about cooking the latter to perfection than the former.

Still, I don't want to undermine anything I learned at that legendary culinary institution. It gave me all the basic tools I needed to set out on a career in food. I particularly remember my thrill at making a pithivier – a sweet version with almond cream – using my own puff pastry. It was the first 'professional'-looking thing I had ever made and I beamed with pride. This savoury version is wonderfully rich and aniseedy and only needs a sharp leafy salad alongside.

Bring the stock to a simmer and add the porcini mushrooms. Remove from the heat and set aside to soften.

Place 1 tablespoon of the oil in a large, heavy-based sauté pan with a third of the butter. Add the shallots and cook on a medium–high heat for 10 minutes, stirring from time to time, until the shallots have softened and coloured all over. Transfer to a bowl and set aside.

Add another tablespoon of oil and half of the remaining butter to the pan. Keeping the pan on a medium–high heat, add the chestnut and shiitake mushrooms and leave them for a minute without stirring. Stir and then cook for another 2 minutes before adding them to the shallots.

Place the remaining oil and butter in the pan and repeat the process with the remaining mushrooms. Return the shallots and cooked mushrooms to the pan, along with the stock, porcini, ¾ teaspoon of salt and a good grind of black pepper. Simmer vigorously for 8 minutes or until the stock has reduced to a third. Reduce the heat to low, add the crème fraîche and cook for another 8 minutes. When just a small amount of sauce is left – about 2–3 tablespoons – add the ouzo or Pernod, tarragon and parsley. Cook for a final minute before transferring the mixture to a bowl and setting aside to cool.

Preheat the oven to 220°C/200°C Fan/Gas Mark 7.

Divide the pastry into 2 blocks and roll each out on a floured work surface to a square roughly 3mm thick. Rest them in the fridge for 20 minutes and then cut into circles: one 28cm in diameter, the other 30cm. Leave them to rest in the fridge again for at least 10 minutes.

Place the smaller circle on a baking sheet lined with greaseproof paper. Spread the mushroom filling on top, leaving 2cm clear around the edge. Brush the edge with egg and place the other circle over the filling, sealing

the two edges together. Use the prongs of a fork to make decorative parallel lines around the edge. Brush the pie with egg and use the blunt side of a small knife to draw circular lines, running from the centre of the pie to the edge. Make sure you just score the pastry without cutting through it.

Place the pithivier in the oven and bake for about 35 minutes or until golden on top and cooked on the bottom. Remove from the oven and leave to rest for at least 10 minutes. Serve warm or at room temperature.

STUFFED PEPPERS WITH FONDANT SWEDE AND GOAT'S CHEESE

This was inspired by a dish that Scully made when we were in the last and very stressful stages of opening NOPI in early 2011. All the decisions and madness surrounding which linen, tables, recipes, cocktails, suppliers, glasses and food processors to choose from stopped just for a second while we all sat and devoured Scully's dish of fondant swede with melted cheese and savoury cabbage. Classic comfort food. Here I use the same method for cooking swede for a rich, unctuous stuffing. You could serve the swede on its own, without the pepper and cheese, as a side to roast beef or pork.

150g unsalted butter
1 large swede, peeled and cut into 1cm dice (1kg)
10g thyme leaves
100g Parmesan, finely grated
2 garlic cloves, crushed
40g capers, roughly chopped
3 small yellow peppers (280g in total)
3 small red peppers (280g in total)
2 tsp olive oil
180g chèvre (goat's cheese) log, broken into 1cm pieces
10g parsley, roughly chopped
salt and black pepper

Melt the butter in a large sauté pan on a medium heat. Add the swede and thyme along with 1½ teaspoons of salt and a good grind of black pepper. Reduce the heat to low and cook, uncovered, for about 50 minutes, spooning the butter over the swede from time to time, until the swede is completely soft and caramelised. Use a slotted spoon to remove the swede from the butter and add it to a large bowl along with the Parmesan, garlic and capers. Set aside until needed. (The leftover butter can be used for cooking carrots or courgettes, if you like.)

Preheat the oven to 250°C/230°C Fan/Gas Mark 9 (or to its highest setting).

Cut the peppers in half, lengthways, keeping the stalks on. Remove the seeds and white flesh and place on a large baking parchment-lined baking tray, cut side up. Drizzle over the oil, sprinkle with a pinch of salt and roast in the oven for 30–35 minutes, until the peppers are slightly charred and the flesh is completely soft. Remove the peppers from the oven and reduce the oven temperature to 220°C/200°C Fan/Gas Mark 7.

Spoon the swede mix into each pepper and dot the goat's cheese on top. Return to the oven for a further 10–15 minutes, so that the cheese gets some colour. Remove from the oven and allow to cool for about 5 minutes before serving warm or at room temperature, with a sprinkle of parsley on each.

BAKED ARTICHOKE AND PEARLED SPELT SALAD

3 large globe artichokes
  (1.2kg in total)
100ml lemon juice (about 2
  large lemons)
2 bay leaves
2 thyme sprigs
4 garlic cloves, thinly sliced
125ml white wine
60ml olive oil
150g peas, fresh or frozen
100g pearled spelt or barley,
  rinsed
20g parsley, roughly
  chopped
1 Gem lettuce, cut in half
  lengthways, each half cut
  into 3–4 wedges (140g)
1½ tsp Urfa chilli flakes or
  ½ tsp normal chilli flakes
salt and black pepper

The pearling that gives this spelt its name is the process of polishing off the outer bran layer of the nutty plump grains. You can buy spelt whole or semi-pearled, but for a clean and silky-smooth texture (and much quicker cooking time) pearled spelt works best. It is often confused with farro (see page 151), which is the Italian word for emmer wheat. The conflation is an easy one to make – both are ancient wheat varieties with a nutty al dente bite – but spelt has a higher protein content, which makes it a favourite of those who watch their intake of wheat. Either way, both are great – hugely versatile and very happy to be paired with robust flavours.

Urfa chilli flakes are a Turkish variety, mild on heat but big on aroma. They are sweet and smoky, have a fantastically dark, purplish-red colour, and go well with almost anything. They are widely available online but can be substituted with other types of chilli flakes.

Preheat the oven to 220°C/200°C Fan/Gas Mark 7.

To clean the artichokes, cut off most of the stalk and start removing the tough outer leaves by hand. Once you reach the softer leaves, take a sharp serrated knife and trim off 2–3cm from the top. Cut the artichoke in half lengthways so you can reach the heart and scrape it clean with a small knife. Rub the clean heart with a teaspoon of lemon juice to stop it discolouring. Cut each artichoke half into slices 0.5cm thick. Place in cold water and stir in 1 tablespoon of lemon juice.

Drain the artichoke and spread out on a baking tray, about 21cm x 23cm. Add the remaining lemon juice, bay, thyme, garlic, wine and olive oil. Cover with foil and bake for 30–35 minutes or until tender. Remove the foil and set aside until cool.

Fill a medium saucepan with plenty of cold water and bring to the boil. Add the peas and blanch for 30 seconds. Use a slotted spoon to plunge them immediately into cold water – you want to reuse the boiling water – then drain and leave to dry. Add the spelt or barley to the pan and simmer gently until al dente – spelt will take 20 minutes; barley will take 30. Drain, refresh under cold water and set aside.

Drain the artichokes, preserving the cooking juices in a small bowl. Place the artichokes, along with 4 tablespoons of their liquid, in a large mixing bowl. Add the peas, spelt or barley, parsley and lettuce, along with ¾ teaspoon of salt and a good grind of black pepper. Toss gently, adding a tablespoon or two more of the cooking juice if the salad needs it, sprinkle with the chilli flakes and serve.

WINTER SAFFRON GRATIN

SERVES FOUR

generously

Different combinations of seasonal vegetables can be used in this recipe. The blend I chose has a balance of textures and sweetness that I love, but feel free to add, omit or substitute as you like using carrots, turnips, salsify, celeriac, beetroot or sweet potato; just remember to keep the total weight of the vegetables the same as listed.

250g Jerusalem artichokes, peeled and thinly sliced
250g swede, peeled and thinly sliced
250g kohlrabies, peeled and thinly sliced
250g parsnips, peeled and thinly sliced
100ml full-fat milk
½ tsp saffron strands
30g unsalted butter, plus extra for greasing the dish
35g plain flour
150ml double cream
60g parsley, chopped
60g basil, chopped
2 tbsp chopped tarragon
90g Parmesan, coarsely grated
15g panko breadcrumbs
salt and white pepper

Preheat the oven to 180°C/160°C Fan/Gas Mark 4.

Bring a large pan of water to the boil, add the sliced vegetables and blanch for a minute. Drain in a colander and set aside.

Put the milk and 300ml of water in a small saucepan, add the saffron and place on a medium heat. Cook for about 4 minutes, until warmed through but not boiling. Set aside to infuse for 5 minutes.

Place the butter in a small saucepan on a medium heat. Add the flour and stir to form a paste. Cook gently for 2 minutes, stirring the whole time. Pour in the saffron-infused milk and water and beat with a whisk as the liquid thickens. Continue cooking and stirring for another 2 minutes before removing from the heat.

Stir in the double cream and then add the chopped herbs, 60g of the Parmesan, ¾ teaspoon of salt and ¼ teaspoon of white pepper. Stir until smooth and then pour the sauce over the vegetables. Mix well and then pour the vegetables and sauce into a greased ovenproof dish (20cm x 20cm). Don't try to level out the mixture too much: it should look rustic. Cover the dish with foil and place in the oven for 40 minutes. Remove the foil, mix the remaining cheese with the breadcrumbs and scatter on top. Increase the oven temperature to 210°C/190°C Fan/Gas Mark 6½ and return to the oven for about 15 minutes, until the crust is golden brown. Remove from the oven and set aside for 10 minutes before serving.

TOMATO AND ALMOND TART

140g unsalted butter, at
  room temperature

2 eggs, beaten

65g fresh breadcrumbs

80g ground almonds

2 garlic cloves, crushed

100g ricotta

20g Parmesan, finely grated

15g thyme leaves

375g all-butter puff pastry

plain flour, for dusting

sunflower oil, for greasing

1kg medium tomatoes
  (about 10 tomatoes), cut
  widthways into 1cm slices

24 black wrinkly olives
  (50g), pitted

2 tbsp olive oil

salt and black pepper

This is a savoury version of the ubiquitous French fruit and frangipane tart. Just as in the sweet variation, the almond paste soaks up the juices and flavours of the fruit to create the most luscious layer of rich, nutty sweetness. It's perfect for a lunch party, along with the Spring Salad (see page 40) or another green leaf salad. Anchovies can be used instead of the olives.

Preheat the oven to 240°C/220°C Fan/Gas Mark 9.

Beat the butter using an electric mixer until light and aerated. Add the eggs slowly with the machine running on a medium speed. If the mixture splits, add some breadcrumbs to bring it back together, and keep on adding the eggs. Stop the machine, add the breadcrumbs, almonds and garlic and work until everything is just combined.

Remove the bowl from the mixer and add the ricotta, Parmesan, half the thyme leaves and ¼ teaspoon of salt. Fold gently until just combined and set aside.

Roll the pastry on a floured work surface into 2 rectangular sheets about 20cm x 30cm, 2mm thick. Grease 2 baking trays with a little bit of sunflower oil and lay your pastry pieces on top. Use a palette knife to spread the almond mix evenly over the pastries, leaving a 2cm border around the edge. Lay the tomato slices on top of each rectangle in 3 long rows, with a fair amount of overlap in the rows and between them. Sprinkle over the olives and remaining thyme. Drizzle the tomatoes with half the olive oil and season with ¼ teaspoon of salt and a good grind of black pepper.

Place the tarts in the oven and bake for 15 minutes. Reduce the temperature to 200°C/180°C Fan/Gas Mark 6 and continue cooking for another 8–10 minutes, until the base is golden-brown. If cooking in a conventional oven, swap the trays round to ensure the tarts colour evenly. Once cooked, remove from the oven and allow to cool slightly. Drizzle over the remaining olive oil and serve.

RICOTTA AND ROSEMARY BREAD PUDDING

SERVES FOUR

The straightforward list of ingredients here masks the number of times this was tried and tested before we were happy with the result. Just when we were quietly wondering whether it was all worth it, the dish came together and sang. Raise a Bloody Mary to the power of perseverance whenever you serve this with Sunday lunch. It works well as a vegetarian main course but would not say no to being accompanied by a lemony roasted chicken. The turnips add a nice peppery touch but you can leave them out, if you like.

400g white sourdough, cut into 2cm slices

800ml full-fat milk

250ml double cream

2 rosemary stalks, plus 1½ teaspoon chopped rosemary

1 large onion, peeled and quartered (160g)

¼ tsp freshly grated nutmeg

8 eggs

2 medium turnips, peeled and cut into 1cm slices (260g)

200g ricotta

90g Parmesan, coarsely grated

20g chives, finely chopped

olive oil, to finish

salt and white pepper

Preheat the oven to 100°C/80°C Fan/Gas Mark ¼.

Spread the sourdough slices out on a baking tray and bake in the oven for 30 minutes, turning once, until dry.

Place the milk, cream, rosemary stalks, onion and nutmeg in a medium saucepan and bring to a gentle simmer, then remove from the heat and set aside to cool. Once tepid, strain and discard the onion and rosemary. Put the eggs in a bowl and whisk as you pour the mixture over them, to form a smooth custard, along with ½ teaspoon of salt and ¼ teaspoon of white pepper.

Meanwhile, blanch the turnip slices in boiling water for 2 minutes. Strain, refresh under cold water, drain and dry. Layer them to cover the base of an ovenproof dish, roughly 22cm x 30cm.

Mix together the ricotta, Parmesan, chopped rosemary and chives and spread over one side of each toasted bread slice. Place the slices in the dish, slightly overlapping, with the cheese facing upwards. Spoon the custard over the bread and gently press down so that the bread is immersed and soaks up the custard well. Leave to sit for about 1½ hours, gently pressing the bread down from time to time.

Preheat the oven to 200°C/180°C Fan/Gas Mark 6.

Cover the pudding with foil and bake for 20 minutes. Remove the foil and continue cooking for about 30 minutes, until golden-brown and crusty. Poke a knife into the centre and gently press down; if no cream surfaces the pudding is ready. Allow to sit for 10 minutes before brushing the top with oil and serving.

BAKED ORZO WITH MOZZARELLA AND OREGANO

100ml olive oil

1 large aubergine, cut into
2cm dice (300g)

4 medium carrots, peeled
and cut into 1.5cm dice
(300g)

4 celery stalks, cut into
1.5cm dice (200g)

1 large onion, finely diced
(170g)

3 garlic cloves, crushed

250g orzo pasta, rinsed

1 tsp tomato purée

380ml vegetable stock

3 tbsp fresh oregano,
chopped, or 1½ tbsp
thyme leaves

grated zest of 1 lemon

120g hard mozzarella, cut
into 1cm dice

40g Parmesan, grated

3 medium tomatoes, cut
into 1cm-thick slices
(400g)

1 tsp dried oregano

salt and black pepper

Even the most standard of pasta bakes will always hold a place in my heart, for they comfort me and remind me of my father's cooking. This is no sentimental journey, though; it's a proud, sophisticated and rather luxurious take on the bake. People can get a bit sniffy about the firm, low-moisture mozzarella sold in blocks. If eaten by itself it's a very different beast from the buffalo, but it works brilliantly for grating or finely dicing in a dish or bake like this.

Preheat oven to 200°C/180°C Fan/Gas Mark 6.

Heat the olive oil in a large sauté pan and add the aubergine. Cook for 8 minutes on a medium–high heat, stirring occasionally, until golden-brown. Remove with a slotted spoon to kitchen paper and set aside. Add the carrot and celery to the pan and fry for 8 minutes. Transfer to kitchen paper. Reduce the heat to medium and add the onion and garlic. Cook for 5 minutes, stirring often. Add the orzo and tomato purée and cook for a further 2 minutes.

Remove the pan from the heat and pour in the stock, fresh oregano or thyme and lemon zest. Add the cooked vegetables, mozzarella, Parmesan, 1 teaspoon of salt and ½ teaspoon of pepper. Mix well and transfer to a rectangular ovenproof dish, 21cm x 27cm, or a round one, 27cm in diameter. Arrange the tomatoes on top and sprinkle with the dried oregano, along with ¼ teaspoon of salt and a grind of pepper.

Bake in the oven for 40 minutes, or until all the liquid has been absorbed and the pasta is cooked through. Remove from the oven, leave to settle for 5 minutes and serve.

TALEGGIO AND SPINACH ROULADE

Dough
160ml full-fat milk
2 tsp dried active yeast
350g strong white bread
 flour, plus extra for
 dusting
1 tsp caster sugar
50ml sunflower oil, plus
 extra for brushing
1 egg and 1 egg yolk
salt

Filling
80g crème fraîche
100g baby spinach leaves
20g basil leaves
100g pecorino cheese,
 coarsely grated
250g Taleggio cheese,
 broken into 2cm chunks
150g semi-dried tomatoes,
 drained (or 400g fresh
 cherry tomatoes,
 baked in the oven – see
 introduction)

To finish
1 egg, beaten
2 tsp poppy seeds

Not all cheeses are born equal, at least when it comes to melting. The queen of them all, in this department at least, is definitely Taleggio, an Italian cow's milk variety with a hefty aroma and the most soothing and creamy of textures, particularly when melted. This is a bread loaf with a built-in filling. Serve it warm and you've got a hearty cheese toastie, or at room temperature for a portable sandwich. You can make your own semi-dried tomatoes by halving some cherry tomatoes and spreading them out on a baking tray with the cut side facing up. Drizzle them with olive oil and some salt and bake in a medium oven (190°C/170°C Fan/Gas Mark 5) for about 50 minutes. Alternatively, buy them, marinated in oil labelled 'sun-blushed' or 'semi-dried' tomatoes.

Place the milk in a saucepan and warm through very slightly, to reach just about 30°C. Add the yeast, stir to dissolve and set aside for 10 minutes.

Place the rest of the ingredients for the dough in the bowl of an electric mixer, with ½ teaspoon of salt. Add the milk and yeast and work with a dough hook on a slow speed for about 2 minutes. Increase the speed to high and knead for another 7 minutes, by which point the dough should turn into a smooth shiny ball. You can also do this by hand: you'll just need to knead the dough for an extra 5 minutes.

Transfer the dough to a large bowl brushed with a little oil, cover the bowl with a clean wet tea towel and set aside somewhere warm. After about 45 minutes, once the dough has doubled in size, line a 30cm x 40cm baking tray with greaseproof paper. Transfer the dough to a lightly floured work surface and roll it out thinly so it reaches the size of the tray. Line the tray with the dough, pulling it right into the corners. Cover with a tea towel and leave for 30 minutes.

Once the rolled-out dough has risen slightly, cover it with the filling. Use a palette knife to spread the crème fraîche all over the surface, sprinkle over ½ teaspoon of salt and then scatter over the spinach, basil, pecorino, taleggio and semi-dried tomatoes. Carefully pick up one of the longer sides of the dough and roll it all up into a neat spiral log shape. Stand the log on the seam so it doesn't unravel when baked. Cover the tray with the tea towel again and leave for another 30 minutes.

Preheat the oven to 220°C/200°C Fan/Gas Mark 7. Brush the roulade's surface gently with the beaten egg and then scatter over the poppy seeds. Bake for 10 minutes, then reduce the oven temperature to 180°C/160°C Fan/Gas Mark 4 and continue baking for another 25 minutes. Don't worry if the roulade breaks or cracks a little. When ready, it should have taken on a nice dark brown colour. Stick a sharp knife inside to check: it should come out with some melted cheese but not any dough. Remove the roulade from the oven and allow it to cool down a little before cutting into thick slices. Alternatively, allow to cool completely and slice as needed.

BATATA HARRA

1kg Charlotte potatoes,
peeled and cut into 2cm
dice

2 tbsp olive oil

2 tbsp sunflower oil

6 large garlic cloves,
crushed

1 tsp pul biber (Turkish
chilli flakes) or
½ tsp of normal dried
chilli flakes

2 large red peppers, cut into
2cm dice (260g)

30g coriander, chopped

grated zest of 1 lemon and
1 tbsp lemon juice

salt and black pepper

This Lebanese and Syrian dish is probably my favourite way with potatoes. Simple, spicy and soothing all at the same time, it is wonderful on its own or as a side dish, along with grilled fish or something yoghurt-based such as the Mixed Vegetables and Yoghurt with Green Chilli Oil (see page 205) or the Yoghurt and Kaffir Lime Leaf Spread (see page 246). You can adjust the degree of heat to suit your threshold; just remember, it is meant to be pretty spicy. Chilli flakes vary widely, so you may want to assess how hot yours are before adding the full amount.

Preheat the oven to 260°C/240°C Fan/Gas Mark 9 (or to its highest setting).

Bring a large pan of salted water to the boil, add the potatoes and cook for 3 minutes. Drain in a colander and set aside until completely dry.

Line a medium roasting tray with tin foil and spread out the potatoes. Pour over both oils, along with 1½ teaspoons of salt and some black pepper. Mix gently, then roast in the oven for 10 minutes. Add the garlic, chilli flakes, red pepper and half the coriander and return to the oven for a further 25 minutes, stirring once halfway through, until the potatoes are nicely coloured and completely tender.

Remove the potatoes from the oven and transfer to a large mixing bowl. Add the lemon zest and juice and give everything another gentle stir. Serve warm or at room temperature, stirring in the remaining coriander at the last minute.

BAIGAN CHOKA

After all these years of cooking and writing recipes, I am still amazed every time I notice how even the minutest of variation in technique can make a spectacular difference. This Trinidadian aubergine dip, served with roti or naan, was introduced to me by my ex-colleague Tricia Jadoonanan. In theory, it is not all that different from baba ghanoush or other Middle Eastern aubergine salads that I've cooked over the years. This recipe, however, uses hot oil flavoured with onion, and some vigorous whisking to achieve a wonderful creaminess and subtlety miles away from the intensity of those old favourites. To make it even milder, leave out the garlic and use less chilli, if you like. Serve it as a dip, with bread, or as a condiment alongside to roasted lamb, chicken or pumpkin.

3 medium aubergines (900g in total)
1 mild red chilli
½ tbsp olive oil
½ tbsp sunflower oil
½ small onion, thinly sliced (50g)
1 garlic clove, crushed
1 tbsp chopped chives
salt

To cook the aubergines on a gas hob, which is the best way to get a smoky flavour, line the area around the hob heads with foil and place the aubergines directly on three medium flames. Roast for about 15 minutes, turning frequently with metal tongs, until the skin is burnt all over. Burn the chilli on a flame for just a minute or two, until it blisters and chars.

To cook the aubergines in the oven, prick them in several places with a sharp knife. Put on a foil-lined tray and place directly underneath a hot grill. Cook for 1 hour 10 minutes, turning every 20 minutes, until the aubergines have deflated and their skin is charred and burnt all over. Add the chilli to the tray for the last 10 minutes so that it too gets charred.

Remove the aubergines from the heat and leave to cool a little before scraping out the flesh and discarding the skin. Place the flesh in a colander to drain for at least 30 minutes. Peel the skin off the chilli, remove the seeds and finely chop the flesh.

Place the aubergine and chilli flesh in a large mixing bowl and whisk vigorously for 2–3 minutes so that it turns light and creamy; you can also use a hand-held electric whisk.

Meanwhile, heat both oils in a small pan and add the onion. Fry on a high heat for 2 minutes, stirring often, in order to cook the onion just a little: you want it to remain slightly crunchy. Pour the hot oil and onion into the bowl with the aubergine and keep on whisking for another minute. Add the garlic and chives, along with ½ teaspoon of salt, and whisk a little longer. Taste, adding more salt if you like, and serve.

ROOT VEGETABLE PIES

240g plain flour, plus extra
    for dusting
190g unsalted butter, fridge-
    cold, diced
60g soured cream
3 tbsp olive oil
1 tsp curry powder
2 tsp caraway seeds
2 tsp black mustard seeds
½ tsp ground cardamom
1 large onion, roughly
    chopped (180g)
1 green chilli, deseeded and
    finely chopped
1 tbsp thyme leaves,
    chopped
2 garlic cloves, crushed
1 small baking potato,
    peeled and cut into 2cm
    dice (160g)
1 medium carrot, peeled
    and cut into 2cm dice
    (100g)
1 medium parsnip, peeled
    and cut into 2cm dice
    (100g)
250ml vegetable stock
½ small butternut squash,
    peeled and cut into 2cm
    dice (250g)
¼ tsp caster sugar
120g mature Cheddar,
    coarsely grated
15g coriander, chopped
1 egg, beaten
salt and black pepper

Serve these with a green salad for lunch or eat them as they are, as a snack. The filling is also delicious on its own, as a vegetarian rice topping. These are also great reheated and eaten the next day, so don't be afraid to make the whole batch if there aren't six of you to eat them first time around. With thanks to Helen Goh.

Place the flour, butter and soured cream in a food processor, with 1 teaspoon of salt, and work until the mixture comes together. Transfer to a lightly floured work surface and gently knead for 1 minute, adding a little flour if needed, until soft and malleable. Wrap in cling film and leave to rest in the fridge for 30 minutes.

Place a large lidded sauté pan on a medium–high heat. Add 2 tablespoons of the oil and, once hot, add the curry powder, caraway seeds, mustard seeds and cardamom. Cook for just a few seconds, stirring and making sure the spices don't burn, before adding the onion, chilli and thyme. Cook for another 4 minutes, add the garlic and cook for another minute, stirring. Add the potato, carrot and parsnip, stir and then pour in the stock. Reduce the heat to medium, cover and cook for 5 minutes. Add the squash, sugar, ¾ teaspoon of salt and a generous grind of black pepper and continue to simmer, covered, for 10 minutes, stirring from time to time, until the vegetables are cooked through and most of the liquid has evaporated: you should have about 3 tablespoons of liquid left; add a little water if needed. Uncover, remove from the heat and set aside to cool totally before stirring in the cheese and coriander.

Preheat the oven to 200°C/180°C Fan/Gas Mark 6.

Use the remaining oil to brush the sides and bases of an extra-large 6-hole muffin tin (each hole should be 6cm wide and 4cm deep). Line the bases with circles of baking parchment and place the tin in the fridge. Roll out the pastry 2–3mm thick, cut out 6 circles, 14cm in diameter, and press down into the tin. Trim the edges, reusing the spare pastry to roll out for a second time. Cut out 6 more circles, 8cm in diameter – these will form lids.

Fill each pie with about 120g of filling, brush the rims with egg and place the lids on top. Pinch the edges together securely, brush the lids with the remaining egg and prick each pie with a fork in a few places. Allow to rest in the fridge for 10 minutes. Place in the oven and bake for 30–35 minutes, until golden-brown. Remove from the oven and set aside for 5 minutes before serving warm or at room temperature.

SWEETENED

BLACKCURRANT FRIANDS

125g unsalted butter,
  melted, plus an extra 20g
  for brushing the tin
60g plain flour, plus extra
  for dusting
60g blanched almonds
50g unsalted pistachios,
  plus 1 tsp, chopped, to
  garnish
¼ tsp ground cinnamon
200g caster sugar
grated zest of 1 lemon
1 tbsp mashed banana
3 egg whites (100g)
120g fresh (or frozen and
  defrosted) blackcurrants,
  tossed in 2 tsp flour, plus
  extra to decorate
salt

Lemon glaze (optional)
50ml lemon juice
200g icing sugar

The number of recipes I write means that I am incredibly systematic about the way they are filed. Yet no sooner was this recipe perfected than it slipped, mysteriously, through the filing system net, only to be remembered years later. It's like when you find money in your jeans pocket that has been there for weeks: rediscovery feels like a gift, even though it was yours in the first place. Friands are small French cakes, popular in Australia and New Zealand as well as, of course, throughout France. The French word friand means 'dainty' or a 'gourmet who delights in delicate tastes'. I'd like to extend the definition, in this case, to anyone with a distinguished sweet tooth in need of the royal treatment. (Also pictured overleaf.)

Preheat the oven to 200°C/180°C Fan/Gas Mark 6.

Place a large 6-hole muffin tray (each section 6cm wide by 4cm deep) in the freezer for 10 minutes. Melt the 20g of butter before brushing it generously over the tin moulds and dusting with flour. Place a circle of greaseproof paper at the bottom of each mould, to prevent the cakes from sticking to the tin, and return to the freezer.

Put the nuts, flour, cinnamon and all except 2 tablespoons of the sugar into a food processor bowl. Work to a coarse, breadcrumb-like texture. Tip the nut mix into a mixing bowl and add the melted butter, lemon zest and mashed banana. Stir to combine.

Whisk the egg whites with ⅛ teaspoon of salt and the remaining 2 tablespoons of sugar until the whites form soft peaks; around 6 minutes with an electric whisk. Gently fold a third into the nut and banana mixture. Once incorporated, gently fold in another third, along with the berries. Finally, fold in the remainder of the egg whites.

Pour the batter into the muffin tins so that it comes two-thirds of the way up the sides. Place in the oven and bake for 20–25 minutes, until a skewer inserted into the centre comes out clean. Remove from the oven and leave to cool. To un-mould, run a sharp knife along the edges of the friands and gently tip the tin over.

Once the friands have cooled, make the glaze, if using. (You can otherwise simply dust with icing sugar.) Whisk together the lemon juice and icing sugar in a small bowl, adding more lemon juice or sugar if needed, to make a thick yet easily pourable glaze. Spoon it liberally over the friands, letting the icing drip down the sides. Sprinkle with the chopped pistachios and put 3–4 blackcurrants on top of each friand, if you have them to spare.

BAKED RHUBARB WITH SWEET LABNEH

I am slightly obsessive about labneh. I like it on its own, spread on a plate, drizzled with olive oil, sprinkled with za'atar and chilli flakes and served with a warm pitta. I also have it with grilled vegetables or dotted in a fresh tomato and cucumber salad. I serve it with roasted lamb cutlets or fried fish and even as a dessert, sweetened with icing sugar and orange blossom syrup and accompanied by baked fruit.

To those of you who haven't been following my pontificating about the merits of strained yoghurt – which is essentially what labneh is – I warmly invite you to join the fan club. Super-popular around the whole of the Eastern Mediterranean, you can buy it from many Arab grocers', either as small white balls marinated in olive oil, to add to savoury dishes, or as a thick and creamy yoghurt sold at the cheese counter or in chilled tubs.

The best, though, is to make your own by draining the yoghurt overnight to reach a rich and creamy texture (although 4–6 hours will just about do). Squeeze the yoghurt bundle a couple of times while it's draining to speed up the process. Plain Greek yoghurt will work well if that's easier: the finished dish won't be as rich but it will still be wonderfully fresh.

800g natural yoghurt
80g icing sugar
400g trimmed rhubarb
100ml muscat (or another dessert wine)
70g caster sugar
½ vanilla pod, split lengthways, seeds scraped
1 lemon, rind shaved in strips from half, zest grated from the other half
20g unsalted pistachios, coarsely chopped
salt

Put the yoghurt in a medium bowl with the icing sugar and ¼ teaspoon of salt. Mix well and transfer to the middle of a clean muslin or J-cloth. Tie into a bundle using an elastic band or string and hang it over a bowl in the fridge for up to 18 hours, squeezing the bundle from time to time.

Preheat the oven to 200°C/180°C Fan/Gas Mark 6.

Cut the rhubarb into 6cm lengths and mix with the muscat, caster sugar, vanilla pod and seeds and lemon strips. Put in an ovenproof dish just large enough to accommodate the rhubarb snugly. Roast, uncovered, for 20 minutes or until the rhubarb is tender but not mushy. Set aside to cool.

Just before serving, take the strained yoghurt from the fridge and give it a good squeeze to release any extra water. Remove from the cloth and place in a bowl. Stir in the grated lemon zest and spoon into serving dishes. Spoon the rhubarb on top with some of the cooking juices and sprinkle over the pistachios.

QUINCE POACHED IN POMEGRANATE JUICE

2 large quinces, peeled and
  quartered (850g)
800ml pomegranate juice
70g caster sugar
1 vanilla pod, split
  lengthways, seeds scraped
shaved rind of 1 large
  orange, plus 50ml juice
  (about ½ orange)
2 star anise
65g pomegranate seeds
  (seeds from about ½
  pomegranate)
120g clotted cream
2 tsp freshly shredded mint
  leaves (optional)

This is a glorious and festive dessert and, if I may say so without enraging too many traditionalists, undeniably superior to the old Christmas pud. It also has the further advantage that Christmas pudding is incongruous 364 days of the year while quinces appear from October onwards and stick around until after the last mince pie has been eaten.

Quinces take on a wonderful red colour while poaching in the pomegranate juice. In the past, quince varieties sold in shops would take hours to cook and this would cause them to go red naturally due to the sugars slowly caramelising. Today's quinces normally take less than half an hour to cook and stay pale; that is, unless they are cooked in pomegranate juice.

Remove the core from the quince quarters. Discard half of them and tie the remainder in a bundle using a tea towel or muslin. Place the quince in a heavy-based saucepan and add the pomegranate juice, sugar, vanilla pod and seeds, orange rind and juice and star anise. Add the wrapped-up cores and bring to the boil. Reduce to a gentle simmer, cover the pan and cook for about 20 minutes, until the quince is soft.

Use a slotted spoon to remove the quince quarters and set aside. Keep the lid off the pan, increase the heat and simmer the sauce for a further 20 minutes or so, until thick and syrupy. You should be left with about 75ml.

Just before serving, squeeze all the thick juices out of the tea towel or muslin before discarding the core bundle, orange peel, star anise and vanilla. Return the quince to the syrup and gently warm through. Place two quince quarters on each plate, pour over some syrup and serve with a sprinkle of pomegranate seeds, a dollop of clotted cream and a sprinkle of mint, if using.

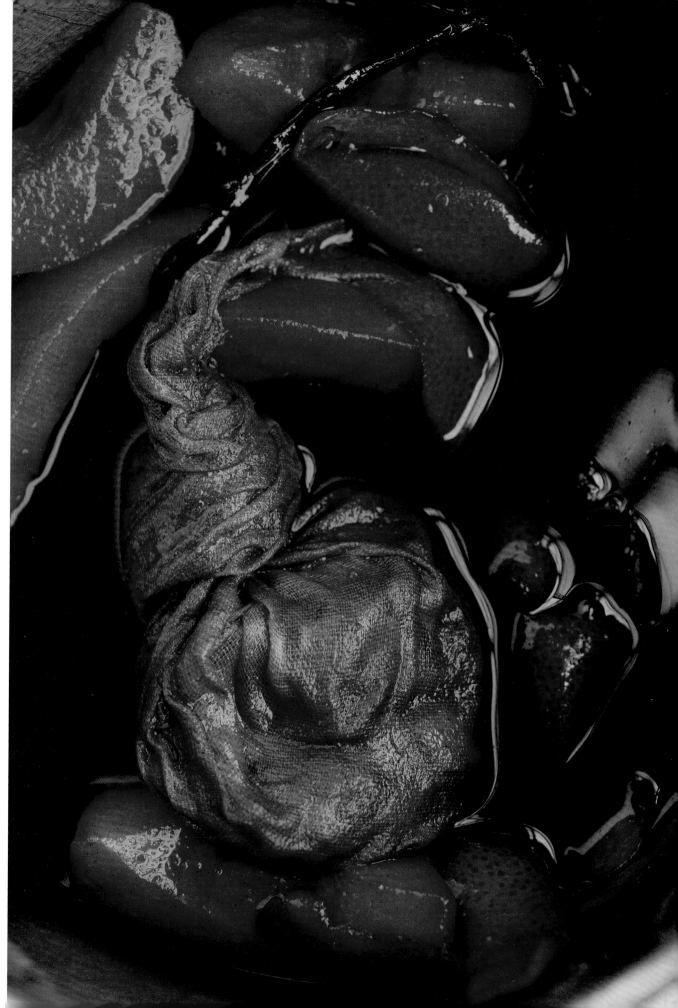

BITTER FROZEN BERRIES WITH WHITE CHOCOLATE CREAM

SERVES SIX

Years ago, when I was the pastry chef at Kensington Place restaurant in west London, one of my colleagues in the kitchen 'leaked' the recipes from the pastry book of the legendary Ivy restaurant. This highly coveted document, of which I only caught an irritatingly short glimpse, included the recipe for the celebrated Scandinavian iced berries with white chocolate sauce. This was a myth of a dish among pastry chefs and I couldn't forgive the man for depriving me of the chance of copying the original recipe (obviously, this was well before the age of smartphones and smart cameras). This dish was inspired by the memory of that elusive recipe.

Use a mixture of berries here, either fresh or from a frozen packet, and keep them all in the freezer until you prepare the dish. Make sure you have a sufficient amount of sharp berries – blackcurrants and redcurrants – to balance the sweetness of the white chocolate. The white chocolate ganache needs to be kept cold in the fridge for at least 5 hours before you can whip it up.

90g white chocolate, chips or a block broken into very small pieces
400ml double cream
380g fresh (see introduction) or frozen berries (raspberries, blackberries, blackcurrants and redcurrants)
40ml Angostura bitters, plus a few extra drops to finish
3 tbsp icing sugar
6 biscotti or another hard biscuit, to serve

First prepare a white chocolate ganache. Place the chocolate in a medium heatproof bowl. Pour 160ml of the cream into a small saucepan and bring to the boil, making sure it doesn't spill over. Pour over the chocolate and stir until all the chips have melted. Leave to cool before covering the bowl with cling film and chilling it in the fridge for at least 5 hours, or overnight.

When ready to serve, place the remaining cream in a mixing bowl and add the ganache. Whisk together – by hand or with an electric whisk – to form very runny peaks. Take care not to pass this stage as the cream will split if it's over-whipped.

Put the frozen berries in a plastic bag, place on a flat surface and bash a few times with a rolling pin until the berries are roughly crushed. Pour them into a bowl and mix with the Angostura bitters and icing sugar. Stir until the sugar dissolves and leave to rest for 5 minutes, until the berries are semi-frozen.

Divide the cream between glass bowls and spoon the berries on top. Alternatively, place the cream in a mixing bowl, add the berries and swirl through before spooning into individual bowls. Drizzle over a few drops of the bitters and serve with a biscuit alongside.

CARAMELISED BRANDY PEARS WITH FENNEL SEED CRACKERS

Cracker dough
125g plain flour, plus extra
   for dusting
½ tsp baking powder
1 tbsp olive oil
salt

Cracker topping
60ml olive oil
35g hazelnuts, chopped
2 tbsp fennel seeds, lightly
   crushed
2 tbsp caster sugar

Caramelised pears
½ vanilla pod
40g caster sugar
3 William or conference
   pears, peeled, cored and
   each cut into 8 wedges
   (350g)
15g unsalted butter
3 tbsp brandy
80g mascarpone, to serve

This wintry dessert is quite spectacular. The crackers are optional – shortbread is a good substitute – or, even better, commercial tortas de aceite from Seville, which are the inspiration for these crackers and are available in the UK. In case you do make them, I made sure the dough makes more crackers than you'll need, about 18. You can store them in an airtight container to snack on for a few days, though I doubt that they'll last that long. The pears can be cooked an hour or two in advance and then warmed through just before serving.

Start by making the crackers. Put all the dough ingredients in a large bowl, along with ¼ teaspoon of salt and 65ml of water, and use your hands to bring the mixture together. Knead it on your worktop for a few minutes to form a soft dough. Cover with cling film and leave to rest in the fridge for 1 hour.

Preheat the oven to 240°C/220°C/Gas Mark 9.

Dust some flour on a clean, dry work surface. Pinch pieces of dough weighing roughly 12g – you should make about 18 – and roll out as thinly as possible into long oval shapes, 22cm x 8cm. Dust with flour as you go. Place the crackers on trays lined with baking parchment. Brush with olive oil before scattering over the hazelnuts, fennel seeds and caster sugar. Bake for roughly 6–8 minutes, until crisp and golden. Remove from the oven, leave to cool and then put in an airtight container.

For the pears, place the vanilla pod in a spice grinder with 1 tablespoon of the sugar and blitz until the vanilla is finely ground (alternatively, chop the vanilla pod finely with a sharp knife and use a pestle and mortar to crush it with the sugar, or just use store-bought vanilla sugar). Transfer the mixture to a large bowl with the remaining sugar. Add the pears and toss to coat evenly.

Put a large non-stick frying pan on a high heat and add the butter. Lay the pears, along with any excess sugar in the bowl, in the pan and cook for 3 minutes, turning once, so that the pears get nicely coloured. Reduce the temperature and continue to cook for another 3–5 minutes, stirring, until the pears soften and the sugar turns a golden caramel. Remove the pan from the heat and pour in 2 tablespoons of water. Be careful as it will spit a little.

Return the pan to the heat and, once boiling, add the brandy. Leave this to bubble away for 2–3 minutes. The caramel will thicken slightly to coat the pears. Place a biscuit on each plate and serve the pears and their sauce alongside, with a spoonful of mascarpone on top.

FIG AND GOAT'S CHEESE TART

150g soft goat's cheese,
  skin removed

85g icing sugar

½ tsp grated orange zest

1 tbsp chopped thyme
  leaves, plus extra leaves to
  garnish

2 eggs, beaten

100g ground almonds

600g ripe figs, halved

1 tbsp caster sugar

1½ tbsp lemon juice

Yeasted pastry

265g plain flour, plus extra
  for dusting

50g caster sugar

1 tsp fast-action yeast

grated zest of ½ lemon

2 eggs, beaten

75g unsalted butter, at room
  temperature, cut into 2cm
  cubes

sunflower oil, for greasing

salt

The last time I had to make this tart was in front of two television cameras and amid the most dreadful of hay fever attacks. It was part of my Mediterranean Feast *programme and I was in a bakery in Tel Aviv. I soldiered on and managed to shoot the whole scene, with regular, not-so-charming snivels that were later masterfully edited out. More importantly, the pie looked and tasted fantastic. And if I could make it in that state, anyone can. If you don't have an electric mixer with a dough hook, or don't want to make the yeasted pastry, it can be replaced with a commercial all-butter puff pastry sheet of similar dimensions.*

First make the pastry. Place the flour, sugar, yeast and zest in a mixer bowl and, using the dough hook attachment, stir everything together on a low speed for a minute. Add the eggs and 60ml of water and work for a few seconds on a low speed before increasing to medium and kneading for 3 minutes, until the dough comes together. Add ⅛ teaspoon of salt and the butter, a few cubes at a time, until it all melts into the dough. Continue kneading for about 10 minutes on a medium speed, until the dough is completely smooth, elastic and shiny. You will need to scrape down the sides of the bowl a few times and throw a small amount of flour on the sides of the bowl to prevent the dough sticking. Place the dough in a large bowl brushed with sunflower oil, cover with cling film and leave in the fridge for at least half a day, preferably overnight. It will increase in volume but only by about a quarter.

Place the goat's cheese in a medium bowl with 10g of the icing sugar, the orange zest, thyme and 1½ of the 2 beaten eggs. Whisk until smooth and then stir through the almonds. Mix until you get a smooth consistency.

Lightly flour a clean work surface and roll the pastry into a 0.5cm-thick square, about 28cm x 28cm. Line a baking tray with baking parchment. Rolling the pastry around a rolling pin to help you, transfer the pastry to the tray. Spread the goat's cheese mix on top, leaving a border of about 1.5cm. Brush the remaining egg over the border.

Stand the figs on top of the mixture, cut side facing upwards and slightly overlapping as they will shrink when cooking. Sprinkle the caster sugar over the figs, cover the tart with foil and set aside in a warm place for 20 minutes. Preheat the oven to 190°C/170°C Fan/Gas Mark 5.

Remove the foil and place the tart in the oven. Bake for about 30 minutes, until the figs are caramelised and the base of the pastry is golden-brown.

Whisk the remaining icing sugar with the lemon juice. You want a thick yet spreadable icing, so add extra juice or icing sugar as needed. Remove the tart from the oven and use a spoon to drizzle the icing over the figs. Sprinkle with the thyme leaves and eat warm or at room temperature.

ROASTED FIGS WITH POMEGRANATE MOLASSES AND ORANGE ZEST

I can't emphasise enough how crucial it is to choose good, sweet, squidgy figs, no matter what you do with them. It makes all the difference. These figs are extremely simple to prepare but have a magnificent, deep and rich flavour that surprises me every time I make them.

Place the pomegranate molasses, lemon juice, 1 tablespoon of the sugar, 2 whole thyme sprigs, 1 tablespoon of water and the orange rind strips in a large mixing bowl with a pinch of salt. Mix well to dissolve the sugar and then stir in the figs. Set aside to marinate for 30 minutes.

Place the mascarpone, yoghurt and icing sugar in a small bowl and whisk until smooth. Set aside in the fridge until ready to use.

Remove the figs from the bowl (keeping the marinade) and arrange them snugly, cut-side up, inside a 20cm-diameter shallow ovenproof dish or pan. Sprinkle the figs with the remaining sugar and place under a hot grill: don't put them directly below the grill as they will burn. Grill for 10 minutes, or until the sugar has caramelised and the figs softened.

Meanwhile, pour the marinade into a small saucepan, bring to the boil and simmer for 2–4 minutes, until the sauce is reduced by half and has a consistency of runny honey.

Transfer the hot figs to individual plates and spoon over any leftover syrup from the baking dish. Drizzle over the sauce reduction and sprinkle with the picked thyme leaves. Place a spoonful of the yoghurt cream on top or alongside the figs, sprinkle over the orange zest and serve.

3 tbsp pomegranate molasses
1 tbsp lemon juice
3 tbsp dark muscovado sugar
4 thyme sprigs, 2 whole and 2 with their leaves picked
1 orange, rind shaved into 1 long strip from half; the zest finely grated from the other half
8 ripe figs, cut in half lengthways (400g)
100g mascarpone
100g Greek yoghurt
1 tbsp icing sugar
salt

CHAR-GRILLED STONE FRUIT WITH LEMON GERANIUM WATER

4 peaches and/or
   nectarines, each stoned
   and cut into 6 wedges
   (500g)
6 apricots, halved and
   stoned (200g)
1 tbsp olive oil
3 large ripe figs, torn into 2
   or 3 pieces (180g)
2 tsp aniseed or fennel
   seeds, toasted and finely
   crushed
10g small basil leaves
1 tsp fresh lavender

Scented yoghurt
150g full-fat yoghurt
1½ tbsp thyme flower
   honey or another floral
   honey
1 tbsp lemon geranium
   water or orange blossom
   water
1½ tsp lemon juice

The strength of opinion of online Guardian *readers of my weekly column never fails to surprise (and delight) me. What readers comment most about is my tendency to use obscure ingredients 'just for the heck of it'. 'I'll just nip out to the corner shop for some Iranian limes and barberries', wrote one commentator recently. Others stick up for me with their own brand of parody: 'For god's sake where am I supposed to buy potatoes? Or tomato purée? Bloody elitist London-centric recipes.' I find this banter amusing but I also see it as eye-opening feedback.*

So before I am accused of introducing yet another impossible-to-find ingredient, I would like to say that lemon geranium water is a wonderfully exotic scented liquid that is extremely difficult to find anywhere but in Tunisia, where I first came across it. However, other flower distillations, like orange blossom water or rose water, are perfectly adequate substitutes.

The peaches, apricots and figs were at their height of perfection when I made this dish in Tunisia but you can use any seasonal stone fruit. If they are really soft and juicy, then leave them as they are and just char-grill the harder fruit. Bring this to the table on a large platter at the end of a healthy meal.

Put a large ridged griddle pan on a high heat and leave until it is very hot. In a bowl mix the peaches, nectarines and apricots with the oil. Place them on the griddle pan and cook for 1–2 minutes on each side, until they are charred and slightly softened. Remove and set aside to cool.

Mix the yoghurt with the honey and lemon geranium water. Stir in the lemon juice and refrigerate until needed.

Before serving, arrange the peaches and apricots on a large platter and dot the torn figs on top. Drizzle the yoghurt sauce over the fruit, leaving parts of the fruit exposed. Sprinkle over the ground seeds and scatter with the fresh basil leaves. Finish with the fresh lavender and serve.

STEWED BLACKBERRIES WITH BAY CUSTARD AND GIN

SERVES FOUR

Some puddings have got to be just for the adults, right?! I figure that once you are too old to fit the number of candles your age requires on top of a dessert, it's time to ditch them entirely and douse the whole thing with booze (though I wouldn't go for the lighting-up stage). As well as giving a sense of occasion, a proper boozy soak also introduces an incredible depth of flavour.

480g blackberries

40g caster sugar

1½ tsp rose water

2½ tbsp gin

90g savoiardi biscuits, broken into 2cm pieces

360g vanilla ice cream

Custard

90ml double cream

70ml full-fat milk

3 bay leaves

1 egg yolk

15g caster sugar

First make the custard. Place the cream, milk and bay in a small saucepan and bring to the boil. Remove from the heat immediately. In a small bowl, whisk the egg yolk and sugar until well combined. While whisking, add a little of the milk mix. Slowly add more milk, continuously whisking, until combined. Return the liquid to the saucepan and place on a medium–low heat. Stir continuously for about 10 minutes until the sauce thickens into a custard. Remove from the heat and set aside to cool. Keep in the fridge until ready to use.

Place 300g of the blackberries in a small saucepan along with the sugar and simmer on a medium–low heat for 10 minutes, stirring occasionally, until the berries are soft but still hold their shape and lots of liquid has come out. Remove from the heat and leave to cool.

Strain the juices from the blackberries and stir through the rose water and gin. Soak the biscuits in the juices until the liquid is fully absorbed.

To serve, scoop a large portion of ice cream into four glasses or tumblers. Top with the soaked biscuits and pour over the custard. Add the stewed blackberries and the remaining fresh blackberries and serve.

SET 'CHEESECAKE' WITH PLUM COMPOTE

400g cream cheese

200g mascarpone

125g caster sugar

200ml double cream

grated zest of 1 lemon

2 tbsp olive oil

½ orange, rind shaved in
   strips

500g plums, stoned and cut
   into small cubes

1 tbsp lemon juice

Crumble

60g wholemeal flour

30g soft light brown sugar

50g unsalted butter, cut into
   small dice

50g skinned hazelnuts,
   lightly crushed

20g black sesame seeds

coarse sea salt

*For all of Ottolenghi's manager Cornelia's powers of persuasion, she has not
yet managed to elicit the highly coveted deconstructed cheesecake recipe from
our good friends at Honey & Co. I am still working on Itamar and Sarit to gain
details of their kadafi-based version but, in the meantime, offer my own, which I
used to make in my old days as a pastry chef at Launceston Place and serve with
greengages or gooseberries.*

*Tara's mum has made this so many times that she has, regardless
of where the recipe might have come from, begun to feel very territorial about
it indeed. The cheese mixture needs to set for 24 hours before serving, so it
makes sense to make the compote and crumble a day or two in advance as well,
so that you simply put it together when you're ready to serve. Use greengages
or gooseberries instead of plums when they are in season, for a divine
alternative compote. (Also pictured on page 325, bottom.)*

The day before serving, place the cream cheese, mascarpone and 100g
of the sugar in the bowl of an electric mixer and beat on a medium speed
until soft and smooth. Separately, whisk the cream until soft peaks form.
Fold this into the cream cheese mix, followed by the lemon zest, stirring
until just combined. Transfer to a glass bowl, or even leave in the mixer
bowl, cover with cling film and refrigerate for 24 hours.

Put the oil and orange rind in a small saucepan and place on a medium
heat. When the orange starts to sizzle, remove it from the heat and leave
the oil to cool with the orange rind immersed.

Put the plums, the remaining 25g of sugar and the lemon juice in a medium
saucepan and cook on a medium–low heat for about 30 minutes, until it
has a compote consistency, a bit runnier than jam. Set aside to cool.

Preheat the oven to 190°C/170°C Fan/Gas Mark 5.

To make the crumble, place the flour, sugar, butter and ½ teaspoon of
salt in a small bowl and, using your fingers, rub in the butter to form the
consistency of breadcrumbs. Mix in the hazelnuts and sesame seeds
and spread out on a baking tray in a thin layer. Bake for 15 minutes, until
golden-brown. Remove from the oven and set aside to cool before breaking
the crumble up again with your fingers.

To assemble, spoon the cream mix on to individual plates. Add a dollop
of fruit on the side of the mix, followed by a scatter of the crumble. Drizzle
½ teaspoon of the orange-infused oil over each cheesecake and serve
at once.

APRICOT, WALNUT AND LAVENDER CAKE

185g unsalted butter, at
  room temperature, diced
2 tbsp walnut oil
220g caster sugar
120g ground almonds
4 eggs, beaten
120g walnuts, freshly
  blitzed in a food processor
  to a coarse powder
90g plain flour
½ tsp vanilla extract
grated zest of 1 lemon
1½ tsp lavender, fresh or
  dried
600g fresh apricots, halved
  and stones removed
salt

Icing
50g icing sugar
1 tbsp lemon juice

The combination of walnuts, apricots and lavender is as French as a good baguette with butter and ripe Brie, and it is every bit as invincible. I seriously urge you to try this cake, and not just as a French classic. It has a moist and soft crumb and a delicate fruity topping and it will keep well, covered, for a few days.

Preheat the oven to 190°C/170°C Fan/Gas Mark 5.

Place the butter, oil, sugar and almonds in the bowl of an electric mixer and beat on a medium–high speed until light and fluffy. Add the eggs in small additions and continue to beat until well incorporated. Fold in the walnuts, flour, vanilla, lemon zest, 1 teaspoon of the lavender and ⅛ teaspoon of salt.

Line the base and sides of a 23cm cake tin with baking parchment. Pour in the cake mix and level out the top. Arrange the apricot halves over the top, skin side down and slightly overlapping, right to the edge. Bake in the oven for 70–80 minutes, covering with foil if the top starts to brown too much.

While the cake is baking, make the icing. Whisk together the icing sugar and lemon juice to get a light, pourable icing, adjusting the amount of sugar or juice if needed. As soon as the cake comes out of the oven, brush the icing on top. Sprinkle over the remaining lavender and leave to cool before serving.

ESME'S OLD-FASHIONED APPLE AND RHUBARB PUDDING

100g unsalted butter, at
  room temperature
160g dark muscovado sugar
100g ground almonds
1 egg
700g cooking apples,
  peeled, cored and roughly
  grated (550g)
250g trimmed and sliced
  rhubarb, cut into 2cm
  pieces
50g demerara sugar
40g fresh breadcrumbs
10g sage leaves, roughly
  chopped
250g Greek yoghurt

This hot and sweet pudding, with its super-crusty almond topping, is normally cooked for hours in an Aga using windfall apples. Savour this romantic image even with my real-world adjustments. With thanks to Esme Robinson for remembering this from her childhood, and for letting me shake up the old school with the addition of rhubarb and sage.

Preheat the oven to 170°C/150°C Fan/Gas Mark 3½.

Place the butter and muscovado sugar in the small bowl of a food processor and cream for about 2 minutes, until smooth: you will need to scrape down the sides of the bowl once or twice. Add the almonds and egg – these will almost fill up the bowl but should just fit – and continue to process for 4–5 minutes, until the batter is completely smooth.

Place the apple, rhubarb, demerara sugar, breadcrumbs and sage in a large bowl and mix. Transfer to a round, high-sided ovenproof dish, about 18cm in diameter. Press down firmly with your hands and pour over the batter. Use a spatula to spread it out to form an even covering, about 1.5cm thick.

Place the pudding in the oven, uncovered, for 2 hours, until the batter has formed a thick crust. Remove from the oven and leave to cool down a bit, about 10–15 minutes, before serving with the yoghurt alongside.

RICOTTA PANCAKES WITH GOOSEBERRY RELISH

SERVES FOUR
makes 10–12 pancakes

You need to adjust your expectations slightly before making these. They are not your ordinary fluffy-cakey pancakes, but rather more eggy and cheesy (and comforting, I think), like a cross between cheesecake and French clafoutis. The relish recipe yields more than you'll need here, but because gooseberry season is short and they are so wonderful, I've left some for the fridge. You can spoon this over granola or your breakfast toast. Plums are a good substitute for gooseberries.

750g gooseberries (or plums), fresh or frozen
240g caster sugar
½ orange, rind shaved in strips
10g fresh root ginger, peeled and cut into thin matchsticks
1 cinnamon stick
4 eggs, lightly whisked
500g ricotta
25g potato flour
35g plain flour
¼ tsp vanilla extract
2 tbsp sunflower oil
100g crème fraîche
salt

Place the gooseberries, 180g of the sugar, the orange rind, ginger and cinnamon in a medium saucepan and cook on a medium–low heat for roughly 30 minutes, until a semi-thick compote consistency has formed. Set aside to cool.

In a large bowl, whisk the eggs and ricotta until smooth. Add the flours, remaining sugar, vanilla and ⅛ teaspoon of salt and mix well. Cover and refrigerate for 1 hour.

To cook, put a large frying pan on a medium heat, add 1 teaspoon of the oil and, once hot, reduce the heat to low. Make pancakes 10cm wide by 1cm thick and cook for 3–4 minutes on one side before flipping and cooking for a final minute, until golden-brown on both sides. It is important the pancakes are cooked on a low heat so they start to set on top before being flipped over, or you will end up with splashes of mix all over the pan. Transfer to a plate lined with kitchen paper and keep somewhere warm whilst you repeat with the remaining mix, adding oil as you go.

Serve two warm pancakes on each plate, with the relish and crème fraîche spooned alongside.

WALNUT AND HALVA CAKE

I wondered, for a second, whether it was too much to have two sweet recipes using halva in one book. I then realised that you could have an entire baking book in celebration of the Arab-style sesame halva, so didn't worry about it again. It's one of the ingredients I'd sneak into my treasure box if I were packed off to a desert island, to nibble on with black coffee or to use in my cooking. This cake is a treat for all ages, for teatime fun or served as a dessert, with thick whipped cream.

85g unsalted butter, at room temperature, plus extra for greasing the tin
100g caster sugar
2 eggs, lightly whisked
200g plain flour
¾ tsp baking powder
¾ tsp bicarbonate of soda
130g soured cream
salt

Topping
60g unsalted butter
120g walnuts, roughly chopped
1 tsp ground cinnamon
25g dark muscovado sugar
170g plain sesame halva, broken into 3cm pieces

Preheat the oven to 180°C/160°C Fan/Gas Mark 4. Grease a 900g loaf tin (25cm x 12cm), with a little butter, and line with greaseproof paper so that it comes above the sides.

Start with the topping. Put the butter in a small saucepan and put on a low–medium heat. Melt and then allow it to sizzle for about 3 minutes until light brown and smelling slightly nutty. Remove from the heat and set aside to cool. Once cool, mix the butter, walnuts and cinnamon together. Divide the mixture in two and stir the brown sugar into one of the portions; you may need to use your hands to ensure that the sugar breaks up and spreads evenly through the nuts.

Now for the cake batter. In an electric mixer cream the butter and sugar on a medium speed until the mixture becomes light in colour and the texture is fluffy. Add the eggs, a little at a time, until they are incorporated.

Sift together the flour, baking powder, bicarbonate of soda and a pinch of salt. Add this to the batter, alternating with the soured cream, in a couple of additions: be sure not to over-mix.

Spread half the batter on to the bottom of the loaf tin and scatter the sugarless nut mix evenly over the batter. Dot the halva on top. Spread the remaining batter on top; this may be slightly challenging as the halva drags into the batter but you shouldn't worry about it too much. Finish by sprinkling the sugary nuts on top.

Bake in the oven for 40–45 minutes, or until a skewer inserted in the centre comes out clean. Leave to cool for 20 minutes, then gently remove from the tin by lifting the greaseproof paper. Remove the paper and leave the cake to cool completely on a wire rack (otherwise it might crumble). Wrapped in foil, the cake will keep for a day or two.

HALVA ICE CREAM WITH CHOCOLATE SAUCE AND ROASTED PEANUTS

250ml double cream

350ml full-fat milk

1 vanilla pod, split
lengthways, seeds scraped

2 egg yolks

40g caster sugar

30g tahini paste

100g plain sesame halva,
cut into 0.5cm dice

60g roasted salted peanuts,
roughly chopped (shop-
bought are best)

1 tsp black sesame seeds (or
white, if unavailable)

Chocolate sauce

150ml double cream

80g dark chocolate (70 per
cent cocoa solids), finely
chopped

½ tsp brandy

The flavour of halva works brilliantly in an ice cream. Make it once and you'll go back to it over and over again, even without the chocolate sauce and peanuts. With the two condiments it tastes a bit like a luxurious Snickers ice cream: sweet, nutty and comforting. The chocolate can mask the halva flavour a little, so better not drench it with sauce, just drizzle lightly. With an ice-cream machine, you would need to churn the ice cream at least a few hours ahead of time, preferably a day in advance. If you don't have an ice-cream machine, make this the old-fashioned way, by making the custard and freezing it without churning, beating occasionally for 4–5 hours. Add the halva halfway through. Using this method works well for serving immediately but the next day the ice cream tends to go hard.

Heat the cream, milk, vanilla pod and seeds in a medium saucepan until just coming to the boil. Remove from the heat.

In a medium bowl, whisk the egg yolks and sugar until combined. Use a ladle to spoon a little of the hot cream mix into the egg mix, whisking the whole time. Continue with more cream mix until it is all incorporated. Return to the saucepan and place on a medium heat. Stir with a wooden spoon continuously for 10 minutes, until the sauce thickens to a light custard consistency. Remove from the heat and whisk in the tahini. Leave to cool for 20 minutes, then remove the vanilla pod.

Pour the custard into an ice-cream machine and churn for about 35 minutes, until semi-frozen but creamy. (Alternatively, transfer it to a freezer-proof container and place in the freezer for 4–5 hours, stirring through the halva halfway.) Remove from the machine and stir through the halva pieces. Place in a pre-frozen container and freeze. Remove from the freezer 10 minutes before serving to let it soften.

Make the chocolate sauce just before serving. Place the cream in a small saucepan and bring to a gentle boil. Immediately pour this over the chocolate and stir until soft and uniform. Stir in the brandy. Divide the ice cream into bowls and drizzle over some warm sauce. Sprinkle with the peanuts and sesame seeds and serve immediately.

GRILLED BANANA BREAD WITH TAHINI AND HONEYCOMB

MAKES 1 LARGE LOAF

Telephone calls were put through to the next-door arches when this came together in the test kitchen: 'stop what you are doing, you must come for tea'. This is all about three things: an incredibly perfect banana bread (thank you, Helen), tahini, which is so smooth and nutty you could eat it by the spoon, and arriving at the table with a big cup of tea and a rumbling tummy. I pitched this to the team as my offering for Christmas breakfast. Raised eyebrows relaxed back down once the trilogy was tried.

For me, tahini is the new peanut butter. It is runnier and earthier but has a similarly rich flavour and is completely impossible to resist. In many Middle Eastern cultures it is served not only as a base for hummus and other savoury sauces and dips, but also as a spread served at breakfast with sweet condiments, such as grape or date syrup.

The banana bread can be baked in advance – a day or two, or even more – and then just sliced and grilled when you need it. Drizzle it with tahini as I do here, or leave out the tahini and make do with the butter, honeycomb and salt.

180g pecans
3 large ripe bananas, peeled and mashed (300g)
275g soft light brown sugar
3 eggs, lightly beaten
140ml full-fat milk
70ml sunflower oil
275g plain flour
1 tsp bicarbonate of soda
1½ tsp baking powder
salt

To finish
80g unsalted butter, at room temperature
60g tahini paste
200g honeycomb in honey
¾ tsp coarse sea salt

Preheat the oven to 170°C/150°C Fan/Gas Mark 3½ and line a 900g loaf tin (25cm x 12cm), with baking parchment.

Place the pecans on a baking tray and roast for 10 minutes before roughly chopping them and setting aside.

Place the bananas, sugar and eggs in the large bowl of an electric mixer and beat until combined. With the machine running on a slow speed, add ½ teaspoon of salt, the milk and then the oil. Sift together the flour, bicarbonate of soda and baking powder and, with the machine still running, add this to the mix. Continue to mix on a medium speed for about 5 minutes, until thoroughly combined. Stir through the pecans and then pour the mixture into the loaf tin.

Place in the oven and bake for about 1 hour 10 minutes, until a skewer or knife inserted in the centre comes out clean. Leave aside for 10 minutes before removing the cake from the tin and setting aside on a wire rack until completely cool. You can now wrap the bread in foil and keep for up to 5 days, or freeze for a few weeks.

Set your oven grill to high. Cut the banana bread into 2cm-thick slices and brush with butter. Place under the grill for up to 2 minutes, until lightly toasted on one side, and remove. Drizzle over the tahini, place a chunk of honeycomb on each slice and sprinkle with coarse sea salt. Serve at once.

SUPER FRENCH TOAST

600ml full-fat milk
200ml double cream
1 orange, rind shaved into
   long strips
3 long cinnamon sticks,
   broken in half
1 vanilla pod, split
   lengthways, seeds scraped
400g brioche loaf, crusts
   removed, cut into eight
   2.5cm-thick slices
6 eggs
40g caster sugar
60g unsalted butter
40g icing sugar
240g soured cream
maple syrup, to serve

Last year Sami and I were on a book tour in Toronto and were taken by our 'Canadian mother', Bonnie Stern, to the fantastic Rose and Sons, a restaurant/ diner serving food that is rich in every sense of the word: rich in flavour, rich in tradition, rich in love and rich in calories. It was definitely one of the most memorable meals we have ever had. One of Rose and Sons' most outstanding creations is a cross between a bread pudding and French toast. I reckon their secret involves double-dipping: the bread being soaked in custard once, before it is cooked like a pudding, and then dipped one more time, before it is fried like French toast. I haven't got confirmation for this, but this is my hunch and that's what I do here.

To say that this 'needs' anything extra would, frankly, be decadent but, to elevate it to the realm of the serious brunch, some stewed seasonal fruit or fresh berries would not go amiss. Brioche loaf is available from most supermarkets.

Preheat the oven to 190°C/170°C Fan/Gas Mark 5.

Place the milk, cream, orange rind, cinnamon and vanilla pod and seeds in a medium saucepan. Heat gently on a medium–low heat and remove just before it comes to the boil, about 5 minutes. Set aside for about 20 minutes, for the cream to cool a little and for the flavours to infuse.

Meanwhile, line a 32cm x 22cm baking dish with baking parchment and lay the brioche slices flat in the base.

Place the eggs and sugar in a medium bowl and whisk well. Pour the warm milk gradually into the eggs, continuing to whisk the whole time. Strain the custard and then pour two-thirds of it over the brioche, so that it's fully covered. Place the remaining custard in a wide shallow bowl and set aside.

Place the dish in the oven and bake for 20 minutes, until the custard is cooked through and golden-brown. Set aside to cool and then slice into 8 square pieces.

Place half the butter in a large non-stick frying pan and place on a medium–high heat. Dip half the bread squares into the remaining custard mix, transfer to a plate and sprinkle ½ teaspoon of icing sugar over each square. Put them immediately in the pan, sugar side down, and fry for 30 seconds to 1 minute, to caramelise the sugar. Whilst they are frying, sprinkle ½ teaspoon of icing sugar over each slice. Flip over and cook for the same amount of time, until the sugar is dark brown and crispy. Remove from the pan, rest on a wire rack and repeat with the remaining brioche slices and butter.

To serve, place one slice of toast on each plate with 2 tablespoons of soured cream and as much maple syrup as you like.

RICOTTA FRITTERS WITH ORANGE AND HONEY

470g ricotta

60g caprino goat's cheese, or another soft goat's cheese

3 eggs

60ml full-fat milk

1½ tbsp mint leaves, finely chopped

grated zest of 1 orange

160g plain flour, possibly more

1½ tsp baking powder

50g caster sugar

about 700ml sunflower oil, for frying

4 tbsp clear honey, warmed slightly for drizzling

icing sugar, for dusting

salt

Orange syrup

100g caster sugar

1 orange, rind shaved into long pieces then cut into very thin strips

You know how slightly terrifying certain grandmother figures can be? Well, I had to cook these fritters for one such person. Signora Assunta proved completely harmless in the end (of course) but I was sure she was going to eat me alive if I didn't produce something extra-special for her on a recent visit to Sardinia. Luckily, I did her proud and she even gave me a kiss (I had to promise her husband would never know of it).

Start by making the orange syrup. Place the sugar and 100ml of water in a small saucepan on a medium heat, stirring until the sugar has dissolved. Gently simmer for 3–4 minutes. Add the orange strips and continue cooking for another 2 minutes. Remove from the heat and leave the orange strips to cool down in the syrup.

Place 350g of the ricotta in a medium bowl with the goat's cheese and eggs. Beat until fairly smooth before whisking in the milk, mint and orange zest. Set aside.

In a separate bowl, sift together the flour and baking powder and add the sugar and ¼ teaspoon of salt. Stir the wet ingredients into the dry ingredients to form a batter, adding more flour if necessary, until you reach a dropping consistency. Set aside for 10 minutes to rest.

Heat a small heavy-based saucepan filled with enough sunflower oil so that it comes approximately 4cm up the sides of the pan. When the oil is hot (180°C), gently drop heaped teaspoonfuls of the batter into the oil and cook for 3–4 minutes, turning occasionally, until golden-brown; reduce the temperature if they are browning too quickly. Remove with a slotted spoon and drain on kitchen paper. Continue with the remaining batter.

Pile the fritters on to individual plates and drizzle over the warmed honey. Top with a dollop of ricotta and dust with icing sugar. To finish, spoon orange strips and some of the syrup on top of the ricotta and serve immediately.

POT BARLEY, ORANGE AND SESAME PUDDING

SERVES TWO TO FOUR

This is like rice pudding with texture, for people who don't mind using their teeth for a dessert. It is also fantastically delicious. It works just as well with pearl barley, if that's what you have. Pearl barley won't need the overnight soaking but it will require a little bit more milk – about 100ml extra – and a little bit more cooking (about 20 minutes more) instead.

Start with the orange syrup. Place the shaved strips of orange rind in a small saucepan. Add the caster sugar and pour over 75ml of water. Place on a high heat, bring to the boil and cook for less than a minute, stirring, until the sugar dissolves. Set aside to cool.

Use a small sharp serrated knife to trim the orange, top and bottom. Cut around its sides to remove the white pith and then, over a small bowl, so that you catch the juice, remove the segments by slicing between the membranes. Add the segments and juices to the orange syrup in the pan, along with the orange blossom water, and set aside.

Put the sesame seeds in a mortar with 1 teaspoon of the muscovado sugar. Roughly crush with a pestle and set aside.

Drain and rinse the barley. Place in a medium saucepan with the remaining muscovado sugar, the milk, vanilla pod and seeds, citrus zest and ⅛ teaspoon of salt. Place on a high heat, bring to the boil and then reduce the heat to medium–low. Simmer for 1 hour, stirring occasionally, until the barley is cooked but still has a bite: you might need to add a little bit of milk towards the end if the barley becomes very thick. Allow to cool for 5 minutes before removing the vanilla pod, dividing between bowls and drizzling 1 teaspoon of tahini over each portion. Spoon over the orange segments and syrup, avoiding the skin, sprinkle with the crushed sesame seeds and serve.

½ tbsp white sesame seeds, toasted
½ tbsp black sesame seeds (or white if unavailable), toasted
1½ tbsp dark muscovado sugar
125g pot barley, soaked in plenty of cold water overnight
750ml full-fat milk
½ vanilla pod, split lengthways, seeds scraped
finely grated zest of ½ lemon
finely grated zest of 1 orange
20g tahini paste
salt

Orange syrup
1 medium orange, rind shaved into long strips
40g caster sugar
¼ tsp orange blossom water

TAU FU FA

10 pandan leaves (30g)

1 litre unsweetened soya milk

40g caster sugar

100g palm sugar, crushed into 1cm chunks

5g fresh root ginger, peeled and cut into thin strips

½ small pineapple, peeled, quartered lengthways, core removed, then sliced widthways into 2mm slices (300g)

1¾ tsp Vege-Gel (7g)

2 tbsp coconut cream

salt

I first came across this tofu dish – popular all over East Asia, where it has many variations, sweet and savoury, hot or cold – in a Malaysian food market. It is a bit like crème caramel, but even more silky-smooth. I've used Vege-Gel here, rather than gelatin, to make it vegetarian. This can be found in supermarkets (next to the gelatin) and is very easy to use. Apologies for the awkward quantity needed here though – just over 1 sachet – but you have to be really precise with quantities to get the setting right: 2 teaspoons is too much and 1½ is not enough!

Pandan leaves are widely used in South East Asian cooking to infuse a range of sweet and savoury dishes with their almost grassy fragrance. You'll need to pay a visit to a specialist shop to find them. You can, however, substitute with a scraped vanilla pod, half in the milk and half with the pineapple. (Also pictured overleaf and on pages 324–5.)

Tie half the pandan leaves in a knot and place them in a medium saucepan with the milk and caster sugar. Place on a medium–high heat and cook for about 5 minutes, just until it starts to simmer. Remove from the heat and set aside to cool. Transfer to a medium bowl, cover and leave in the fridge to infuse overnight.

Put the palm sugar, ¼ teaspoon of salt and the ginger in a medium saucepan with 50ml of water. Place on a medium–high heat and cook, stirring from time to time, until the sugar dissolves. Increase the heat and boil for 2 minutes before adding the pineapple and remaining pandan leaves, also tied in a knot. Reduce the heat a little and simmer for 8 minutes, stirring once or twice, until the liquid starts to thicken. Remove from the heat and set aside: it will continue to thicken as it cools. Pour into a medium bowl, cover and leave in the fridge to infuse overnight.

Line a sieve with a clean J-cloth or muslin and strain the soya infusion straight into a medium saucepan. Transfer 3 tablespoons to a small bowl and whisk with the Vege-Gel to combine. Add this to the pan and whisk everything well. Place on a medium–high heat and stir constantly for 5–6 minutes while the milk comes back to a simmer and starts to thicken. Remove from the heat and ladle into 6 individual glasses. Set aside to cool before placing them in the fridge to firm up for at least 1 hour: you want them to be set but still have a good wobble.

Place the coconut cream in a small bowl, add a tablespoon of water and stir until the cream is just runny enough to pour; add more water if you need to. Keep in the fridge until required.

Half an hour before serving, remove the pineapple from the fridge so it's not cold. When ready to serve, spoon 2 tablespoons of the pineapple and sauce on top of the set milk, followed by a drizzle of the coconut cream.

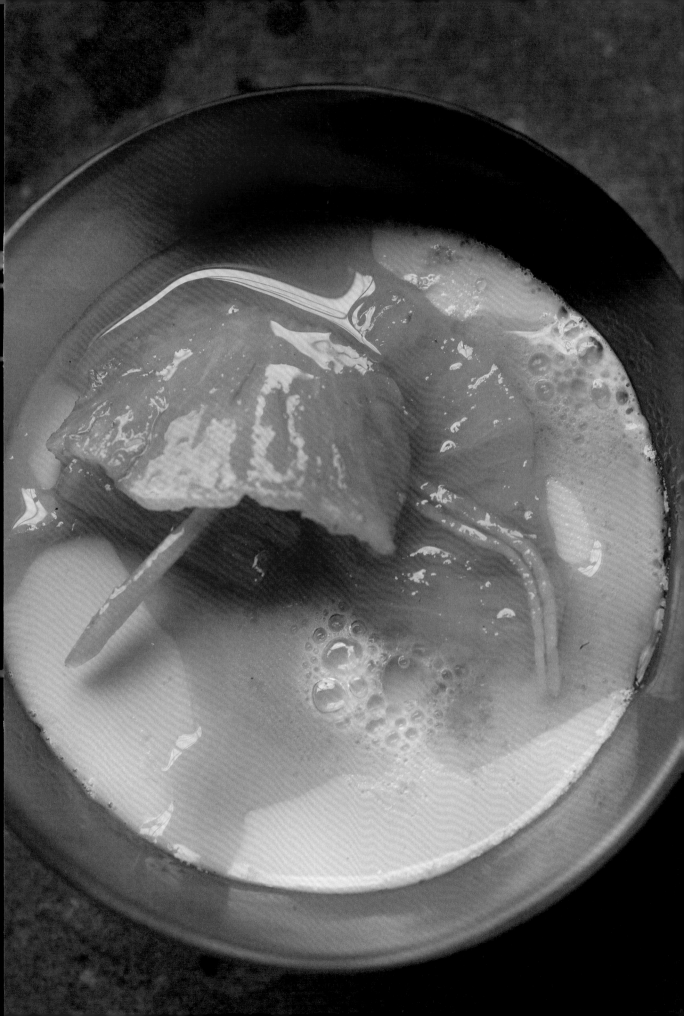

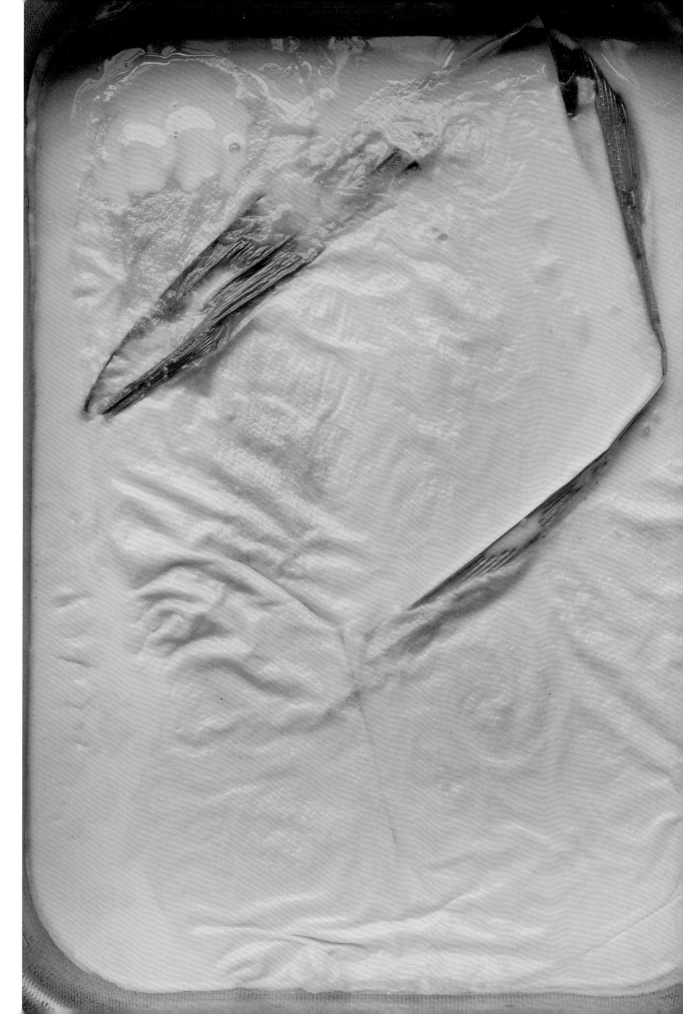

COLD RICE AND PANDAN PUDDING WITH ALPHONSO MANGO AND LIME SYRUP

Pandan, the Asian vanilla, gives a mellow, slightly coconutty aroma to savoury and sweet dishes. If you don't like it or can't get it, half a vanilla pod with the seeds scraped would be a good alternative.

My obsessive adoration for Alphonso mangoes has been established elsewhere (see page 105) but, if needs be, other varieties can be used, as long as they are sweet and ripe.

For the meringues you can easily use shop-bought. If you want to make your own, whisk the 2 egg whites remaining from making the pudding in an electric mixer, adding 120g of caster sugar gradually when the whites froth. Whisk until glossy and firm, about 10 minutes, spread as small discs or nests on baking parchment and bake for about 40 minutes at 120°C/100°C Fan/Gas Mark ½, until completely dry. Use the amount the recipe calls for and keep the rest in a jar for up to a month. (Also pictured on page 324.)

100ml double cream
700ml full-fat milk
1 pandan leaf
100g pudding rice
50g caster sugar
2 egg yolks
30g meringue, broken into pieces
2 passion fruit, pulp spooned out
salt

Lime syrup
70ml lime juice
1 tsp grated lime zest
2 tsp caster sugar
4 Alphonso mangoes or other sweet mangoes, peeled and cut into 1cm dice (400g)

....

Preheat the oven to 150°C/130°C Fan/Gas Mark 2.

Put the cream, milk, pandan leaf and ⅛ teaspoon of salt in a medium saucepan. Place on a medium–low heat and, once it begins to simmer, add the rice. Simmer very gently for 15 minutes, stirring occasionally, until semi-cooked.

Place the sugar and egg yolks in a large bowl and whisk together before slowly pouring in the rice and liquid as you continue to whisk. Transfer to an ovenproof dish (16cm x 26cm) and place in a bain marie (a roasting tin with enough boiling water to reach halfway up the sides of the dish). Transfer carefully to the oven and cook for 55 minutes to 1 hour, until just beginning to set but still a little runny: it will continue to thicken as it cools down. Take everything out of the oven, remove the dish from the tray and leave to cool, then chill for a few hours or overnight.

Meanwhile, make the lime syrup. Put the lime juice, zest and sugar into a small saucepan and place on a medium heat. Stir until the sugar dissolves and then set aside to cool. Transfer to a bowl, add the diced mango and set aside.

Use a fork to mix the cooked rice mixture until loosened and well combined and divide between bowls or shallow plates. Sprinkle the meringue on top before spooning over the mango and syrup. Finish with the passion fruit pulp.

MERINGUE ROULADE WITH ROSE PETALS AND FRESH RASPBERRIES

Meringue
4 egg whites (120g)

250g caster sugar

1 tsp vanilla extract

1 tsp white wine vinegar

1 tsp cornflour

Cream
100g mascarpone

1 tbsp icing sugar, plus
  extra for dusting

1½ tbsp rose water

400ml whipping cream

Filling
150g fresh raspberries

2 tbsp dried rose petals

1 tsp slivered pistachios (or
  regular if unavailable),
  crushed

Light, pretty, festive and special, this can pull off the trick of being either the Christmas Yule log (without the chocolate or the sponge) or the perfect pudding for a midsummer lunch.

Preheat the oven to 160°C/140°C Fan/Gas Mark 3.

Line the base and sides of a 33cm x 24cm Swiss roll tin with greaseproof paper. Allow the paper to come about 1cm above the sides of the tin.

In a large, clean bowl, whisk the egg whites with an electric mixer until they begin to firm up. Add the caster sugar to the whisking whites in spoonfuls or tip into the bowl in a slow stream. Continue whisking until you achieve a firm, glossy meringue. Using a large metal spoon, gently fold in the vanilla essence, vinegar and cornflour. Spread the mixture inside the lined tin and level with a palette knife.

Bake in the oven for 30 minutes, until a crust forms and the meringue is cooked through (it will still feel soft to the touch). Remove from the oven and allow to cool in the tin.

Tip the cooled meringue on to a fresh piece of greaseproof paper. Carefully peel off the lining paper.

Meanwhile, place the mascarpone in a large mixing bowl, along with the icing sugar and rose water. Whisk to combine and become smooth, then add the whipping cream. Whisk by hand for about 4 minutes, until the cream just holds its shape. (You can do this in an electric mixer but keep a close eye on it as it's easy to over-mix.) Spread most of the mascarpone cream over the original underside of the meringue, reserving a few tablespoons. Leave a small border around the edge of the meringue. Scatter most of the raspberries and 1½ tablespoons of rose petals all over the cream.

Use the paper to assist you in rolling up the meringue along its long edge, until you get a perfect log shape. Carefully transfer the log on to a serving dish. Use the remaining cream to create a rough wavy strip along the top of the log. Chill for at least 30 minutes.

When ready to serve, dust the log with icing sugar, scatter the remaining rose petals, along with the pistachios, over the top, and dot with the remaining raspberries.

INDEX

1 3 5 7 9 10 8 6 4 2

Published in 2014 by Ebury Press, an imprint of Ebury Publishing
A Random House Group Company

Text © Yotam Ottolenghi 2014
Photography © Jonathan Lovekin 2014

Yotam Ottolenghi has asserted his right to be identified as the author of this Work in
accordance with the Copyright, Designs and Patents Act 1988

Addresses for companies within the Random House Group can be found at www.
randomhouse.co.uk

A CIP catalogue record for this book is available from the British Library

The Random House Group Limited supports the Forest Stewardship Council® (FSC®),
the leading international forest-certification organisation. Our books carrying the FSC
label are printed on FSC®-certified paper. FSC is the only forest-certification
scheme supported by the leading environmental organisations, including Greenpeace.
Our paper procurement policy can be found at www.randomhouse.co.uk/environment

To buy books by your favourite authors and register for offers visit
www.randomhouse.co.uk

Design: Caz Hildebrand and Sakiko Kobayashi, Here Design
Photography: Jonathan Lovekin
Stylist: Sanjana Lovekin

Colour origination by Altaimage, London
Printed and bound in Italy by Graphicom S.r.l

ISBN 9780091957155

ACKNOWLEDGMENTS

All the dishes in this book have been created under the watchful eyes of Sarah Joseph, Tara Wigley, Esme Robinson and Claudine Boulstridge. Their input is priceless. Tara deserves extra recognition for her enormous contribution in both research and imaginative writing. Noam Bar, as always, was involved throughout, constantly giving his fresh outlook.

Jonathan Lovekin and Caz Hildebrand, my close creative partners, made another book which, in my mind, is unusually beautiful; Felicity Rubinstein and Sarah Lavelle are credited with allowing us to take this thrilling ride and for making it so smooth.

I would also like to thank my family, close friends and colleagues for their on-going support: Karl Allen, Michael and Ruth Ottolenghi, Tirza, Danny and the Florentin family, Pete and Greta Allen, Cornelia Staeubli, Peter Lowe, Sami Tamimi, Jeremy Kelly, Helen Goh, David Kausman, Alex Meitlis, Tamara Meitlis, Garry Chang, Ramael Scully, Lucy Henry, Shachar Argov, Alison Quinn, Maria Mok, Basia Murphy, Heidi Knudsen, Luana Knudsen, Paulina Bembel, Charissa Fraser, Faiscal Barakat, Toni Birbara, Laura Clifford, Angelita Pereira, Francis Pereira, Sarit Packer, Itamar Srulovich, Lingchee Ang, Gemma Bell, Bob Granleese, Merope Mills, Fiona MacIntyre, Sarah Bennie, Mark Hutchinson, Imogen Fortes, Sanjana Lovekin, Keren Margalit, Yoram Ever-Hadani, Itzik Lederfeind, Ilana Lederfeind and Amos, Ariela and David Oppenheim.

Finally, I sincerely thank all the team members at Ottolenghi and NOPI for their endless commitment and hard work.

YOTAM OTTOLENGHI

....

OTTOLENGHI ON THE GO

Lists of ingredients for all our published recipes are available at ottolenghi.co.uk/ingredients